BENSON and HEDGES
SNOOKER YEAR

FIFTH EDITION EDITED BY TERRY SMITH
ASSOCIATE EDITOR DENNIS TAYLOR

PELHAM BOOKS

PELHAM BOOKS

Published by the Penguin Group
27 Wrights Lane, London W8 5TZ, England
Viking Penguin Inc., 40 West 23rd Street, New York, New York 10010, USA
Penguin Books Australia Ltd, Ringwood, Victoria, Australia
Penguin Books Canada Ltd, 2801 John Street, Markham, Ontario, Canada L3R 1B4
Penguin Books (NZ) Ltd, 182–190 Wairau Road, Auckland 10, New Zealand

Penguin Books Ltd, Registered Offices: Harmondsworth, Middlesex, England

First published by Pelham Books simultaneously in hardback and paperback 1988

Typeset, printed and bound in Great Britain by
Hazell Watson & Viney Limited
Member of BPCC plc
Aylesbury, Bucks, England

A CIP catalogue record for this book is available from the British Library

ISBN 0 7207 1830 9

CONTENTS

ACKNOWLEDGEMENTS

Journalism can be a cut-throat business. I am grateful that, in ten years of reporting, I have been able to make so many friends – some of whom have provided invaluable contributions to this fifth edition of the *Benson and Hedges Snooker Year*. My thanks, therefore, go to Alexander Clyde (*Evening Standard*), John Hennessey (*Daily Mail*), Alasdair Ross (*Sun*), Bruce Beckett (Press Association), Gaye Jones and Karen Smyth. Martyn Blake of the WPBSA, David Ford of the B&SCC and international referees Alan Chamberlain and John Street have all been vital sources of help and inspiration. Mark Wildman has again looked with authority at the billiards scene and, last but not least, my associate editor Dennis Taylor has scripted a telling insight into the world of professional snooker. In fact, all players and officials have helped make my task an enjoyable one.

My photographic friends have provided pictures: John Hawken (on page 57); Trevor Jones (on page 61); David Muscroft (on pages 60, 122, 124, 126, 130); Maurice Ward (on page 29); Mike Webster (on page 126).

Of course, Benson and Hedges and Pelham Books are to be thanked for allowing me the privilege of producing this book for the second year.

Twelve months ago I concluded with heartfelt praise for the hard-working ladies of our team. Remarkably, three of them have continued to work with me – my wife, Eileen, who compiled so many of the facts and figures; Pat Mead, who spent numerous hours slaving over a word-processor; and Ruth Baldwin, who again ensured that the book came out on time by reading the original text, sorting out problems with the proofs and making certain that deadlines were adhered to. A new female member of the squad this year is designer Sandie Boccacci, who has produced some enterprising layouts.

BEWARE OF THE 'DIRT DIGGERS'

by Dennis Taylor

Snooker has never been in better shape, even though these days it seems fashionable to knock anything that is successful. In places like America the media people love sporting heroes, but in Britain we seem to enjoy taking a pot at our stars.

It is a proven fact that snooker is the UK's number one television sport. The viewing figures are still high and we are spreading out all over Europe and, indeed, the world. Yet to listen to some people you would think the game was on its last legs. I can't understand why there are always those who have to dig for dirt – even if it is not there.

Steve Davis is one of the greatest sporting ambassadors this country has ever had.

I don't think he played his best snooker last season, but he still recorded his best results. He won four ranking tournaments and that is certainly going to take some beating – even by Steve himself!

I had my greatest season in terms of winning money as I finished third on the cash list, but I won most of that at the start of the season. I was successful in World Series tournaments in Japan and Canada and then I came out on top in the Carling Champions in Dublin and the Matchroom Champion of Champions in Southend. I won £170,000 in ten weeks, then my form started to fall away – don't ask me why, because I usually come good at the end of the season!

Tokyo triumph: Dennis Taylor, complete with a Samurai helmet and a £30,000 cheque after winning the British Caledonian Masters in Japan.

Things began to go wrong at the start of 1988 when I lost 6–2 to Cliff Thorburn in a Rothmans Matchroom League match in Belgium. After that I couldn't seem to do a thing right. I even found myself relegated from the League for this season – and that hurt! It has made me very determined to get back into the League with my performances on the table this season.

I didn't do well in the Benson and Hedges Masters at Wembley, going out to Mike Hallett in the first round. In last year's edition of *Snooker Year* I told you how I used to go out in the opening match at Wembley all the time until I won the title in 1987. Now it was back to my first-round jinx again.

I am often asked how I came to team up with Barry Hearn. It all started in 1984 after I won the Rothmans Grand Prix – my first title after thirteen years as a professional. I had mentioned that I would like to join Barry and he invited me to go to the Far East with him in the summer of 1985, saying we would talk about it then. Of course, I won the world title the same year. Most people probably think that at this point Barry rushed up to me and asked me to sign, but it was not like that at all – in fact, it was much more low-key. Just after I won the title I had to attend a function in London and Barry was there. We simply looked at each other across the room, shrugged our shoulders and decided we might as well get together. It was just what I needed: now I could concentrate on playing snooker. Barry has been good for me, and I hope that I have been good for the Matchroom.

Well done, Steve: Steve Davis after his Benson and Hedges Masters triumph last season. Taylor had been the 1987 Masters winner.

They say that playing a professional sport means a lot of time away from the family. That used to be true in my case, but last summer I asked Barry to cut right back on my exhibition schedule because I wanted to spend much more time with my wife, Pat, and our three children. My exhibition nights now are usually for large companies or Matchroom sponsors. I miss the club evenings because they are the grass roots of snooker. However, something had to go, and though I don't see so many club players these days, I do see a lot more of my family. And anyone who knows me will understand why that means so much.

Who impressed me most last season? I think John Parrott is the man who fits that bill. Parrott burst on to the scene a few years ago and reached the semi-final of the Lada Classic, and everyone was predicting great things for him. But the expected overnight success didn't quite happen – he had to serve his snooker apprenticeship. Last

---

WHO SAID THAT?

'I don't care what they think about me off the table as long as they acknowledge my professional ability. That is what really matters.'

▲

– *Steve Davis after being labelled 'Mr Boring'.*

season, he produced some brilliant performances and so nearly beat Davis in the final of the Mercantile Credit Classic. Now he is firmly established in the top sixteen and is at number 7 for this year. It won't be long before he wins his first title.

What about Stephen Hendry? He is a truly great player and has served his apprenticeship in double-quick time. He must have been disappointed at going out in the second round of the World Championship and I just hope that there is not too much pressure on him. I read that if he didn't win the World Championship this season, it would be a disaster; of course it wouldn't – he would still be only twenty!

I had first-hand experience of how well Hendry played last season in the final of the Rothmans Grand Prix. At one stage I was leading 4–1, but he came back to win 10–7 and fully deserved to become the youngest ever winner of a professional title.

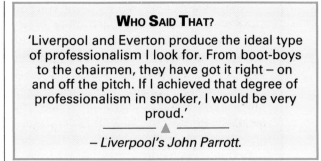

WHO SAID THAT?

'Liverpool and Everton produce the ideal type of professionalism I look for. From boot-boys to the chairmen, they have got it right – on and off the pitch. If I achieved that degree of professionalism in snooker, I would be very proud.'

▲

– Liverpool's John Parrott.

What about Alex Higgins? Well, the Hurricane dropped out of the top sixteen for the first time in his career. He had, by his standards, a terrible season. In the years preceding last season I had been fortunate to skipper Ireland to three successive victories in the World Cup. That all changed in 1987/88, however, and I wasn't too happy with the way the format was altered. Higgins, Eugene Hughes and myself had been together for those three victorious years but, without consultation, they split the Irish team up into Northern Ireland and the Republic of Ireland. Why didn't they ask the opinion of the players concerned or wait until we had lost our title? It seemed very unfair not to give us a chance to make it four wins in a row. As it happened, both Irish teams went out in the first round. Would we have made it four titles? We will never know.

Of course, there are some great young players in the game, but there is still a lot of life left in the over-thirty-fives. Just look at the World Championship last season — there were two forty-year-olds in the semi-final, Cliff Thorburn and Terry Griffiths. There is no substitute for experience, especially in an event like the World Championship. Youngsters like Hendry will make an impact, but don't forget us 'old 'uns'! I reckon I can still win another World Championship.

Of the lighter moments in our year on the snooker road around the world I particularly remember an incident in the

Slick as a Parrott: John Parrott, a young man who impressed Dennis Taylor so much last season.

Foster's World Doubles which made me cry with laughter. I was partnering Thorburn against Eddie Charlton and David Taylor. You probably know that 'Steady' Eddie often makes comments about his run of bad luck in games. Well, when Cliff fluked a snooker, Eddie's bad language just caught a funny spot and all four players cracked up laughing. Then the audience joined in, and before we knew where we were it was going out on television in front of millions of people.

WHO SAID THAT?

'I had a £100,000 deal lined up to play pool all over Australia but it fell through and I had to play more snooker to earn the money – after all, I have got a baby to look after now.'

▲

– *Australian veteran Eddie Charlton after becoming a dad again at fifty-seven.*

A specially memorable experience of the season was when I joined other Matchroom players in a coaching session at London's plush Dorchester Hotel. But this was no ordinary coaching engagement. The man we had to teach was fifteen-year-old Prince Billah, the son of the Sultan of Brunei – the richest man in the world. It was one of the most unusual missions I had ever undertaken and I must admit I was a bit nervous as I made my way into the hotel to the specially prepared room complete with table. But I should not have worried – the Prince was a charming young man and just wanted to know more and more about snooker. I thoroughly enjoyed my few hours with him and it was certainly the experience of a lifetime. My spectacles have become world-famous and the Prince was very interested to see how they worked.

When countries like Brunei are going potty for snooker, the future of the game must be guaranteed. Of course, snooker has a few problems just like any other sport but, as I said earlier, the game has never been in better shape. Let's stop knocking snooker and get on with talking about the good things – and I can assure you that there are plenty of good things to talk about.

WHO SAID THAT?

'It was a pleasure to be involved in such a great final and a great tournament. You won't see much better snooker than that anywhere in the world.'

▲

– *Dennis Taylor after winning the John Labatt Classic Canadian Masters with a 9–7 final success over Jimmy White.*

SPONSOR'S INTRODUCTION

In the last edition of the *Benson and Hedges Snooker Year*, Dennis Taylor, our distinguished Associate Editor, predicted that snooker was ready to become even stronger on a world-wide basis. With the publication of this, our fifth edition, Dennis is being proved right. Snooker is now conquering audiences from Monte Carlo to China and there are major ranking tournaments planned this season in Canada and Belgium. Young stars like Stephen Hendry guarantee that snooker has a bright future, while established professionals like Steve Davis and Jimmy White continue to thrill crowds up and down the country. Snooker has enjoyed rapid growth in popularity, and is now Britain's number 1 television sport.

In this edition we look back over a busy year for snooker and bring you up-to-date on what really happened. In addition we are again including the complete Official Rules for Snooker and Billiards to help answer those difficult technical questions. We are confident that our editor, Terry Smith, has brought together a book that will be both a stimulating review of last season and a valuable reference to help you enjoy the game in the future.

John Slade,
Marketing Manager – Benson and Hedges,
on behalf of the company.

A BAN, BUST-UPS AND BETA-BLOCKERS – AND A PEACE PACT TOO

by Terry Smith

Snooker has been under the media microscope even since it introduced random drug tests in 1985. The many critics, convinced that the sport was riddled with drug takers, waited for a spate of failed tests. That spate never arrived, however, and snooker could be applauded on its positive move. How many other professional sports can boast such a thorough testing procedure?

It was inevitable, though, that someone would fall foul of the test, that there would be an isolated incident that would make front-page headlines across the country. This happened last season when Canadian Cliff Thorburn failed a test at the MIM Britannia Unit Trusts British Open in February. It was a serious matter

Question time: Canada's Cliff Thorburn can still manage a smile at the World Championship despite being questioned about his failed drugs test.

that cast a shadow over snooker. But as the hysteria died down, it paid to examine the facts. This was the *first* positive test from hundreds of samples taken. Does that indicate a sport riddled with drugs? Would other sports and other famous sporting names come out as clean if testing were established for *every* professional sport? I doubt it very much.

Thorburn's sample showed small traces of cocaine and he faced a maximum ban of six ranking tournaments, an £18,000 fine and the deduction of four ranking points. The matter was due to be heard just two days before the Embassy World Championship got under way. Thorburn went to the High Court to obtain an injunction to take part at Sheffield. He won.

After the championship Thorburn appeared before an independent tribunal in front of Gavin Lightman QC – the man who had heard the infamous Alex Higgins head-butting case a year earlier. Lightman had been appointed by the WPBSA.

Following the ninety-minute hearing, Mr Lightman went away to consider his verdict. Thorburn was banned from the first two ranking tournaments this season, fined £10,000 and had two ranking points deducted. Some observers thought the punishment too lenient, but Mr Lightman took into account the fact that Thorburn had not attempted to use the drug to enhance his performance as a player and that he had an unblemished record. Thorburn and his manager, Barry Hearn, stayed silent and the WPBSA stated that there would be no further comment but, despite their assurances, the comments came thick and fast from two of Hearn's rival managers, Howard Kruger, who runs the Framework organization, and Ian Doyle, who manages Stephen Hendry and Mike Hallett. Both were members of the WPBSA board but were making their comments as individual managers rather than board directors.

Kruger stated: 'What Mr Lightman has done is to hand every player a free ticket to drug abuse. Thorburn should have received the maximum punishment for taking hard drugs. The WPBSA should have hit him with everything they could to discredit a man who has set such a terrible example to thousands of kids who look up to sporting idols. I am furious to think that the same man handed out a far heavier sentence to Alex Higgins. I have always believed the punishment should fit the crime, but obviously Mr Lightman doesn't agree. It is a sad and sickening day for snooker.'

Doyle said: 'It is incredible – I am amazed at the decision. Drugs are a worldwide problem and governing bodies have a responsibility. Unless we stand together, the kids of today will suffer. I cannot follow the reasoning that allows Thorburn to keep £8,000 of the prize money and two of the ranking points he earned from the tournament at which he failed the test.'

> **WHO SAID THAT?**
>
> 'It was obviously taken into account that Cliff did this as a social thing and not to enhance his performance. I do not believe drug taking is rife in snooker.'
>
> ▲
>
> *– John Virgo, chairman of the WPBSA, speaking after Canadian Cliff Thorburn was banned and fined for failing a drugs test.*

The decision dropped Thorburn one place in the world rankings to number 6. The season had started, naturally, with the announcement of increases in prize money which, over all the tournaments, totalled more than £3.5 million.

There was also a new format for the Rothmans Matchroom League with Joe Johnson and Stephen Hendry being invited into the £220,000 competition. There was a novel twist in that tale. Matchroom's Barry Hearn said: 'The bottom two will be relegated and I don't care who it is, even if it is Steve Davis or Jimmy White. The League was a tremendous success last season and this relegation issue means that all matches will have needle injected into them. It will be an embarrassment for the players who have to drop out.'

It didn't take long for snooker's internal problems to come into the open when Hearn resigned as a director of the WPBSA. In a letter to the board he stated: 'I have been increasingly concerned about a potential clash of interests because of my many different roles in snooker. But with the launch of the World Series this position has now reached a crisis. There is a distinct

> **WHO SAID THAT?**
>
> 'It is incredible – I am amazed at the decision.'
>
> ▲
>
> *– Ian Doyle after the verdict on Cliff Thorburn who failed a drugs test.*
>
> 'I am disgusted by the decision because I firmly believe Thorburn should have received the maximum punishment for taking hard drugs. The WPBSA should have hit him with everything they could to discredit a man who had set such a terrible example to thousands of kids.'
>
> ▲
>
> *– Howard Kruger talking about the verdict on Cliff Thorburn.*

possibility of clashes between us in the future. The resulting television coverage worldwide of my many involvements could well place me in an embarrassing position with the WPBSA.'

The following day Rex Williams, a close ally of Hearn, refused to resign as chairman of the WPBSA despite being given a 5–1 vote of no confidence at a board meeting where the atmosphere was less than harmonious. 'I have a duty to all members and I plan to continue working for snooker,' he said.

The Board were upset that Williams had been out of the country on a Hearn promotion when a major sponsorship was announced and the boardroom battle had been in the air for many months. Williams was bitter that details of the meeting had leaked out despite an agreement that it should be confidential.

Of course, we couldn't get far into the season without the dreaded subject of beta-blockers rearing its ugly head when the board received a letter from the Sports Council threatening to withdraw their support for the WPBSA drug testing programme. The Council were bitter that the WPBSA had refused to place an outright ban on beta-blocker drugs which were outlawed by the International Olympic Committee (IOC) but have always been permitted in professional snooker when taken by players under proper medical supervision.

Sports Minister Colin Moynihan

stepped in following an inquiry by Sir Arthur Gold, the chairman of the Sports Council. In a letter to the WPBSA, Mr Moynihan stated: 'I am disappointed the WPBSA has not been able to signify to Sir Arthur Gold its willingness to step into line with recognized sports in adopting procedures and practices to ensure an effective system of doping control. I would be grateful for your support for independent random testing based on the IOC guidelines and for an indication that snooker would be prepared to join our initiative against drug abuse.'

If snooker failed to fall into line, no further grants would be available from the Sports Council to continue drugs testing at the Chelsea College. (Each drugs test cost £90 with the Sports Council donating £64.) The WPBSA went away to consider the letter, but finance was hardly the problem. Gordon Ingham, chairman of the WPBSA drugs advisory committee, said: 'If a medical practitioner considers it necessary to prescribe beta-blockers, which are not an illegal drug, to a patient, the opinion of the medical practitioner is accepted, especially in view of the fact that they had been told no evidence exists that suggests any harmful effects and no evidence exists that they are beneficial to a snooker player other than to correct a medical condition.'

The expected resignation of Williams, chairman of the WPBSA for fourteen of the last eighteen years, occurred during the Tennents UK Open. His place was temporarily taken by vice-chairman John Virgo, who later stepped up to chairman.

No tournament seemed safe from controversy and there was hardly an event that went by without behind-the-scenes rows tending to dominate the media headlines. The Mercantile Credit Classic, held just after Christmas at Blackpool's Norbreck Hotel, was no exception. Once again it was beta-blockers that took over the proceedings.

WHO SAID THAT?

'I have stopped taking the beta-blockers – they made me too relaxed. I was shaking inwardly in this game. I still take the tablets for the double vision but it is more important these days that I get a good night's sleep.'

▲

– Veteran John Spencer after his 5–0 win over Dennis Taylor in the MIM Britannia Unit Trusts British Open.

The WPBSA then did an about-turn, the board voting unanimously to accept partially the Sports Council's recommendations. WPBSA solictor John Aucott said: 'We hope that these latest measures satisfy the Sports Council and the Sports Minister, Colin Moynihan.' The Association bowed to mounting Government pressure and banned beta-blockers, with the exception of the heart drug Atenolol. The ban came into effect this season.

An angry Williams declared that he might have to quit the game following the decision. He said: 'I will be taking top legal advice. I am absolutely amazed at the board's decision. We have always agreed that the drug would be allowed as long as it was prescribed medically. I am fortunate as I do not have to play snooker again for financial reasons – other players might not be in that position. What do they do? Go on the dole? Our Association has been

WHO SAID THAT?

'I haven't played my last game of snooker. I haven't investigated the situation about changing my medication.'

▲

– Rex Williams whose type of beta-blocker will be banned this season.

rushed into this decision. Why didn't they get a proper panel of experts to examine the case and then make a decision? I take such a low dosage that it could not possibly affect my performance as a snooker player.'

One day later Williams produced a report from a top London consultant to whom he had been sent for a second opinion on the tablets he was taking. This had been done, he explained, because 'David Forster, the WPBSA medical adviser, said that as chairman I should be seen to be whiter than white.' Williams made public that report from M. H. Lader, a professor of clinical psycho-pharmacology at the University of London. The reported stated: 'Mr Williams has suffered from anxiety problems and has seen specialists for these problems. For the past fifteen years he has been on medications given for anxiety not tremor. They are an entirely appropriate treatment for chronic anxiety and stress. It is my opinion that if the medication was reduced or changed he would run the risk of severe symptoms and anxiety recurring. I do not believe that the medication which Mr Williams is taking is likely to affect his game. It is almost certainly not affecting his skills as a professional snooker player.'

South Africa was the next problem to hit the snooker headlines when Silvino Francisco was omitted from the Benson and Hedges Irish Masters because the sponsors wanted to avoid any possible anti-apartheid demonstration. Francisco, who had been applying for British citizen-

An angry man: Rex Williams, who was amazed at the beta-blocker ban.

ship, was far from happy. 'Why me?' he asked. 'I have been in this country five years. I should have received more support from the WPBSA – if they won't take me, they shouldn't have taken anyone. I am very sore. I have been to Ireland – north and south – on many occasions and never had problems. I have only ever had one incident and that was in Basingstoke in 1983 when a man in the crowd must have thought there were still elephants and lions on the streets in South Africa.'

The sponsors had a contract dated August 1987 which gave them the right to pick and choose whom they wanted. Clearly Francisco was a man who did not fit the bill, and it was a decision that was severely criticised in many places.

The Matchroom and Framework camps had been strangely quiet for a while, but that all changed during the Benson and Hedges Masters at Wembley. The row involved the Kent China Cup to be held in Peking. Hearn's Matchroom organization had travelled to the Chinese capital in 1987, but Kruger's Framework team secured the 1988 event which would be worth £120,000 in prize money.

Hearn said: 'I have been turned over and I am cheesed off. We were just too expensive. I don't believe what is in Kruger's press release. Are they playing for prize money? Is this a proper tournament? We were offered the same money as in the press release.'

Kruger joined in the war of words: 'Every time I put on the TV Hearn is voicing his opinion. There are 128 professionals but he only seems interested in eight of them. I keep hearing of a split within snooker, but if he wants a confrontation I will meet him head on.'

Kruger had been far from happy when Hearn's World Series had been postponed until 1989 with Hearn saying that he had lost nearly £100,000. Kruger said: 'I cannot guarantee that Joe Johnson and Tony Knowles will be available next year. I will

have to look into the compensation aspect.'

Snooker was full of rumours of a possible split between Hearn and the WPBSA and of Hearn's intention to set up a rival camp, but he denied this, saying: 'That would be lunacy – none of my players will be leaving. There is more than £3 million worth of prize money to be won out there.'

Hardly a week went by without yet another bust-up and now it was again the turn of poor old Kirk Stevens, one of the most likeable players on the circuit. Stevens once admitted to 'being hooked on cocaine', and it was announced that he would be missing from the MIM Britannia Unit Trusts British Open because he was receiving treatment in a Toronto clinic which specialized in drug rehabilitation. He eventually spent thirty days in the clinic and came out saying, 'I have had my problems and Alcoholics Anonymous have

Welcome back: Kirk Stevens returns to World Championship action after a month-long stay in a Toronto drugs rehabilitation clinic.

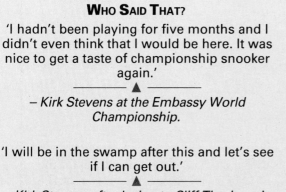

saved my life. I am just glad to be playing again.'

Surely there could be no worries as the snooker circuit headed down to the south coast and sleepy Bournemouth, home of the retired? There were!

The WPBSA had decided to split the Ireland team, winners for the past three years, into Northern Ireland and the Republic of Ireland for the Fersina Windows World Cup. Dennis Taylor, who had captained the side for three years, was not pleased. 'I am disgusted that we have not been offered the chance to defend the title,' he complained. 'No one even bothered to talk to us about it – they just went ahead and did it.' Both Irish teams went out quickly.

The tournament stage switched to Derby for the MIM British Open and immediately there seemed to be a plethora of press conferences. As one pressroom wit saw it: 'We will soon be having more press conferences than days of real snooker!'

Hearn started the ball rolling by joining up with boxing promoter Frank Warren and Trans World International, the television arm of Mark McCormack's International Management Group, to promote two major tournaments. These were the World Matchplay Championship, being held this season with a record price of £100,000 for the winner, followed by a World Open next year including men's and women's singles and mixed and men's doubles and a junior event. Hearn said: 'It will be seen that our announcements will bring us into conflict with the WPBSA but we certainly hope they realize the validity of our promotional plans and can work in commercial harmony with us.'

John Virgo, who had been unanimously elected WPBSA chairman a couple of months earlier, said: 'This is typical Barry Hearn. He won't be happy until he controls the game or ruins it. He is just a money-making machine. These tournaments do not create interest.'

The World Matchplay was then planned to include the eight players who had produced the best performances of the season, which meant places for John Parrott, a member of the Framework squad, and Stephen Hendry, a member of Ian Doyle's Scottish-based outfit. Doyle, a director of the WPBSA, said, 'I don't see any reason why Stephen shouldn't take part,' while Kruger took the opposite view, saying, 'Does Hearn have a sponsor? He keeps on coming up with ideas but I have this vision of him sitting with a load of jamboree bags and hoping something pops out.'

The bitter battle continued the next day when Virgo announced that he had been promised that Parrott and now Hendry would not be appearing in the World Matchplay. Hearn hit back by saying that Steve Davis and Jimmy White would not be taking part in a new WPBSA event scheduled for December and designed to include the top sixteen players with the best records from one season. Then Doyle retaliated: 'Hearn wants to make up his mind whether he is a snooker manager, snooker promoter, boxing manager, boxing promoter or an entrepreneur.'

The next day Hearn withdrew Dennis

The opposing camps: (above) Frank Warren, Bill Sinrich and Barry Hearn announce their World Matchplay event; (below) Ian Doyle, John Virgo, Ray Reardon and Howard Kruger announce their opposition to the World Matchplay. A peace pact was later signed between the 'warring' groups.

Taylor and Cliff Thorburn from the WPBSA tournament. Virgo's response to this was instant. 'Hearn is just cocking a snook at everything the WPBSA has been working at for years,' he declared.

Hearn, Warren and Bill Sinrich, representing Trans World International, the television arm of IMG, hopped on a train to Derby for yet another press conference. The press corps trooped over to a hotel near Derby station and we waited for the latest verbal battle.

Hearn began: 'I would like to apologize to MIM Britannia, the sponsors of the British Open, for everything that has happened this week during their tournament. I pledge the support of my players for their event in the years to come.

'The World Matchplay will not go away – we are here to stay and we are not a novelty event. It will be seen in forty-two countries all over the world including many countries who have never seen the sport before.

'There is no conflict and we hope that all invited players will eventually take part.'

Warren also suggested that the WPBSA was not the governing body of the sport but was merely a limited company geared to making a profit.

Then the verbal exchanges became more personal with Hearn blasting out at Doyle. He said: 'He has known what has been going on for many weeks. I flew to Scotland to see Doyle and he has telephoned me virtually every day to discuss the event. We spoke recently and the last thing he said was to request an entry form for Hendry for the World Matchplay as soon as possible. I can't believe he has changed his mind.'

Over to Doyle who didn't call a press conference but issued a statement saying: 'My meeting with Mr Hearn was at his request. He made a number of proposals to me and requested my support in a break-away ruling body to be headed by Rex Williams. I categorically refused.'

Meanwhile, Jimmy White, the world number 2, was fined £100 and ordered to write an apology for swearing at referee John Smyth during the Foster's World Doubles.

Then the real bombshell hit snooker as it was revealed that Cliff Thorburn had failed a drugs test at the MIM Britannia British Open. The tabloid newspapers had a field day as headlines like 'Cocaine Shock' and 'Drugs Shame' waited for us on our breakfast tables. One week later WPBSA chairman John Virgo admitted to a Sunday newspaper that he had once smoked 'pot' in the 1970s.

Snooker always seems to run headlong into a crisis just before the World Championship: this time there were two issues to deal with. Thorburn was allowed, after an appearance in the High Court to obtain an adjournment, to compete in the Championship. But at least during the tournament there was some good news as the WPBSA and Hearn patched up their differences and the Association sanctioned Hearn's World Matchplay Championship.

The WPBSA also granted Hearn and his syndicate the television rights while dropping their own sixteen-man invitation tournament and abandoning the World Doubles. Hearn agreed to increase the field from eight to twelve players in return for the WPBSA sanctions, which also included the World Open scheduled for 1989.

As the season finished there was just time for one minor ripple. Channel Four announced that they were dropping their snooker coverage because, chief executive Michael Grade claimed, 'Snooker boosts our viewing figures but it damages the image of the Channel. We will replace it with programmes for people that hate snooker.'

Roll on next season!

WHERE THE ACTION IS FOR 1988/89 IN SNOOKER AND BILLIARDS

PROPOSED SNOOKER TOURNAMENT DATES

DATES	EVENT	VENUE
1988		
Jun 13–14	Fidelity Unit Trusts International (Prelims)	Norbreck Castle Hotel, Blackpool
Jun 15–16	Rothmans Grand Prix (Prelims)	Norbreck Castle Hotel
Jun 17–20	Tennents UK Open (Prelims)	Norbreck Castle Hotel
Jun 21–22	Mercantile Credit Classic (Prelims)	Norbreck Castle Hotel
Aug 28–31	Fidelity Unit Trusts International (Last 64)	Trentham Gardens, Stoke-on-Trent
Sept 2–11	Fidelity Unit Trusts International (Last 32, TV stages)	Trentham Gardens, Stoke-on-Trent
Sept 17–18	Norwich Union European Grand Prix	Brussels
Sept 21–23	Canadian Masters (Prelims)	Norbreck Castle Hotel
Sept 24–25	European Open (Prelims)	Norbreck Castle Hotel
Sept 26–27	British Open (Prelims)	Norbreck Castle Hotel
Oct 1–2	Norwich Union European Grand Prix	Amsterdam
Oct 3–5	Foster's Champions	RTE Studios, Dublin
Oct 4–9	LEP Matchroom Champion of Champions	Cliffs Pavilion, Southend
Oct 10–13	Rothmans Grand Prix (Last 64)	Hexagon Theatre, Reading
Oct 15–23	Rothmans Grand Prix (Last 32, TV Stages)	Hexagon Theatre, Reading
Oct 26–27	Canadian Masters (Last 32)	Toronto
Oct 28–Nov 5	Canadian Masters (Last 16, TV stages)	Toronto
Nov 11–16	Tennents UK Open (Last 64)	Guild Hall, Preston
Nov 12–13	Norwich Union European Grand Prix	Madrid
Nov 19–27	Tennents UK Open (Last 16, TV stages)	Guild Hall, Preston
Dec 2–10	World Matchplay Championship	Brentwood
Dec 3–4	Norwich Union European Grand Prix	Milan
Dec 12–18	English Professional Championship (Prelims)	Venue to be announced
Dec 17–18	Norwich Union European Grand Prix (Finals)	Monte Carlo

DATES	EVENT	VENUE
1989		
Jan 1–4	Mercantile Credit Classic (Last 64)	Norbreck Castle Hotel, Blackpool
Jan 6–15	Mercantile Credit Classic (Last 32, TV stages)	Norbreck Castle Hotel, Blackpool
Jan 22–29	Benson and Hedges Masters	Wembley Conference Centre, London
Jan 30–Feb 2	European Open (Last 64)	Venue to be announced
Feb 4–11	European Open (Last 16, TV stages)	Venue to be announced
Feb 12–18	National Championships: English, Irish, Scottish, Welsh	Venues to be announced
Feb 19–22	British Open (Last 64)	Assembly Rooms, Derby
Feb 24–Mar 5	British Open (Last 32, TV stages)	Assembly Rooms, Derby
Mar 21–24	Fersina Windows World Cup	Bournemouth International Centre
Mar 22–Apr 4	Embassy World Championship (Prelims)	Guild Hall, Preston
Mar 28–Apr 2	Benson and Hedges Irish Masters	Goffs, County Kildare, Ireland
Apr 15–May 1	Embassy World Championship (Last 32, TV stages)	Crucible Theatre, Sheffield

PROPOSED BILLIARDS TOURNAMENT DATES

DATES	EVENT	VENUE
1988		
Nov 6–10	Strachan UK Championship	Marton Country Club, Middlesbrough
1989		
Jan 17–21	Yorkshire Bank Professional Players' Tournament	Venue to be announced
Mar 6–10	BCE World Championship	Marton Country Club, Middlesbrough
May 28–Jun 4	BCE European Open Championship	Venue to be announced

All dates and venues may be subject to change without prior notification.

THE RANKINGS AND HOW THEY EARN POINTS

Snooker's top professionals will this season have eight ranking tournaments counting towards their place in the world ranking list. This is an increase of two tournaments on last year and shows the game's commitment in moving the top events into new overseas markets. The two new tournaments are the Canadian Masters in Toronto from 28 October to 5 November and the European Open from 30 January to 11 February.

Until this season a player's ranking has been determined by the points picked up in the events in the preceding two years – that is, it has been based on twelve tournaments. During the 1988/89 season this will obviously change to include the six tournaments of 1987/88 and the eight tournaments of 1988/89. These fourteen tournaments will then be analysed and the points accumulated will give the player his ranking for the 1989/90 season.

A problem will occur in the 1989/90 season when the WPBSA propose ten ranking tournaments with the creation of two more foreign events – probably in Australia and Hong Kong, though at the time of going to press dates have yet to be finalized. The WPBSA are aware that with ten ranking tournaments per season, the system might become too unwieldy. There is a train of thought in the Association that a player's ranking should be restricted to the results of just one season.

Players keep the same ranking all season and, unlike players of other sports, do not change their position from tournament to tournament. This is because the qualifying rounds of the majority of snooker tournaments all take place during the summer and it would be impossible to update them at the start of each individual event.

The six ranking tournaments in the 1987/88 season counted towards a player's ranking in the current season of 1988/89. Those tournaments were the Fidelity Unit Trusts International, the Rothmans Grand Prix, the Tennents UK Open, the Mercantile Credit Classic, the MIM Britannia Unit Trusts British Open and the Embassy World Championship. Points were awarded in most tournaments as follows:

Winner	6	points
Runner-up	5	points
Losing semi-finalist	4	points
Losing quarter-finalist	3	points
Fifth-round loser	2	points
Fourth-round loser	1	point
Third-round loser	1	merit point
Second-round loser	1	'A' point
First-round loser	Frames won in match	

The World Championship is the most prestigious tournament of the season and higher points are awarded, as follows:

Winner	10	points
Runner-up	8	points
Losing semi-finalist	6	points
Losing quarter-finalist	4	points
Second-round loser	2	points

Gunning for the top: Jimmy White (left), the world number 2, who is chasing Steve Davis, the world number 1.

First-round loser	1 ranking point unless member of top sixteen who receive 2 merit points
Fourth-round prelim-round loser	2 merit points
Third-round prelim-round loser	1 merit point
Second-round prelim-round loser	1 'A' point
First-round prelim-round loser	Frames won in match

In the event of ties on ranking points, the player who has picked up most ranking points in the most recent season is allocated a higher placing. If there is still a tie, the player with the greatest number of merit points is given the higher placing. If scores are still equal, the number of merit points in the preceding season applies. In the unlikely event that players are still level, their positions are decided on 'A' points, followed by frames won. If, by a remote chance, the players still cannot be separated, their performances in the preceding World Championship will determine their ranking order; and, if this method fails, the other ranking tournaments are worked through in reverse order until the players' positions can be established.

THE WPBSA OFFICIAL WORLD RANKING LIST 1988/89

(Previous season's position in brackets)

POSITION	NAME	R	M	A	F	POSITION	NAME	R	M	A	F
1 (1)	S. Davis (Eng)	59	1	–	–	43 (40)	D. Fowler (Eng)	5	7	3	–
2 (2)	J. White (Eng)	44	1	–	–	44 (39)	W. King (Aust)	5	4	3	9
3 (3)	N. Foulds (Eng)	34	3	–	–	45 (–)	Gary Wilkinson (Eng)	4	2	1	–
4 (23)	S. Hendry (Scot)	33	2	1	–	46 (48)	G. Cripsey (Eng)	4	10	1	–
5 (6)	T. Griffiths (Wales)	33*	–	–	–	47 (33)	W. Werbeniuk (Can)	4	8	1	–
6 (4)	C. Thorburn (Can)	31*	3	–	–	48 (30)	M. Macleod (Scot)	4	11	–	–
7 (13)	J. Parrott (Eng)	30	2	–	–	49 (46)	A. Jones (Eng)	4	7	3	–
8 (7)	A. Knowles (Eng)	28	3	–	–	50 (37)	S. Duggan (Eng)	4	5	5	–
9 (16)	M. Hallett (Eng)	24	3	–	–	51 (58)	A. Chappel (Wales)	3	11	1	–
10 (8)	Dennis Taylor (NI)	23	3	1	–	52 (54)	M. Bennett (Wales)	3	6	2	12
11 (5)	J. Johnson (Eng)	23	2	–	–	53 (52)	K. Owers (Eng)	3	5	4	2
12 (10)	S. Francisco (SA)	22	2	–	–	54 (43)	P. Browne (Rep Ire)	3	2	8	–
13 (11)	W. Thorne (Eng)	19	4	–	–	55 (59)	R. Edmonds (Eng)	2	5	6	6
14 (18)	P. Francisco (SA)	18	3	–	–	56 (99)	N. Gilbert (Eng)	2	3	5	10
15 (19)	J. Virgo (Eng)	17	–	–	–	57 (82)	D. Gilbert (Eng)	2	2	7	–
16 (17)	C. Wilson (Wales)	16	3	–	–	58 (92)	M. Fisher (Eng)	2	1	5	13
17 (9)	A. Higgins (NI)	14	4	–	–	59 (64)	P. Houlihan (Eng)	2	1	4	16
18 (12)	R. Williams (Eng)	13	9	–	–	60 (57)	R. Bales (Eng)	2	–	10	–
19 (26)	E. Charlton (Aust)	12	6	2	–	61 (53)	J. Wright (Eng)	2	7	3	2
20 (32)	A. Drago (Malta)	12	4	–	–	62 (51)	L. Dodd (Eng)	2	5	5	–
21 (24)	E. Hughes (Rep Ire)	12	7	–	–	63 (42)	M. Gauvreau (Can)	2	5	6	–
22 (15)	D. Reynolds (Eng)	12	7	–	–	64 (50)	J. McLaughlin (NI)	2	5	5	–
23 (35)	D. O'Kane (NZ)	11	1	6	–	65 (68)	G. Miles (Eng)	1	7	4	–
24 (14)	D. Mountjoy (Wales)	11	5	–	–	66 (79)	R. Foldvari (Aust)	1	6	6	–
25 (45)	S. Newbury (Wales)	10	8	2	–	67 (78)	C. Roscoe (Wales)	1	5	4	7
26 (29)	B. West (Eng)	10	4	–	–	68 (67)	P. Medati (Eng)	1	5	7	–
27 (28)	J. Spencer (Eng)	10	8	–	–	69 (98)	P. Gibson (Eng)	1	3	6	10
28 (25)	David Taylor (Eng)	10	6	–	–	70 (90)	B. Rowswell (Eng)	1	3	7	1
29 (41)	R. Chaperon (Can)	9	6	–	–	71 (72)	V. Harris (Eng)	1	3	5	10
30 (31)	S. Longworth (Eng)	9	5	–	–	72 (107)	M. Smith (Eng)	1	2	3	22
31 (20)	A. Meo (Eng)	9	8	–	–	73 (–)	J. Chambers (Eng)	1	1	2	5
32 (66)	S. James (Eng)	8	2	4	7	74 (87)	J. Donnelly (Scot)	1	–	7	15
33 (22)	J. Campbell (Aust)	8	6	2	–	75 (56)	M. Bradley (Eng)	1	7	5	–
34 (34)	W. Jones (Wales)	8	5	2	–	76 (47)	M. Wildman (Eng)	1	6	5	–
35 (55)	J. O'Boye (Rep Ire)	7	7	2	–	77 (49)	R. Harris (Eng)	1	6	6	–
36 (27)	D. Martin (Eng)	7	9	–	–	78 (62)	G. Foulds (Eng)	1	3	7	1
37 (21)	K. Stevens (Can)	7	6	–	–	79 (63)	R. Grace (SA)	1	2	5	13
38 (36)	J. Wych (Can)	7	4	1	–	80 (65)	A. Kearney (Rep Ire)	1	1	8	10
39 (83)	D. Roe (Eng)	6	6	5	–	81 (69)	John Rea (Scot)	–	9	2	5
40 (38)	R. Reardon (Wales)	6	6	1	–	82 (77)	M. Morra (Can)	–	7	3	–
41 (–)	M. Clark (Eng)	5	2	–	8	83 (61)	F. Davis (Eng)	–	6	7	10
42 (44)	T. Murphy (NI)	5	8	2	–	84 (84)	B. Oliver (Eng)	–	6	6	7

POSITION	NAME	R	M	A	F
85 (76)	E. Sinclair (Scot)	—	6	4	11
86 (86)	J. Bear (Can)	—	5	4	2
87 (71)	J. van Rensburg (SA)	—	5	6	—
88 (70)	M. Gibson (Scot)	—	5	6	7
89 (80)	I. Williamson (Eng)	—	4	6	4
90 (60)	G. Scott (Eng)	—	4	8	—
91 (85)	G. Rigitano (Can)	—	3	6	11
92 (103)	J. Dunning (Eng)	—	2	5	12
93 (—)	E. Lawlor (Eng)	—	2	1	9
94 (91)	J. Meadowcroft (Eng)	—	2	7	9
95 (96)	Glen Wilkinson (Aust)	—	2	5	10
96 (74)	I. Black (Scot)	—	2	6	7
97 (73)	B. Mikkelsen (Can)	—	2	5	—
98 (113)	P. Watchorn (Rep Ire)	—	1	6	14
99 (111)	Jack Rea (NI)	—	1	5	16
100 (89)	M. Darrington (Eng)	—	1	3	24
101 (115)	T. Whitthread (Eng)	—	1	3	19
102 (—)	A. Robidoux (Can)	—	1	—	—
103 (75)	P. Fagan (Rep Ire)	—	1	6	10
104 (93)	G. Jenkins (Aust)	—	1	5	13
105 (97)	P. Burke (Rep Ire)	—	1	4	16
106 (95)	F. Jonik (Can)	—	1	3	20
107 (100)	I. Anderson (Aust)	—	1	3	4
108 (81)	M. Watterson (Eng)	—	1	—	20
109 (101)	J. Rempe (USA)	—	1	7	4
110 (102)	B. Kelly (Rep Ire)	—	—	7	18
111 (105)	D. Hughes (Eng)	—	—	5	12
112 (110)	D. Chalmers (Eng)	—	—	5	30
113 (116)	F. Ellis (SA)	—	—	4	19
114 (88)	J. Fitzmaurice (Eng)	—	—	4	16
115 (94)	D. Sheehan (Rep Ire)	—	—	4	35
116 (—)	A. Harris (Eng)	—	—	3	9
117 (—)	S. Meakin (Eng)	—	—	3	9
118 (—)	J. Smith (Eng)	—	—	2	17
119 (—)	R. Marshall (Eng)	—	—	2	6
120 (112)	C. Everton (Wales) (NT)	—	—	2	14
121 (114)	D. Mienie (SA) (NT)	—	—	2	19
122 (104)	J. Hargreaves (Eng) (NT)	—	·	2	14
123 (—)	D. Heaton (Eng) (NT)	—	—	1	13
124 (109)	P. Thornley (Can) (NT)	—	—	1	13
125 (117)	D. Greaves (Eng) (NT)	—	—	1	28
126 (119)	M. Hines (SA) (NT)	—	—	1	6
127 (122)	M. Parkin (Eng) (NT)	—	—	—	21
128 (120)	B. Demarco (Scot) (NT)	—	—	—	17
129 (123)	B. Bennett (Eng) (NT)	—	—	—	14
130 (118)	J. Caggianello (Can) (NT)	—	—	—	7
131 (106)	E. McLaughlin (Scot) (NT)	—	—	—	1
132 (127)	S. Mizerak (USA) (NT)	—	—	—	—
133 (108)	G. Watson (Can) (NT)	—	—	—	—
134 (121)	P. Morgan (Aust) (NT)	—	—	—	—
135 (124)	J. Giannaros (Aust) (NT)	—	—	—	—
136 (125)	L. Condo (Aust) (NT)	—	—	—	—
137 (126)	M. Francisco (SA) (NT)	—	—	—	—
138 (128)	W. Saunderson (Can) (NT)	—	—	—	—
139	S. Campbell (Eng)	—	—	—	—
140	C. Edwards (Eng)	—	—	—	—
141	I. Graham (Eng)	—	—	—	—
142	M. Johnston-Allen (Eng)	—	—	—	—
143	D. Morgan (Wales)	—	—	—	—
144	M. Price (Eng)	—	—	—	—
145	M. Rowing (Eng)	—	—	—	—
146	N. Terry (Eng)	—	—	—	—
147	T. Wilson (Eng)	—	—	—	—

* Deducted two points for failing drugs test.

Key to table
R – ranking points
M – merit points
A – 'A' points
F – frames
NT – non-tournament status

NATIONALITIES
Aust – Australia
Can – Canada
Eng – England
Malta – Malta
NI – Northern Ireland
NZ – New Zealand
Rep Ire – Republic of Ireland
Scot – Scotland
SA – South Africa
Wales – Wales
USA – United States of America

WHO MOVED WHERE IN THE RANKINGS

Stephen Hendry, as expected, was the player to make the biggest impact as he moved up nineteen places to number 4 in the rankings for the current season. But he will have been disappointed at his 13–12 defeat by Jimmy White in the Embassy World Championship at Sheffield. If Hendry had gone on to win the final, he would have taken over the number 2 slot from White. Even so, this young man from Edinburgh is no doubt delighted by his dramatic move up the rankings.

World champion Steve Davis maintained his number 1 position and holds a fifteen-point lead over Jimmy White.

Canada's Cliff Thorburn, under so much pressure at the end of last season, dropped one place to number 6, while the ever-consistent Welshman, Terry Griffiths, rose by one place to 5th. Liverpool's John Parrott was disappointed that his best ever season did not culminate in at least one major title. At one stage, Parrott had risen to number 5 on the provisional rankings but finally had to settle for a rise of six places to number 7. Hendry's stablemate, Mike Hallett, built on his arrival into the top sixteen last season by establishing a top ten place at number 9.

There was a disappointing drop of six places for former world champion Joe Johnson and there was also movement down the rankings by Tony Knowles, Dennis Taylor, Silvino Francisco and Willie Thorne. Peter Francisco finally made it into the top sixteen at number 14 and the elite group was completed by John Virgo (number 15) and Cliff Wilson (number 16).

Alex Higgins, now at number 17, was banned from the first two ranking tournaments of last season and that was one of

Flower power: (left) Stephen Hendry, after winning the MIM Britannia Unit Trusts British Open, which helped him move nineteen places up the rankings; (right) stablemate Mike Hallett – who moved into the top ten for the first time at number 9 – pictured with his girlfriend, Jan Herring.

the reasons for his disappearance from the top sixteen for the first time in his career. Three other players also lost their top sixteen place – Rex Williams, Dean Reynolds and Doug Mountjoy.

They say that snooker is a young man's game, but try telling that to Australian grandad Eddie Charlton. He moved over to England to compete full-time on the circuit after a sponsorship deal fell flat back home and, as well as helping Australia to the final of the World Cup, came back into the top twenty at number 19, a lift of seven places.

Malta's only professional, Tony Drago, was rewarded for a quarter-final place in the World Championship by moving up twelve places to number 20. But there was disappointment for Dene O'Kane despite his twelve-place jump to number 23. Before the World Championship, O'Kane was at number 21 and poised for a move into the top sixteen, but he was sent tumbling out of the second qualifying round.

Welshman Steve Newbury, semi-finalist in the Mercantile Credit Classic, produced a twenty-place move to number 25, while 'golden oldie' John Spencer made a modest improvement of one place to number 27. The top thirty-two will be exempt from the qualifying rounds this season and Tony Meo, despite his poor season, was happy to hang on at number 31. Canada's Bob Chaperon moved into the top thirty-two at number 29, while Steve James, who joined the professional ranks only two years ago, took the final place of number 32 after a leap of thirty-four places.

Ireland's Joe O'Boye was another twenty-place mover to number 35, though he had been hoping for a better World Championship and a place in the top thirty-two. Three years ago Canada's Kirk Stevens was in the top ten but problems off the table saw him fall to number 21 last season and he could manage only 37th place this time.

Martin Clark and Gary Wilkinson both

On the move: Gary Wilkinson, an impressive performer in his first professional season.

made their debuts in the professional rankings last season. Clark got off to a tremendous start with victories over Dennis Taylor and Neal Foulds, but his game tailed off towards the end of the campaign. Even so, his first-time placing of number 41 proved that he is ready for a charge on the top sixteen this time. Wilkinson did not produce the same spectacular results but was probably more consistent and started the year at number 45.

The two Gilberts, Nigel and Dave, both made significant improvements this season, Nigel moving up forty-three places to number 56 and Dave going up twenty-five places to number 57. Mick Fisher also finally made an impact, going up from number 92 to number 58. Martin Smith shot up thirty-five places to number 72, while Jimmy Chambers, in his first year as a professional, came in at number 73.

Canada's Alain Robidoux needed to win two qualifying matches in the World Championship to earn full professional status. In the event he did not even have to play one match as his two prospective opponents both withdrew, leaving him at number 102 without hitting a ball.

THE NEW NAMES FOR 1988/89

Young talent is the life-blood of any sport and snooker's future is assured with so many top-class players in the amateur ranks. Professional snooker guarantees that the best young amateurs have a chance to win their place in the pro ranks with a series of pro ticket tournaments. The top eight at the end of the series joined the world amateur champion and the English amateur champion and have the right to challenge the bottom ten in the professional rankings for their places. If successful, the amateurs become professionals and the professionals step down – usually to non-tournament status which means that they can still play in the Embassy World Championship.

Last season three professionals – John Hargreaves, Bert Demarco and Mike Hines – opted for non-tournament status without taking part in the play-offs. Because of this, world amateur champion Darren Morgan, English amateur champion Mark Rowing and Mark Johnston-Allen, who finished second in the pro ticket events, automatically gained their professional status. Morgan also finished top of the pro ticket. Seven professionals took part in the play-off matches with only one, Exeter's Robert Marshall, maintaining his full place as a professional. Marshall took on Dartmouth's Darren Clarke who finished ninth in the pro ticket series, but Clarke, who survived a motorbike accident in 1987, was unable to overcome Marshall and went down 10–5. If Clarke had won, he would have become the world's current youngest professional at eighteen.

DARREN MORGAN

Date of birth: 3 May 1966   *Star sign:* Taurus

Darren Morgan, from Cwmfelinfach, South Wales, finished top of the pro ticket series but he had already earned his right to become a professional by winning the World Amateur Championship in India in 1987. Morgan's talents have already been recognized by Ian Doyle who looks after Stephen Hendry and Mike Hallett. Doyle signed Morgan in February 1988 and the Scottish businessman is convinced that Morgan has a great future. 'It is a fantastic feeling to know I have made it – to become a professional,' said a happy Morgan.

MARK ROWING

Date of birth: 24 March 1966   *Star sign:* Aries

Doncaster's Mark Rowing overcame Coventry's Sean Lanigan 13–11 in the final of the BCE English Amateur Championship in 1987. That put Rowing in the professional ranks. A former world amateur champion, he took up the game seriously only five years ago when he left school. 'I dreamed of winning the English Amateur but that final was a real struggle,' he said. Now he can embark on his professional career with confidence.

NICK TERRY

Date of birth: 15 September 1967   *Star sign:* Virgo

Nick Terry won the final pro ticket event which took him into third place in the series. He had to face a play-off match with Maurice Parkin but came home a convincing 10–5 winner. Terry is certainly a celebrity back home in his native Dagenham as they have named a snooker club the Nick Terry Social and Snooker Centre. He is a director and the centre boasts ten tables on the second floor and one special table in the lounge with a plaque bearing the name of world number 1, Steve Davis. Davis, who comes from the nearby Matchroom stable, is certainly a hit with Terry who said, 'I love to watch Steve as you can learn so much from him. I have never played him but it would be a privilege to be beaten by him and give me the experience that all players coming into the game need.'

Happy trio: Nick Terry celebrates another victory with his proud parents.

STEVE CAMPBELL

Date of birth: 7 March 1966   *Star sign:* Pisces

Steve Campbell, from Birmingham, recorded his best performance in the pro ticket events at Brean Sands in June 1987 when he finished runner-up. 'This was the second occasion that I entered the pro ticket tournament and I was determined to do well,' he said. Campbell is a resident professional at the Kings Winsford Snooker Club and had to tackle Canadian Paul Thornley in the play-offs. He marched into an 8–1 lead, at which point Thornley had had enough and conceded the match.

IAN GRAHAM

Date of birth: 17 February 1967   *Star sign:* Aquarius

Ian Graham did not win any of the pro ticket events but was consistent enough to force a place in the play-offs. This young player from Watford obtained four points at Prestatyn's spring tournament, six at Puckpool, four at Brean Sands and six at Prestatyn's autumn get-together. His play-off was against Welshman Clive Everton and Graham was delighted with his 10–1 hammering of the BBC commentator.

TONY WILSON

Date of birth: 12 February 1964   *Star sign:* Aquarius

Hertfordshire's Tony Wilson, originally from the Isle of Man, has achieved his place in the pro ranks. He is nicknamed 'the Wall', but this 15½-stone young man recovered from a bone marrow disease called osteomyelitis, discovered when he was twelve. At school he was pushed down the stairs, which started the progression of the disease. Eventually he had to have 3 inches taken off both his legs and now has several pins holding his legs together. Despite that, he still stands tall at 6 feet 4 inches.

'At school I played a lot of football, tennis and athletics, but because of the disease I could not carry on,' he said. 'I decided to start playing snooker and I am delighted I did just that.'

Wilson plays at the Greyfriars Snooker Club in Bedford which is owned by fellow professional Mick Fisher; another pro, Nigel Gilbert, also plays at the club.

South African Derek Mienie was Wilson's play-off opponent and Wilson came home a 10–8 winner.

CRAIG EDWARDS

Date of birth: 23 December 1968   *Star sign:* Capricorn

Craig Edwards, from Cleethorpes, finished fifth in the series and has a reputation for setting a target and achieving it. In the 1987 pro ticket tournaments he came through with great pride. He only started playing when he was fifteen and a half, which means that natural ability has played a great part in his progress. 'It was watching snooker on television that convinced me that I wanted to be part of the game. If I can achieve what Steve Davis has done, I will be more than happy,' said a positive-thinking Edwards. 'Snooker is a

career that gives a lot of satisfaction as well as a very good living.'

Edwards's play-off opponent was Derek Heaton who had earned his professional place just one year earlier. But Edwards's dream looked in tatters as Heaton seemed certain to cling on to his professional status when he opened a 8–1 lead. However, he remarkably captured seven frames in a row to draw 8–8 before a bewildered Heaton edged back in front at 9–8. Then Edwards captured the final two frames for a tremendous 10–9 victory.

MARK JOHNSTON-ALLEN

Date of birth: 28 December 1968   *Star sign:* Capricorn

This Bristol youngster has been winning titles for years, including the Avon County Championship for three successive seasons. He has been English junior and senior international champion and, according to his father, David, 'Our house is full of Mark's trophies but we do not

mind the extra dusting.' Younger brother Craig is also progressing well and won the Under-16 title in Pontin's Brean Sands tournament in 1987. Who knows? – Mark and Craig could follow in the footsteps of another brother combination, Joe and Fred Davis.

MICK PRICE

Date of birth: 2 June 1966   *Star sign:* Gemini

Nuneaton's Mick Price finished fourth in the series and, wearing his Dennis Taylor 'upside-down' glasses, has earned several titles. But none of those victories has given him as much pleasure as turning professional. 'I have been playing snooker since I was five and now I have achieved my goal – to play against all top-class players I have admired for years,' he said. Price's final hurdle was in the play-offs against Blackpool's David Greaves, a professional since 1973. But Price was always on top and came home 10–4.

Taylor-made: (right) Mick Price, complete with his Dennis Taylor-style 'upside-down' glasses.

Making his mark: (below) Mark Johnston-Allen prepares for his first professional season.

	Winfield Masters	Carling Champions	Langs Supreme Scottish Masters	Fidelity Unit Trusts International	Rothmans Grand Prix	Dutch Open	World Series	Matchroom Champion of Champions	Tennents UK Open
1 S. Davis	–	–	–	40,000 4,000(HB)	4,500	–	47,000	12,500	70,000
2 S. Hendry	21,800	5,825	3,125	12,000	60,000	–	19,000	–	1,531.25
3 Dennis Taylor	–	12,500 2,000(HB)	3,125 1,500(HB)	1,937.50	36,000	–	63,000	50,000 2,500(HB)	3,390.62
4 J. White	–	–	5,000	3,000	2,906.25	–	33,000	7,500	42,000 7,000(HB)
5 T. Griffiths	–	–	10,000	1,937.50	4,500	–	27,000	7,500	10,500
6 J. Parrott	4,367	–	–	3,000	18,000 6,000(HB)	909	–	–	10,500
7 C. Thorburn	4,367	–	5,000	24,000	2,906.25	–	13,000	–	10,500
8 M. Hallett	13,100	–	–	12,000	1,312.50	–	–	–	10,500
9 N. Foulds	–	5,825	3,125	1,937.50	1,312.50	–	20,000	12,500	1,531.25
10 W. Thorne	–	–	–	1,937.50	9,000	–	11,000	25,000	21,000 6,750(HB)
11 J. Johnson	4,367	8,500	16,000	875	2,906.25	–	5,000	–	21,000
12 A. Knowles	2,183	–	–	3,000	9,000	–	5,000	–	5,250
13 A. Higgins	8,743 1,310(HB)	–	3,125	–	–	1,818	–	–	5,250
14 D. Reynolds	2,183	–	–	875	1,312.50	606	–	–	1,531.25
15 A. Meo	–	–	–	1,937.50	1,312.50	–	7,000	7,500	3,390.62
16 P. Francisco	–	–	–	875	18,000	–	–	–	3,390.62
17 A. Drago	–	–	–	875 1,000(HB)	4,500 1,500(HB)	–	–	–	1,531.25
18 E. Charlton	7,424	–	–	6,000	4,500	–	–	–	1,531.25
19 S. James	–	–	–	3,000	1,312.50	–	–	–	–
20 S. Francisco	–	–	–	3,000	2,906.25	–	–	–	5,250
21 E. Hughes	2,183	–	–	6,000	1,312.50	606	–	–	3,390.62
22 M. Clark	–	–	–	3,000	2,906.25	–	–	–	–
23 S. Newbury	–	–	–	1,937.50	9,000	–	–	–	1,531.25
24 R. Williams	–	–	–	875	1,312.50	–	–	–	1,531.25
25 J. Campbell	2,183	–	–	875	1,312.50	–	–	–	5,250
26 D. Mountjoy	–	–	–	875	1,312.50	–	–	–	1,531.25
27 J. Virgo	–	–	–	6,000	2,906.25	–	–	–	3,390.62
28 C. Wilson	–	–	–	1,937.50	4,500	–	–	–	3,390.62
29 D. O'Kane	2,183	–	–	875	–	–	–	–	5,250
30 M. Macleod	–	–	–	875	1,312.50	–	–	–	1,531.25
31 B. West	–	–	–	875	1,312.50	–	–	–	3,390.62
32 R. Chaperon	–	–	–	1,937.50	9,000	–	–	–	1,531.25
33 D. Roe	–	–	–	1,937.50	2,906.25	–	–	–	5,250
34 J. O'Boye	–	–	–	6,000	–	–	–	–	1,531.25
35 W. King	2,183	–	–	875	–	–	–	–	1,531.25
36 J. Wych	–	–	–	1,937.50	2,906.25	–	–	–	3,390.62
37 D. Martin	–	–	–	875	1,312.50	–	–	–	1,531.25
38 W. Jones	–	–	–	1,937.50	1,312.50	–	–	–	1,531.25
39 S. Longworth	–	–	–	1,937.50	1,312.50	–	–	–	3,390.62
40 J. Spencer	–	–	–	1,937.50	1,312.50	–	–	–	1,531.25
41 A. Chappel	–	–	–	875	2,906.25	–	–	–	5,250
42 David Taylor	–	–	–	1,937.50	1,312.50	–	–	–	3,390.62
43 K. Stevens	–	–	–	875	2,906.25	–	–	–	3,390.62
44 T. Murphy	–	–	–	875	–	–	–	–	3,390.62
45 G. Cripsey	–	–	–	875	4,500	–	–	–	1,531.25
46 W. Werbeniuk	–	–	–	1,937.50	2,906.25	–	–	–	1,531.25
47 D. Fowler	–	–	–	875	1,312.50	–	–	–	5,250
48 R. Foldvari	4,367	–	–	1,937.50	1,312.50	–	–	–	–
49 John Rea	–	–	–	875	1,312.50	–	–	–	1,531.25
50 Gary Wilkinson	–	–	–	875	4,500	–	–	–	1,531.25

*Fined £10,000 for failing drugs test at this event.
HB=high break

Money Last Season

Foster's World Doubles	Mercantile Credit Classic	Benson and Hedges Masters	National Titles	MIM Britannia Unit Trusts British Open	Fersina Windows World Cup	Benson and Hedges Irish Masters	Kent China Cup	Embassy World	Rothmans Matchroom League	TOTAL
1,217	50,000	56,000 5,000(HB)	–	1,312.50	13,333.33	25,748.86	–	95,000	70,000	495,611.69
30,000 3,125(HB)	7,500	–	9,000 1,250(HB)	60,000 6,000(HB)	4,166.66 1,666.66(HB)	–	–	7,125	30,000	283,114.57
17,500	7,500 5,000	6,000	2,750 350(HB)	2,906.25	2,500	3,969.62	–	7,125	9,000	240,553.99
1,217	3,750	12,000	1,187.50 250(HB)	9,000	13,333.33	6,437.22	–	28,500	17,000	193,081.30
4,375	7,500	12,000	9,000 1,000(HB)	2,906.25	2,500	10,728.69 3,004.01(HB)	–	57,000	15,000	186,451.45
4,375	30,000	18,000	1,187.50	18,000	–	–	35,000 5,000(HB)	7,125	–	161,463.50
17,500	2,421.87	12,000	2,830.18 235.84(HB)	8,000*	2,500	6,437.22	–	28,500	13,000	153,198.36
30,000 3,125(HB)	1,093.75	32,000	2,375	36,000	–	–	–	7,125	–	148,631.25
4.375	2,421.87	6,000	9,000	4,500	13,333.33	15,449.32	–	14,250	20,000	135,560.77
1,217	2,421.87	6,000	2,375	4,500	–	3,969.62	–	7,125	25,000	127,295.99
4,375	2,421.87	18,000	4,750	4,500	–	6,437.22	8,750	7,125	5,000	120,007.34
4,375	15,000	6,000	2,375	2,906.25	–	6,437.22	12,500	14,250	–	88,276.47
2,187.50	3,750	12,000	625	1,312.50	2,500	10,728.69	8,750	4,007.81	–	66,107.50
4,375	2,421.87	6,000	15,000	1,312.50	–	–	12,500	4,007.81	–	52,124.93
1,217	2,421.87	–	2,375	1,312.50	–	–	–	3,117.19	11,000 5,000(HB)	47,584.18
8,750	3,750	–	–	2,906.25	–	–	–	4,007.81	–	41,679.68
1,217	2,421.87	–	–	1,312.50	4,166.66	–	8,750	14,250	–	41,524.28
2,187.50	1,093.75	–	1,333.33	1,312.50	8,333.33	–	–	7,125	–	40,840.66
8,750	1,093.75	–	–	2,906.25	–.	–	–	14,250 9,500(HB)	–	40,812.50
8,750	3,750	6,000	–	2,906.25	4,166.66	–	–	4,007.81	–	40,736.97
2,187.50	1,093.75	–	150	1,312.50	2,500	3,969.62	8,750	3,117.19	–	36,572.68
2,187.50	3,750	–	562.50	1,312.50	–	–	20,000	1,632.81	–	35,351.56
1,217	15,000	–	625	1,312.50	–	–	–	3,117.19	–	33,740.44
2,187.50	1,093.75	6,000	1,187.50	9,000	–	3,969.62	–	4,007.81	–	31,164.93
2,187.50	1,093.75	–	888.89	2,906.25	8,333.33	–	–	4,007.81	–	29,038.03
2,187.50	2,421.87	6,000	2,250	1,312.50	2,500	–	–	7,125	–	27,515.62
2,187.50	3,750	–	1,187.50	2,906.25	–	–	–	4,007.81	–	26,335.93
2,187.50	2,421.87	–	2,250	2,906.25	2,500	–	–	4,007.81	–	26,101.55
4,375	–	–	–	9,000	4,166.66	–	–	–	–	25,849.66
2,187.50	1,093.75	–	4,500	4,500	4,166.66 1,666.66(HB)	–	–	3,117.19	–	24,950.51
1,217	3,750	–	4,750 1,250(HB)	2,906.25	–	–	–	4,007.81	–	23,459.18
1,217	1,093.75 1,250(HB)	–	471.70	2,906.25	–	–	–	4,007.81	–	23,415.26
8,750	–	–	–	4,500	–	–	–	–	–	23,343.75
1,217	1,093.75	–	1,250	9,000	2,500	–	–	–	–	22,592.00
2,187.50	–	–	2,222.22 222.22(HB)	–	8,333.33	–	–	4,007.81	–	21.562.33
4,375	–	–	801.89	1,312.50	2,500	–	–	1,632.81	–	18,856.57
1,217	7,500	–	1,187.50	1,312.50	–	–	–	3,117.19	–	18,052.94
2,187.50	–	–	5,500	1,312.50	–	–	–	4,007.81	–	17,789.06
1,217	2,421.87	–	1,187.50	1,312.50	–	–	–	4,007.81	–	16,787.30
1,217	2,421.87	–	562.50	4,500	–	–	–	3,117.19	–	16,599.81
1,217	1,093.75	–	625	1,312.50	–	–	–	3,117.19	–	16,396.69
2,187.50	2,421.87	–	562.50	1,312.50	–	–	–	3,117.19	–	16,242.18
2,187.50	1,093.75	–	1,037.74	–	–	–	–	4,007.81	–	15,498.67
1,217	3,750	–	625	1,312.50	2,500	–	–	1,632.81	–	15,302.93
1,217	1,093.75	–	–	2,906.25	–	–	–	3,117.19	–	15,240.44
1,217	1,093.75	–	–	–	2,500	–	–	4,007.81	–	15,193.56
1,217	–	–	1,187.50	1,312.50	–	–	–	4,007.81	–	15,162.31
1,217	–	–	888.89	1,312.50	–	–	–	3,117.19	–	14,152.58
150	1,093.75	–	2,250	–	4,166.66 1,666.66(HB)	–	–	–	–	13,045.82
–	–	–	562.50	4,500	–	–	–	–	–	11,968.75

	Winfield Masters	Carling Champions	Langs Supreme Scottish Masters	Fidelity Unit Trusts International	Rothmans Grand Prix	Dutch Open	World Series	Matchroom Champion of Champions	Tennents UK Open
51 G. Miles	–	–	–	–	1,312.50	–	–	–	3,390.62
52 A. Jones	–	–	–	–	1,312.50	–	–	–	1,531.25
53 R. Reardon	–	–	–	875	1,312.50	–	–	–	1,531.25
54 R. Edmonds	–	–	–	–	2,906.25	–	–	–	3,390.62
55 M. Bennett	–	–	–	875	1,312.50	–	–	–	–
56 P. Browne	–	–	–	–	–	–	–	–	–
57 M. Smith	–	–	–	–	–	–	–	–	3,390.62
58 F. Davis	–	–	–	–	–	–	–	–	1,531.25
59 M. Morra	–	–	–	875	–	–	–	–	–
60 J. Bear	–	–	–	–	1,312.50	–	–	–	1,531.25
61 J. McLaughlin	–	–	–	–	1,312.50	–	–	–	–
62 L. Dodd	–	–	–	–	1,312.50	–	–	–	1,531.25
63 K. Owers	–	–	–	875	–	–	–	–	–
64 J. Chambers	–	–	–	–	2,906.25	–	–	–	1,531.25
65 D. Gilbert	–	–	–	3,000	–	–	–	–	–
66 J. Wright	–	–	–	875	1,312.50	–	–	–	–
67 S. Duggan	–	–	–	–	–	–	–	–	1,531.25
68 B. Oliver	–	–	–	–	–	–	–	–	1,531.25
69 N. Gilbert	–	–	–	3,000	–	–	–	–	1,531.25
70 P. Gibson	–	–	–	875	2,906.25	–	–	–	–
71 J. van Rensburg	–	–	–	–	1,312.50	–	–	–	–
72 M. Bradley	–	–	–	875	–	–	–	–	–
72 M. Wildman	–	–	–	875	–	–	–	–	–
74 C. Roscoe	–	–	–	875	–	–	–	–	–
75 P. Houlihan	–	–	–	–	2,906.25	–	–	–	–
76 M. Gauvreau	–	–	–	–	1,312.50	–	–	–	1,531.25
77 M. Fisher	–	–	–	–	4,500	–	–	–	–
78 R. Harris	–	–	–	–	–	–	–	–	–
79 Glen Wilkinson	2,183	–	–	–	1,312.50	–	–	–	–
80 R. Bales	–	–	–	–	2,906.25	–	–	–	–
81 B. Rowswell	–	–	–	–	–	–	–	–	–
82 E. Sinclair	–	–	–	875	–	–	–	–	–
83 M. Gibson	–	–	–	–	–	–	–	–	–
84 J. Donnelly	–	–	–	–	–	–	–	–	–
85 E. Lawlor	–	–	–	–	–	–	–	–	1,531.25
86 V. Harris	–	–	–	–	–	–	–	–	3,390.62
87 I. Williamson	–	–	–	875	–	–	–	–	–
88 R. Grace	–	–	–	875	–	–	–	–	–
89 P. Medati	–	–	–	–	–	–	–	–	–
90 J. Dunning	–	–	–	–	–	–	–	–	1,531.25
91 B. Kelly	–	–	–	–	–	–	–	–	–
92 P. Morgan	2,183	–	–	–	–	–	–	–	–
93 P. Watchorn	–	–	–	–	–	–	–	–	1,531.25
94 A. Kearney	–	–	–	–	1,312.50	–	–	–	–
95 G. Rigitano	–	–	–	–	–	–	–	–	–
96 A. Robidoux	–	–	–	–	–	–	–	–	–
97 M. Darrington	–	–	–	–	–	–	–	–	–
97 J. Meadowcroft	–	–	–	–	1,312.50	–	–	–	–
99 I. Black	–	–	–	–	–	–	–	–	–
100 B. Demarco	–	–	–	–	–	–	–	–	–
101 G. Scott	–	–	–	–	–	–	–	–	–
101 T. Whitthread	–	–	–	–	–	–	–	–	–
103 Jack Rea	–	–	–	875	–	–	–	–	–
104 J. Caggianello	–	–	–	–	–	–	–	–	–
104 F. Jonik	–	–	–	–	–	–	–	–	–
104 G. Watson	–	–	–	–	–	–	–	–	–
107 E. McLaughlin	–	–	–	–	–	–	–	–	–
108 D. Greaves	–	–	–	–	–	–	–	–	–
108 R. Marshall	–	–	–	–	–	–	–	–	–
110 G. Jenkins	–	–	–	–	–	–	–	–	–
111 B. Mikkelsen	–	–	–	–	–	–	–	–	–
112 D. Hughes	–	–	–	–	–	–	–	–	–
112 J. Smith	–	–	–	–	–	–	–	–	–
114 I. Anderson	–	–	–	–	–	–	–	–	–
115 W. Saunderson	–	–	–	–	–	–	–	–	–
115 P. Thornley	–	–	–	–	–	–	–	–	–
117 L. Condo	–	–	–	–	–	–	–	–	–
118 P. Burke	–	–	–	–	–	–	–	–	–
118 P. Fagan	–	–	–	–	–	–	–	–	–
118 J. Fitzmaurice	–	–	–	–	–	–	–	–	–
118 G. Foulds	–	–	–	–	–	–	–	–	–
118 A. Harris	–	–	–	–	–	–	–	–	–
118 D. Heaton	–	–	–	–	–	–	–	–	–
118 D. Sheehan	–	–	–	–	–	–	–	–	–

Foster's World Doubles	Mercantile Credit Classic	Benson and Hedges Masters	National Titles	MIM Britannia Unit Trusts British Open	Fersina Windows World Cup	Benson and Hedges Irish Masters	Kent China Cup	Embassy World	Rothmans Matchroom League	TOTAL
2,187.50	–	–	–	1,312.50	–	–	–	1,632.81	–	9,835.93
1,217	1,093.75	–	–	4,500	–	–	–	–	–	9,654.50
1,217	1,093.75	–	625	2,906.25	–	–	–	–	–	9,560.75
1,217	1,093.75	–	–	–	–	–	–	–	–	8,607.62
150	2,421.87	–	625	–	–	–	–	3,117.19	–	8,501.56
150	–	–	1,250	2,906.25	2,500	–	–	1,632.81	–	8,439.06
1,217	1,093.75	–	562.50	–	–	–	–	1,632.81	–	7,896.68
–	1,093.75	–	562.50	1,312.50	–	–	–	3,117.19	–	7,617.19
150	1,093.75	–	1,037.74	1,312.50 1,500(HB)	–	–	–	1,632.81	–	7,601.80
150	–	–	1,650.94	1,312.50	–	–	–	1,632.81	–	7,590.00
150	1,093.75	–	5,000	–	–	–	–	–	–	7,556.25
1,217	1,093.75	–	562.50	–	–	–	–	1,632.81	–	7,349.81
1,217	2,421.87	–	1,187.50	–	–	–	–	1,632.81	–	7,334.18
2,187.50	–	–	562.50	–	–	–	–	–	–	7,187.50
1,217	1,093.75	–	562.50	1,312.50	–	–	–	–	–	7,185.75
150	1,093.75	–	562.50	–	–	–	–	3,117.19	–	7,110.94
1,217	–	–	562.50	–	–	–	–	3,117.19	–	6,427.94
150	1,093.75	–	–	–	–	–	–	3,117.19	–	5,892.19
–	– –	–	–	1,312.50	–	–	–	–	–	5,843.75
150	–	–	–	–	–	–	–	1,632.81	–	5,564.06
–	1,093.75	–	3,056	–	–	–	–	–	–	5,462.25
1,217	1,093.75	–	–	–	–	–	–	1,632.81	–	4,818.56
1,217	1,093.75	–	–	–	–	–	–	1,632.81	–	4,818.56
–	2,421.87	–	–	1,312.50	–	–	–	–	–	4,609.37
–	–	–	–	–	–	–	–	1,632.81	–	4,539.06
1,217	–	–	471.70	–	–	–	–	–	–	4,532.45
–	–	–	–	–	–	–	–	–	–	4,500.00
1,217	–	–	–	–	–	–	–	3,117.19	–	4,334.19
150	–	–	555.56	–	–	–	–	–	–	4,201.06
1,217	–	–	–	–	–	–	–	–	–	4,123.25
–	1,093.75	–	–	2,906.25	–	–	–	–	–	4,000.00
150	–	–	1,250	–	–	–	–	1,632.81	–	3,907.81
150	–	–	2,250	1,312.50	–	–	–	–	–	3,712.50
–	2,421.87	–	1,250	–	–	–	–	–	–	3,671.87
150	–	–	562.50	1,312.50	–	–	–	–	–	3,556.25
150	–	–	–	–	–	–	–	–	–	3,540.62
1,217	–	–	–	1,312.50	–	–	–	–	–	3,404.50
150	–	–	2,083	–	–	–	–	–	–	3,108.00
150	–	–	–	2,906.25	–	–	–	–	–	3,056.25
–	–	–	–	1,312.50	–	–	–	–	–	2,843.75
–	–	–	150	–	–	–	–	2,375(HB)	–	2,525.00
–	–	–	333.33	–	–	–	–	–	–	2,516.33
–	–	–	625	–	–	–	–	–	–	2,156.25
–	–	–	625	–	–	–	–	–	–	1,937.50
150	1,093.75	–	471.70	–	–	–	–	–	–	1,715.45
–	–	–	–	–	–	–	–	1,632.81	–	1,632.81
150	–	–	–	1,312.50	–	–	–	–	–	1,462.50
150	–	–	–	–	–	–	–	–	–	1,462.50
150	–	–	1,250	–	–	–	–	–	–	1,400.00
–	–	–	1,250	–	–	–	–	–	–	1,250.00
150	1,093.75	–	–	–	–	–	–	–	–	1,243.75
150	1,093.75	–	–	–	–	–	–	–	–	1,243.75
–	–	–	150	–	–	–	–	–	–	1,025.00
–	–	–	801.89	–	–	–	–	–	–	801.89
–	–	–	801.89	–	–	–	–	–	–	801.89
–	–	–	801.89	–	–	–	–	–	–	801.89
–	–	–	750	–	–	–	–	–	–	750
150	–	–	562.50	–	–	–	–	–	–	712.50
150	–	–	562.50	–	–	–	–	.–	–	712.50
150	–	–	555.56	–	–	–	–	–	–	705.56
150	–	–	471.70	–	–	–	–	–	–	621.70
–	–	–	562.50	–	–	–	–	–	–	562.50
–	–	–	562.50	–	–	–	–	–	–	562.50
–	–	–	555.56	–	–	–	–	–	–	555.56
–	–	–	471.70	–	–	–	–	–	–	471.70
–	–	–	471.70	–	–	–	–	–	–	471.70
–	–	–	333.33	–	–	–	–	–	–	333.33
–	–	–	150	–	–	–	–	–	–	150.00
–	–	–	150	–	–	–	–	–	–	150.00
150	–	–	–	–	–	–	–	–	–	150.00
150	–	–	–	–	–	–	–	–	–	150.00
150	–	–	–	–	–	–	–	–	–	150.00
150	–	–	–	–	–	–	–	–	–	150.00
–	–	–	150	–	–	–	–	–	–	150.00

THE TOP THIRTY-TWO – A LOOK AT LIFE ON AND OFF THE TABLE

STEVE DAVIS

World ranking: number 1   *Prize money:* £495,611.69

Full name: Steve Davis
Date of birth: 22 August 1957
Star sign: Leo
Height: 6 feet 1½ inches
Weight: 11½ stone
Colour of eyes: Grey
Family: Mum Jean, dad Bill and brother Keith
Home: 200-acre farm in Essex
Turned pro: 1978
Hobbies: Record collecting and being interesting
Music: Rhythm and blues, soul
Car: None
Favourite food: Marmite
Favourite drink: Kronenbourg 1664
Greatest achievement: Winning my first world title in 1981
Biggest disappointment: Losing 18–17 on the black ball in the final frame of the world final to Dennis Taylor in 1985
Ambition: Never had one
Favourite TV: Any good comedy series
Whom do you most admire? People who can sing well
Favourite holiday spot: My favourite as a kid was Hemsby near Great Yarmouth
Previous jobs: None
Do you collect anything? Records
Favourite author: Tom Sharpe

Country boy: Steve Davis relaxes on his Essex farm.

One wish: what would it be? To be able to sing like Solomon Burke
Nickname: The Nugget, Ginger Magician, Interesting
Dislikes: Dirty glasses – it ruins the beer

Last season, it was easier to list the titles Davis didn't win as he embarked on another trophy-hunting campaign that earned him seven individual titles, a share of the World Cup and, to round it off, a £50,000 necklace in a promotional challenge match, the Heritage Classic. Davis set a new record in winning four ranking tournaments in one season, including the World Championship. He also won the two Benson and Hedges titles and the Rothmans Matchroom League, and there was another record when his total earnings of £495,000 easily eclipsed the £367,000 he had earned twelve months earlier. He also branched out as a music promoter, bringing French group Magma over to the UK for a short series of concerts. The perfect ambassador for the sport, he still lives with his mum and dad on a 200-acre estate in Essex. His one disappointment was losing the Foster's World Doubles title with regular partner Tony Meo.

JIMMY WHITE

World ranking: number 2   *Prize money:* £193,081.30

Full name: James Warren White
Date of birth: 2 May 1962
Star sign: Taurus
Height: 5 feet 9 inches
Weight: 11 stone 10 lbs
Colour of eyes: Blue
Family: Wife Maureen and daughters Lauren and Ashley
Home: Town house in Wimbledon
Turned pro: 1981
Hobbies: Golf and horse racing
Music: Eric Clapton, most good music
Car: BMW
Favourite food: Seafood
Favourite film star: Jack Nicholson, Bob Hoskins, Robert De Niro, Al Pacino
Favourite colour: Ocean blue
Greatest achievement: Winning the world amateur title at eighteen
Biggest disappointment: Losing the 1984 Embassy World final 18–16 to Steve Davis
Ambition: To win the world title and be world number 1 at the same time; to play football for Chelsea
Favourite TV: Any comedy
Whom do you most admire? Sugar Ray Leonard
Favourite holiday spot: Like to explore
Do you collect anything? Trophies
Favourite author: Stephen King
One wish: what would it be? A more peaceful world
Nickname: The Whirlwind
Dislikes: Snakes

Jimmy White confessed before the World Championship that he had had a bad season, reaching only one major final – the Tennents UK Open where he was beaten 16–14 by Steve Davis. White has a habit of playing in classic matches and losing them, but that changed at the World Championship when, after one of the most exciting encounters for many years, he overcame Scottish teenager Stephen Hendry 13–12 in the second round. He went on to reach the semi-final where he lost to Terry Griffiths. At sixteen he was the youngest English amateur champion and at eighteen the youngest world amateur champion. White is taking over the mantle from Higgins as the 'People's Champion', and if he were to win the World Championship it would be one of the most popular successes of all time. Last season wife Maureen presented him with their second daughter, Ashley. Off the circuit, Jimmy has become a golf fanatic.

NEAL FOULDS

World Ranking: number 3   *Prize money:* £135,560.77

Full name: Neal Robert Foulds
Date of birth: 13 July 1963
Star sign: Cancer
Height: 6 feet 2 inches
Weight: 14 stone
Colour of eyes: Blue
Home: Perivale
Turned pro: 1983
Hobbies: Racing greyhounds and playing cricket
Music: Elvis Costello, Morrisey, Roger Waters
Car: Sierra Cosworth
Favourite food: Indian
Favourite film star: Jack Nicholson
Favourite colour: Black
Greatest achievement: Winning the BCE International in 1986
Biggest disappointment: Losing the final of the Dulux British Open in 1987
Ambition: To be world champion
Favourite TV: Any sports programmes
Whom do you most admire? Anyone at the top of their sport
Favourite holiday spot: USA
Previous jobs: Worked in an office for one year after leaving school
Do you collect anything? Parking tickets!
One wish: What would it be? To give up my obsession for parking on yellow lines!

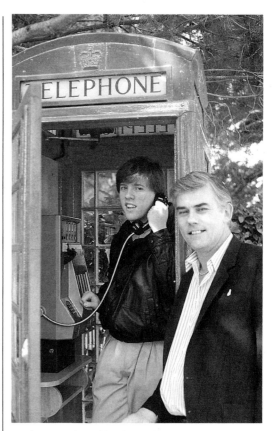

Buzby: Neal Foulds phones home watched by dad Geoff.

Nickname: Buzby (I'm always on the telephone)
Dislikes: Very good snooker players, traffic wardens

Neal Foulds enjoyed a spectacular rise to fame in the 1986/87 season with a jump of ten places to number 3. He stays at number 3 this season but was disappointed with his overall performances in the major ranking tournaments when, apart from in the World Championship, he never progressed past the fifth round. He is a young man of immense talent and his form improved towards the end of the season as he finished runner-up in the English Championship and the Benson and Hedges Irish Masters, and then earned a quarter-final placing in the World Championship. Away from snooker Foulds has an intense love of greyhound racing and is a cricket enthusiast. His father Geoff is also a professional snooker player.

STEPHEN HENDRY

World ranking: number 4   *Prize money:* £283,114.57

Full name: Stephen Gordon Hendry
Date of birth: 13 January 1969
Star sign: Capricorn
Height: 5 feet 11 inches
Weight: 9 stone
Colour of eyes: Blue
Family: Mum Irene, dad Gordon and brother Keith
Home: Semi-detached villa
Turned pro: 1985
Hobbies: Golf and music
Music: Simple Minds, Phil Collins
Car: Mercedes 190E 2.3
Favourite food: Chinese
Favourite film star: Rutger Hauer
Favourite colour: Black
Greatest achievement: Beating Steve Davis in the Rothmans Grand Prix in 1987
Biggest disappointment: Losing to Joe Johnson 13–12 in the quarter-finals of the World Championship in 1987 and to Jimmy White by the same score in 1988
Ambition: To be world champion and number 1
Favourite TV: 'Comic Relief'
Whom do you most admire? Phil Collins
Favourite holiday spot: Anywhere without a snooker table
Do you collect anything? Records and tapes
Nickname: Spike
Dislikes: Photography sessions

Stephen Hendry was the highest-paid teenage sportsman in Britain last season with estimated earnings of £600,000. He drives a £35,000 Mercedes, but manager Ian Doyle ensures that money doesn't go to his head by giving him a weekly allowance. Hendry entered the snooker record books at the Rothmans Grand Prix when he became the youngest ever winner of a professional title at eighteen by beating Dennis Taylor in the final. He then went on to win the MIM Britannia Unit Trusts British Open but was upset at his World Championship performance when he lost 13–12 to Jimmy White in the second round. He continued his meteoric rise up the rankings – last year he moved twenty-eight places and this season has jumped from number 23 to number 4. Last season's target was a place in the top eight – now White's number 2 spot will be his minimum ambition. He also won the Foster's World Doubles with stablemate Mike Hallett.

TERRY GRIFFITHS

World ranking: number 5   *Prize money:* £186,451.45

Full name: Terence Martin Griffiths
Date of birth: 16 October 1947
Star sign: Libra
Height: 5 feet 10 inches
Weight: 11 stone
Colour of eyes: Green
Family: Wife Annette and two sons
Home: Pembrey
Turned pro: 1978
Hobbies: Golf
Music: Dire Straits
Car: Citroen

Fan appeal: World finalist Terry Griffiths and a present from an admirer.

Favourite food: Chips (although I'm always watching my weight)
Favourite colour: Blue
Greatest achievement: Winning the world title at my first attempt in 1979
Ambition: None
Favourite TV: Sport
Whom do you most admire? My wife
Favourite holiday spot: Florida

Previous jobs: Miner, bus conductor, postman, insurance agent
Do you collect anything? Disappointments
Favourite author: Sidney Sheldon
One wish: what would it be? Happiness
Nickname: Snowy
Dislikes: Incompetent people

Terry Griffiths has enjoyed a busy year. Not only has he produced his normal consistent performances on the table but he has also opened a brand-new snooker club in Llanelli and has had a new house built in nearby Pembrey. Just for good measure he reached the final of the Embassy World Championship for the first time since his remarkable triumph in 1979 in his first year as a professional, but had to settle for runner-up spot at Sheffield after losing 18–11 to Steve Davis. Arguably the most dedicated practice player on the circuit, he will lock himself away for hours to improve his game. Amazingly Griffiths's last title was in 1982 but he has maintained his position in the world top ten. Last season he won the Welsh title for the third time in four years.

CLIFF THORBURN

World ranking: number 6   *Prize money:* £153,198.36

Full name: Clifford Charles Devlin Thorburn
Date of birth: 16 January 1948
Star sign: Capricorn
Height: 6 feet 2 inches
Weight: 12 stone 10 lbs
Colour of eyes: Blue
Family: Wife Barbara and two sons Jamie and Andrew
Home: House in North London
Turned pro: 1973
Hobbies: Golf, chess, reading spy and mystery novels, tennis
Music: Rhythm and blues
Car: Mercedes

Favourite food: Fish
Greatest achievement: Winning the world title in 1980 and scoring the first 147 in the World Championship in 1983
Biggest disappointment: Losing the World Championship final to Steve Davis in 1983
Whom do you most admire? Jack Nicklaus
Favourite holiday spot: Mexico
Previous jobs: None
One wish: what would it be? Happiness for the family
Nickname: The Grinder, the Methodical Mountie

Cliff Thorburn missed the first two ranking tournaments this season after being banned, fined £10,000 and deducted two ranking points after small traces of cocaine were found during his drugs test at last season's British Open. The loss of those ranking points meant that Thorburn changed places with Terry Griffiths and slipped one place to number 6. Thorburn played in the World Championship last season and reached the semi-final after he went to the High Court to get an adjournment on the disciplinary hearing into his failed drugs test. He won the world title in 1980 and then in 1983 went into the record books as the only player to score a 147 in the World Championship. He remains the only overseas player to win the world title.

JOHN PARROTT

World ranking: number 7   *Prize money:* £161,463.50

Full name: John Stephen Parrott
Date of birth: 11 May 1964
Star sign: Taurus
Height: 6 feet 2 inches
Weight: 13½ stone
Colour of eyes: Blue-green
Family: Confirmed bachelor
Home: Gateacre, Liverpool
Turned pro: 1982
Hobbies: Watching football, horse racing, golf (I'm a seven handicapper)

Music: Funk, soul
Car: BMW
Favourite food: Chinese
Favourite film star: Humphrey Bogart, Woody Allen
Favourite colour: Blue
Greatest achievement: Reaching the final of the 1988 Mercantile Credit Classic
Biggest disappointment: Missing a vital red when I was 11–10 ahead in that final against Steve Davis

Ambition: To be continuously happy in life
Favourite TV: 'Cheers', 'Bread'
Whom do you most admire? Steve Davis
Favourite holiday spot: Barbados
Previous jobs: None. I never did a stroke
Do you collect anything? Colds
Favourite author: Many – Robert Ludlum, Agatha Christie
Nickname: JP
Dislikes: Smoking, ignorant people

Going places: John Parrott and manager Phil Miller.

John Parrott last season emerged as a player of true international class. He seemed to be stuck on the brink of the world's top sixteen for a couple of seasons but this year he is firmly established at number 7. Last season was one of total consistency as he reached the last sixteen of the Fidelity Unit Trusts International, the semi-finals of the Rothmans Grand Prix, the MIM Britannia Unit Trusts British Open and the Benson and Hedges Masters, and also the final of the Mercantile Credit Classic. The Classic final, his first as a professional, so nearly earned him the title. But after leading Davis 11–10, he missed a red and Davis recovered to take the crown 13–11. He was being tipped as a possible world champion, but a marathon match saw him go out 13–10 to Canadian Cliff Thorburn in the second round. Parrott has a ready wit and sparkling personality and will be looking for a place in the top four at the end of this season. He lives in Liverpool with his father and is a keen soccer fan.

TONY KNOWLES

World ranking: number 8   *Prize money:* £88,276.47

Smart boy: Tony Knowles, immaculate as ever.

Full name: Anthony Knowles
Date of birth: 13 June 1955
Star sign: Gemini
Height: 6 feet 2 inches
Colour of eyes: Brown
Home: Ambleside, Cumbria
Turned pro: 1980
Hobbies: Waterskiing and tennis
Music: Soul
Car: Granada 2.8 Ghia XI, Ford Cabriolet
Favourite food: Anything and everything
Favourite film star: Robert De Niro
Favourite colour: Burgundy

Greatest achievement: Winning my first major title – the Jameson International Open in 1982
Biggest disappointment: Losing
Ambition: To become world champion
Favourite TV: 'Dallas'
Whom do you most admire? Walter Lindrum
Favourite holiday spot: Marbella
Previous jobs: Far too many to mention
Do you collect anything? Old records, but I'm not an avid collector
Nickname: TK
Dislikes: Inferior playing conditions, sensational journalism

Tony Knowles has dropped just one place on the world rankings after another consistent but unspectacular season. His best performance came in the Mercantile Credit Classic when a semi-final appearance ended with a 9–4 defeat by John Parrott. The World Championship has often been a happy hunting ground for him and he reached the last eight yet again before going down 13–6 to Jimmy White. Knowles likes nothing better than getting back to the seclusion of his country home on the banks of Lake Windermere, though he is also a sun lover and regularly visits his apartment in the Canary Islands. He will be looking this season for his first major title since 1983.

MIKE HALLETT

World ranking: number 9   *Prize money:* £148,631.25

Full name: Michael William Hallett
Date of birth: 6 July 1959
Star sign: Cancer
Height: 5 feet 9 inches
Weight: 12 stone
Colour of eyes: Hazel
Family: Dad Charles and sister Ann
Home: Detached villa in Grimsby
Turned pro: 1979
Hobbies: Golf
Music: Charts, disco
Car: Mercedes 190
Favourite food: Chinese
Favourite film star: Clint Eastwood, Jacqueline Bissett
Favourite colour: Blue
Greatest achievement: Winning the Foster's World Doubles with Stephen Hendry in 1987
Biggest disappointment: Losing to Steve Davis in the final of the Benson and Hedges Masters in 1988
Ambition: To be successful in snooker
Favourite TV: Alternative comedy
Whom do you most admire? Ian Doyle
Are you superstitious? Sometimes
Favourite holiday spot: Mediterranean – Greece
Previous jobs: I was a shipping clerk from the age of sixteen to seventeen
Do you collect anything? Records
One wish: what would it be? To become a millionaire
Nickname: Hammer
Dislikes: Ignorant people

Mike Hallett, who turned professional in 1979, finally made the top sixteen last season. Now, after enjoying the best season of his career, he has made a big step up to the top ten at number 9. He reached the first finals of his career in the Benson and Hedges Masters and the MIM Britannia Unit Trusts British Open but suffered heavy defeats, first at the hands of Steve Davis and then by his stablemate Stephen Hendry. Hallett was one of the most successful men on the circuit and also reached the semi-final of the Fidelity Unit Trusts International and the quarter-finals of the Tennents UK Open. He joined forces with Hendry to take the Foster's World Doubles title – the last time that this event will be played. In the World Championship he was beaten 13–1 by Davis in the second round, but will be hoping to claim his first title this season.

DENNIS TAYLOR

World ranking: number 10   *Prize money:* £240,553.99

Full name: Dennis James Taylor
Date of birth: 19 January 1949
Star sign: Capricorn
Height: 5 feet 9½ inches
Weight: 13 stone
Family: Wife Pat and three children
Home: Detached house in Blackburn
Turned pro: 1971
Hobbies: Golf
Music: Any good music
Car: BMW 750 IL
Favourite food: Cantonese and Indian

Favourite film star: Paul Newman
Favourite colour: Black
Greatest achievement: Winning the world title in 1985
Ambition: Health and happiness for the family
Favourite TV: 'Auf Wiedersehen Pet'
Whom do you most admire? The Pope
Favourite holiday spot: Spain
Previous jobs: Office clerk in transport firm, sales rep for a papermill
Dislikes: Arrogant people

Dennis Taylor made a slight drop down the rankings of two places to number 10. At one stage, at the start of the season, he had won tournaments in Japan, Canada, Ireland and England that gave him £170,000 earnings in just ten weeks. That included a final appearance in the Rothmans Grand Prix where he was beaten 10–7 by Stephen Hendry. In the World Championship he was hammered by Malta's Tony Drago and he was also disappointed at losing his Benson and Hedges Masters title. Of course, the major landmark in Taylor's career was his 1985 World Championship success with an 18–17 last-frame black-ball success over Steve Davis at 12.23 in the morning. Last season he was particularly upset, however, at the way the format was changed for the Fersina Windows World Cup which cost Ireland the chance of winning the title four times in a row. Taylor remains one of the most popular men on the circuit but likes nothing better than to spend a day with his family or on the golf course.

JOE JOHNSON

World ranking: number 11   *Prize money:* £120,007.34

Full name: Joseph Johnson
Date of birth: 29 July 1952
Star sign: Leo

Height: 5 feet 8 inches
Weight: 13 stone
Colour of eyes: Deep brown

Family: Wife Terryll and six children
Turned pro: 1979
Hobbies: Singing with my group, Made in Japan
Music: Older types of music, especially musicals
Car: Mercedes
Favourite food: Indian
Favourite colour: Red
Greatest achievement: Winning the World Championship in 1986
Ambition: To make a hit record
Favourite TV: World Snooker Championships
Whom do you most admire? Elvis Presley
Favourite holiday spot: Disneyworld, Florida
Previous jobs: Office clerk, gas board service layer
Nickname: The Shoe

Sing-along Joe: Joe Johnson.

Whatever Joe Johnson achieves in his career, he will never forget his 18–12 win over Steve Davis in the final of the 1986 World Championship. But Johnson was unhappy with his overall form last season as he reached just one semi-final and slipped down six places to number 11. That semi-final was the Tennents UK Open, but in the previous round he had suffered a heart scare when beating Mike Hallett 9–7. The scare thankfully turned out to be a trapped nerve. Johnson also reached one other World Championship final in 1987, when Davis got his revenge by an 18–14 margin. Johnson made his debut in the Rothmans Matchroom League last season but finished rock bottom after getting just one point from his nine matches and ended up being relegated. Johnson has a great love of singing and appears regularly with his group, Made in Japan.

SILVINO FRANCISCO

World ranking: number 12   *Prize money:* £40,736.97

Full name: Silvino Francisco
Date of birth: 3 May 1946
Star sign: Taurus
Height: 6 feet
Weight: 13½ stone
Colour of eyes: Dark brown
Family: Wife Denise and children Silvino jnr, Stephen and Ashley Dominic
House: Four-bedroomed detached house in Chesterfield
Turned pro: 1978
Hobbies: Scuba diving and fishing
Music: All the latest pop music
Car: BMW

Favourite food: Chinese
Greatest achievement: Winning the Dulux British Open in 1985
Ambition: To win the world title
Favourite TV: 'Only Fools and Horses'
Whom do you most admire? Steve Davis – he is phenomenal
Are you superstitious?: Sometimes
Previous jobs: Oil salesman, production manager in Thurston's Sports
Favourite author: Alistair MacLean

Cheers: Silvino Francisco.

Silvino Francisco, one of the game's most consistent performers, suffered a first-round reversal in the Embassy World Championship to Australian Eddie Charlton. He reached the last sixteen in three of the four ranking tournaments last season, while the highlight of his career came in 1985 when he captured the Dulux British Open title. Francisco was unhappy about not being invited to the Benson and Hedges Irish Masters last season because of his South African connections and he spoke out firmly against that decision. Together with nephew Peter he reached the semi-final of the Foster's World Doubles.

WILLIE THORNE

World ranking: number 13   *Prize money:* £127,295.99

The Great WT: Willie Thorne.

Full name: William Joseph Thorne
Date of birth: 4 March 1954
Star sign: Pisces
Height: 6 feet 2 inches
Weight: 15 stone 4 lbs
Colour of eyes: Brown
Family: Wife Fiona and twin sons
Turned pro: 1976
Hobbies: Golf, football and racing
Music: Anything
Car: Mercedes 500 SEL
Favourite food: Indian
Favourite film star: Clint Eastwood
Favourite colour: Black
Greatest achievement: Winning the 1985 Mercantile Credit Classic
Biggest disappointment: Losing
Ambition: To win the World Championship
Favourite TV: 'Minder'
Whom do you most admire? Gary Lineker
Do you collect anything? Money

Nickname: The Great WT | *Dislikes:* Big-headed people

Willie Thorne slipped two places down the rankings to number 13 but achieved a semi-final placing in the Tennents UK Open before losing 9–2 to Steve Davis. Thorne, also nicknamed Mr Maximum for his impressive number of 147s which now total more than eighty, finally achieved a 147 in tournament play during the Tennents UK Open. Unfortunately, he made the maximum when the television cameras were not in position and that cost him £50,000, but he still became the fourth player to score a 147 under tournament conditions. Thorne remains one of the most respected professionals on the circuit but he still has only one major title to his name – the Mercantile Credit Classic in 1985. Willie finished third in the Rothmans Matchroom League. He loves a day at the races and has just become involved with a horse racing syndicate company.

PETER FRANCISCO

World ranking: number 14   Prize money: £41,679.68

Full name: Manuel Peter Francisco
Date of birth: 14 February 1962
Star sign: Aquarius
Height: 6 feet 2 inches
Weight: 13½ stone
Colour of eyes: Green
Family: Wife Colleen and two sons, Jason and Darren
Home: Village near Clacton
Turned pro: 1984
Hobbies: Golf, aqualung diving, angling
Music: Dire Straits, ZZ Top
Car: BMW
Favourite food: Lobster, paella, macaroni cheese
Favourite film star: Clint Eastwood, Charles Bronson
Favourite drink: Sweet cider, whisky
Greatest achievement: Getting into the top sixteen and beating Alex Higgins 5–4 during the 1986 BCE International
Biggest disappointment: Having just two hours' sleep after a bomb scare and losing the semi-final of the Rothmans Grand Prix last season
Ambition: To be world champion
Favourite TV: 'Auf Wiedersehen Pet', 'Go Fishing'

Fishing Fan: Peter Francisco.

Whom do you most admire? My father, Manny
Are you superstitious? Yes. I'll always get out of bed the same side I got in
Favourite holiday spot: The Wild Coast near Cape Town

Previous jobs: Four years in the army
Favourite author: I'm a bookworm – Wilbur Smith, Jack Higgins, Desmond Bagley

One wish: what would it be? To play one of my kids in the world final
Nickname: Guy the Gorilla
Dislikes: Spiders and snakes

Peter Francisco finally achieved his aim of making it into the top sixteen, going up four places to number 14. Many observers thought that Francisco should have attained this position earlier in his career as he is one of the best players on the circuit. He reached the semi-final of the Rothmans Grand Prix, but after just two hours' sleep because of a bomb scare at the hotel he crashed out to Dennis Taylor 9–4. Francisco's uncle, Silvino, is also a snooker professional. Surprisingly, Francisco made his debut at Sheffield's Crucible Theatre only last season and went out in the first round to Willie Thorne – a defeat that stopped him moving higher up the rankings. He is a golf fanatic.

JOHN VIRGO

World ranking: number 15   *Prize money:* £26,335.93

Full name: John Trevor Virgo
Date of birth: 4 March 1946
Star sign: Pisces
Height: 6 feet 4 inches
Weight: 14 stone 4 lbs
Colour of eyes: Brown
Family: Wife Avril and daughter Brook Leah
Home: Rambling house in Surrey
Turned pro: 1976
Hobbies: Horse racing, golf
Music: Folk, rock
Car: Volvo Estate and Executive BMW
Favourite food: Roast beef and Yorkshire pudding, home-made steak and kidney pie

Favourite film star: Gene Wilder
Favourite colour: Black
Greatest achievement: Winning the Coral UK in 1979
Biggest disappointment: Winning the Professional Snooker League in 1983/84 and not receiving any prize money
Ambition: To be world champion
Whom do you most admire? Barry McGuigan
Favourite holiday spot: Marbella
Previous jobs: Clerical officer for a steel company
Nickname: Bugsy
Dislikes: Animal hairs around the house

It was a momentous season for John Virgo. He became chairman of the WPBSA and regained his place in the world's top sixteen. But he was also at the centre of controversy when he 'naïvely' revealed to a Sunday newspaper that he had once smoked cannabis. The board of the WPBSA stood behind him during this crisis. Virgo enjoyed a consistent season but made a first-round exit in the World Championship at the hands of Steve Davis. However, he had Davis rattled and could have produced the shock result of the tournament. He is a member of the BBC's commentary team.

CLIFF WILSON

World ranking: number 16   *Prize money:* £26,101.55

Full name: Clifford John Wilson
Date of birth: 10 May 1934
Star sign: Taurus
Height: 5 feet 11 inches
Weight: 15 stone
Colour of eyes: Blue
Family: Wife Val and four sons
Home: Bungalow
Turned pro: 1979
Hobbies: Gambling, fishing
Music: Hot Chocolate
Car: Ford Granada
Favourite food: King prawns in garlic butter
Favourite film star: Charles Bronson

Favourite colour: Blue
Greatest achievement: Marrying the Dragon (his wife Val!)
Favourite TV: 'Tom and Jerry'
Whom do you most admire? Denis Thatcher
Favourite holiday spot: Puerto Rico, Gran Canaria
Previous jobs: Thirty years in a steel works (twenty years as a shop steward)
Do you collect anything? Betting slips
Favourite author: Oliver Strange, Hannon Swaffer
One wish: what would it be? £1 million
Dislikes: Hot food on cold plates

Cliff Wilson finally made it into snooker's top sixteen despite going out of the World Championship in the first round at the hands of Joe Johnson. Wilson has often laughed at his own misfortunes, particularly his terrible eyesight that made him quit the game for fifteen years. He always keeps the crowd entertained whether he wins or loses and still appears regularly at club exhibition engagements, particularly in his native Wales.

ALEX HIGGINS

World ranking: number 17   *Prize money:* £66,107.50

Full name: Alexander Gordon Higgins
Date of birth: 8 March 1949
Star sign: Pisces
Height: 5 feet 9½ inches
Weight: Varies a lot
Colour of eyes: Grey-green
Family: Two children from my second marriage
Turned pro: 1971
Hobbies: Golf, horse racing
Music: Blues, Motown, Carly Simon, Elkie Brooks
Car: Mercedes sports
Favourite food: Chinese
Favourite film star: Paul Newman

Slipping down: Alex Higgins.

Favourite colours: Blue, green, red
Greatest achievement: Winning world title at first attempt in 1972
Biggest disappointment: Not playing golf every day
Ambition: To play golf every day
Favourite TV: Documentaries
Whom do you most admire? George Best, Cassius Clay
Are you superstitious? Yes
Favourite holiday spot: Spain, Portugal, Far East
Previous jobs: Salesman, apprentice jockey
Do you collect anything? Antiques
Favourite author: Robert Ludlum, Stephen King
One wish: what would it be? To be happy
Nickname: The Hurricane, Sandy (at home in Belfast)
Dislikes: Too many

Alex Higgins missed the first two ranking tournaments of last season while serving a ban for the now-infamous head-butting incident in 1986. That cost him dear in terms of prize money and ranking points and he disappeared from the world's top sixteen for the first time. He was not at his best in the remaining ranking tournaments and went out in round one of the World Championships – 10–2 – at the hands of Malta's Tony Drago. But Higgins, twice a world champion in 1972 and 1982, still remains one of the greatest names in the game. He lost his 'Hurricane' title as he slowed his game down in an attempt to capture former glories. 'I shall return' was his catch phrase last season. Only time will tell if he is right, but it certainly seems strange, when looking at the top sixteen, not to see the name of Higgins in a prominent position.

REX WILLIAMS

World ranking: number 18   *Prize money:* £31,164.93

Full name: Desmond Rex Williams
Date of birth: 20 July 1933
Star sign: Cancer
Height: 5 feet 9 inches
Weight: 12 stone
Colour of eyes: Brown
Family: Wife Loretta and two daughters
Turned pro: 1952
Hobbies: Fishing and golf
Music: Frank Sinatra
Car: Jaguar, Range Rover
Favourite food: French
Favourite film star: Humphrey Bogart
Favourite colour: Blue
Greatest achievement: Catching my first salmon, taking Rex Williams Leisure to the Stock Exchange
Biggest disappointment: Never winning the World Snooker Championship
Ambition: To continue living a happy and healthy life
Favourite TV: Wildlife programmes
Whom do you most admire? Winston Churchill
Favourite holiday spot: South Africa, Australia
One wish: what would it be? To see snooker expand worldwide as it has in Britain
Dislikes: Moody and mean people

Rex Williams had to endure a traumatic season. He resigned as chairman of the WPBSA for health and family reasons while the beta-blockers controversy still raged around him. Williams has never been one to shy away from the major issues affecting snooker,

but his forthright opinions often brought him into conflict with his colleagues on the board. However, there is no doubt that during his fourteen years in charge of the WPBSA he was a major influence on the continued popularity of the sport. His lack of form saw him drop to number 18 in the ranking list, although he did reach the quarter-final of the MIM Britannia Unit Trusts British Open. In the World Championship he was beaten by unseeded Steve James in the first round.

It's a whopper: Rex Williams and a salmon he caught on the River Wye.

EDDIE CHARLTON

World ranking: number 19 | *Prize money:* £40,840.66

Full name: Edward Francis Charlton
Date of birth: 31 October 1929
Star sign: Scorpio
Height: 5 feet 10 inches
Weight: 13½ stone
Colour of eyes: Blue
Family: Wife Robyn and son Andrew
Home: Flat in Sheffield
Turned pro: 1960
Hobbies: Surfing, diving
Music: Anything by Barbra Streisand
Car: Toyota
Favourite food: Chinese
Favourite film star: Edward G. Robinson, Spencer Tracy
Favourite colour: Blue
Greatest achievement: Defeating Ray Reardon in the World Matchplay Championship in 1976

Biggest disappointment: Losing to Ray Reardon 31–30 in the World Championship final in 1975
Ambition: To win 100 tournaments before retiring (current score 90)
Favourite TV: Australia's 'Junior Talent Time'
Whom do you most admire? My wife and son
Are you superstitious? Yes
Favourite holiday spot: Cairns, North Queensland
Previous jobs: Coal miner
Do you collect anything? Only money
Favourite film: 'Crocodile Dundee'
One wish: what would it be? Always to have good health

Eddie Charlton did not think he would be competing full-time on the British circuit last season. But then a lucrative contract to play pool back home in his native Australia fell through and Charlton moved his family to a flat in Sheffield to concentrate on the UK season. He might be one of the game's senior professionals but that did not stop him rejoining snooker's top twenty at number 19 – a jump of seven places. Eddie, who has always been an all-round sportsman and a keep-fit fanatic, reached the last sixteen of the World Championship before losing to Tony Knowles. The highlight of his year was helping Australia through to their first final in the Fersina Windows World Cup, which they lost 9–7 to England.

TONY DRAGO

World ranking: number 20   *Prize money:* £41,524.28

Taking it easy: Tony Drago.

Full name: Tony Drago
Date of birth: 22 September 1966

Star sign: Virgo
Height: 6 feet
Weight: 13 stone
Colour of eyes: Brown
Family: Mother and father, two brothers and two sisters
Turned pro: 1985
Hobbies: Watching movies, relaxing
Music: Any disco
Favourite food: Chinese
Favourite film star: Sylvester Stallone
Greatest achievement: Beating Alex Higgins and Dennis Taylor in the World Championship in 1988
Biggest disappointment: Missing an easy yellow to beat Steve Davis in the 1986 Tennents UK Open quarter-final
Ambition: To be world champion
Favourite TV: Snooker
Whom do you most admire? Jimmy White
Favourite holiday spot: Malta
One wish: what would it be? To be world champion
Nickname: Tornado
Dislikes: The English climate

Tony Drago is Malta's sole professional player but he became the hero of the George Cross island with his breath-taking performances in the Embassy World Championship. In the first round he knocked out Alex Higgins and then despatched another Irishman, Dennis Taylor, to go through to the quarter-finals. There he came unstuck 13–4 against Steve Davis, but was still happy with his dramatic rise to number 20 on the ranking list.

He remains one of the most exciting players in the game and his Sheffield performances were rewarded by an invitation to compete in the eight-man Continental Airlines London Masters in the plush surroundings of the Cafe Royal this season.

EUGENE HUGHES

World ranking: number 21   *Prize money:* £36,572.68

Full name: Eugene Hughes
Date of birth: 4 November 1955
Star sign: Scorpio
Height: 5 feet 9 inches
Weight: 12 stone 10 lbs
Colour of eyes: Hazel
Family: Wife Susan and children Stuart and Suzanne
House: Barking, Essex
Turned pro: 1981
Hobbies: Manchester United – they're a passion of mine; also watching videos – I'm an addict
Music: Simply Red, U2, Pet Shop Boys, Simple Minds
Car: Jaguar XJS
Favourite food: Chinese and my wife's cooking
Favourite film star: James Cagney, Harrison Ford, Mickey Rourke, John Wayne
Favourite colour: Blue
Greatest achievement: Winning the World Team Cup with Dennis Taylor and Alex Higgins for the first time in 1985
Biggest disappointment: Losing 10–9 to Ray Reardon in the first round of the 1985 Embassy World Championship
Ambition: Like every player I'd love to win the world title
Favourite TV: 'Minder', 'Hill Street Blues', 'Only Fools and Horses'
Whom do you most admire? Ray Reardon
Are you superstitious? Touch wood, no!
Favourite holiday spot: Malta
Previous jobs: I did anything and everything to earn a few quid.
Do you collect anything? Compact discs, videos
Favourite author: Stephen King
One wish: what would it be? That my family wouldn't want for anything
Nickname: Houdini
Dislikes: Gamesmanship, playing cards with Tony Knowles

Eugene Hughes was hoping for a much-improved season after dropping down to number 24. There was improvement but not as spectacular as he had wished, although he did rise three places this season to number 21. A major disappointment for this young man from Ireland came in the World Cup when the Irish team was split up and he lost his chance of joining Alex Higgins and Dennis Taylor in chasing their fourth successive title.

DEAN REYNOLDS

World ranking: number 22   *Prize money:* £52,124.93

Full name: Dean Michael Reynolds
Date of birth: 11 January 1963
Star sign: Capricorn
Height: 5 feet 8 inches

Weight: 11½ stone
Colour of eyes: Blue
Family: Wife Joanne
Home: Great Coates, South Humberside
Turned pro: 1981
Hobbies: Golf, fishing (I love the outdoor life)
Music: Disco, Motown, easy listening
Car: Ford Orion Ghia 1600
Favourite food: Traditional English, e.g. roast beef and Yorkshire pudding
Favourite film star: Michael Caine, Jack Nicholson
Favourite colour: Blue
Greatest achievement: Winning the English Championship in 1988
Biggest disappointment: Not becoming world champion by the time I was twenty-two
Ambition: To be the best player in the world and world champion before I'm ninety-two!
Favourite TV: 'A Question of Sport', 'Neighbours'
Whom do you most admire? Alex Higgins: he's my favourite player
Are you superstitious? Extremely: I wouldn't walk under a ladder, I wear lucky clothes and collect lucky charms
One wish: what would it be? To be successful
Nickname: Deano (but Framework call me Haddock)
Dislikes: Eggs, aggressive people

Dean Reynolds claimed his first major title when a victory over Neal Foulds gave him the English Championship and his biggest ever payday of £15,000. But despite that victory, Reynolds will be disappointed with his brief stay in the world's top sixteen as he slipped down seven places to number 22. That was due to below-par performances in the ranking tournaments and he was a first-round casualty in the World Championship against Stephen Hendry. However, Reynolds knows that luck did not favour him against the young Scot and the result could easily have been reversed.

DENE O'KANE

World ranking: number 23   *Prize money:* £25,849.66

Full name: Dene Philip O'Kane
Date of birth: 24 February 1963
Star sign: Pisces
Height: 5 feet 10 inches
Weight: 9½ stone
Colour of eyes: Blue
Home: Flat in London; family house in Auckland, New Zealand
Turned pro: 1984
Hobbies: Skin-diving, nature watching, country walks
Music: All sorts (except opera) from classical to Elvis Presley; Pet Shop Boys, T'Pau
Car: Honda Accord
Favourite food: Gourmet vegetarian

Kiwi king: Dene O'Kane.

Favourite film: 'Fatal Attraction'
Favourite colours: Gold and purple
Greatest achievements: Beating three former world champions – Cliff Thorburn, Dennis Taylor and Joe Johnson – in ranking tournaments; reaching the last eight of the 1987 World Championship
Biggest disappointment: Failing to qualify for the final stages of the 1988 World Championship
Ambition: To be world champion

Favourite TV: Nature programmes, 'Hill Street Blues'
Whom do you most admire? Maharaji (leader of The Knowledge)
Favourite holiday spot: Surfer's Paradise, Australia
Previous jobs: Shipping clerk for nine weeks after leaving school
One wish: what would it be? To enjoy life
Nickname: The Doctor
Dislikes: Opera, New Zealand drivers

Dene O'Kane finally made a major impact on the world rankings, coming in at number 23 for the current season. This slimly-built young New Zealander knew he was in with a chance for a top-sixteen place if he hadn't failed in the World Championship in his first qualifying match as he went down 10–9 to Scotland's Eddie Sinclair. But he can look back on a superb performance in the MIM Britannia Unit Trusts British Open when he reached the last eight after a victory over former world champion Joe Johnson, O'Kane, who used to enjoy snooker's good life, has cut out the nightclub visits to concentrate on his profession. He is another young player looking for a move into the top sixteen.

DOUG MOUNTJOY

World ranking: number 24   *Prize money:* £27,515.62

Full name: Douglas James Mountjoy
Date of birth: 8 June 1942
Star sign: Gemini
Height: 5 feet 9 inches
Weight: 12 stone
Colour of eyes: Hazel
Family: Wife, son and daughter
Home: Bungalow
Turned pro: 1976
Hobbies: Golf
Music: Welsh choirs
Car: Mercedes
Favourite food: Indian
Favourite film star: Paul Newman

Favourite colour: Yellow
Greatest achievement: Winning the UK in 1978
Biggest disappointment: Losing the World Championship final in 1981
Ambition: To win
Favourite TV: Sport
Whom do you most admire? Steve Davis
Favourite holiday spot: Home
Previous jobs: Miner, factory worker
Do you collect anything? No (would like to collect money)
One wish: what would it be? To be rich
Dislikes: Being broke

Welshman Doug Mountjoy, a former miner, has dropped out of the world top sixteen to number 24. That fall came even though he reached the second round of the World Championship before losing to Neal Foulds. Mountjoy, who has now sold his pub on the Welsh border, only reached the fourth round of just one other ranking tournament – the Mercantile Credit Classic. At one time he was about to drop out of the top thirty-two as he battled to cope with a complete change of style. But he is determined to persevere and will be looking for a quick return to the top sixteen.

STEVE NEWBURY

World ranking: number 25   *Prize money:* £33,740.44

Going up: Steve Newbury.

Full name: Stephen William Newbury
Date of birth: 21 April 1956
Star Sign: Taurus
Height: 6 feet 1 inch
Weight: 13 stone

Colour of eyes: Green
Family: Wife Kathryn and two sons
Home: Three-bedroom semi-detached
Turned pro: 1985
Hobbies: Golf, music, cars, car racing
Music: Soul, funk, pop
Car: Fiat Turbo-Diesel
Favourite food: Cantonese, English grills
Favourite film star: John Wayne
Favourite colour: Blue
Greatest achievement: Reaching the semi-final of the Mercantile Credit Classic in 1988 and the final of the Welsh Championship
Biggest disappointment: Losing snooker matches
Ambition: To become the world number 1
Favourite TV: Science-fiction
Whom do you most admire? Steve Davis
Favourite holiday spot: Magaluf
Previous jobs: Furnace operator in a cast-iron foundry, process operator in an oil refinery
One wish: what would it be? To have total peace of mind
Dislikes: Smoking

Welshman Steve Newbury made a jump of twenty places up the rankings but he knows that climb could have been even more spectacular. He slotted in at number 25 on the list but was desperately disappointed with his World Championship performance when he was beaten 10–8 by Barry West in the final qualifying round. Newbury's best performance was in getting to the semi-final of the Mercantile Credit Classic before losing 9–2 to eventual champion Steve Davis. In the Classic, Newbury scored an impressive 5–3 win over Canadian Cliff Thorburn – the man he beat 5–0 in the Rothmans Grand Prix. Newbury's revitalized performances should see him pushing for a place in the top sixteen.

BARRY WEST

World ranking: number 26   *Prize money:* £23,459.18

English success: Barry West.

Barry West left school at sixteen not knowing if he had passed his examinations. But it didn't really matter as he had already decided to concentrate full-time on snooker. This season he has moved up three places to number 26 and experienced his biggest ever payday – he earned £4,750 – when he reached the semi-final of the English Professional Championship and made a break of 134 which proved to be the biggest of the tournament. West reached round one of the World Championship but came unstuck against Welshman Doug Mountjoy.

JOHN SPENCER

World ranking: number 27   *Prize money:* £16,599.81

Full name: John Spencer
Date of birth: 15 September 1935
Star sign: Virgo
Height: 6 feet 1 inch
Weight: 11 stone 7 lbs
Colour of eyes: Blue
Home: Detached bungalow in Radcliffe
Turned pro: 1967
Hobbies : Golf
Music: Background and quiet music, ballads
Car: Mercedes 500
Favourite food: Plain English cooking

Favourite colour: Red or black
Greatest achievement: Winning world title three times
Ambition: To keep playing to the best of my ability
Favourite TV: Sport and comedies
Are you superstitious? Just a little
Favourite holiday spot: I like exploring new places
Previous jobs: Settler in betting office, driver/bookkeeper in Jewish bakery
Nickname: Sniffer, Spenny
Dislikes: Ignorant people

John Spencer's career has been written off many times but that was mainly due to a serious eye problem that threatened his career. In years gone by, Spencer's prowess on the table was regarded by many to be the greatest ever seen. He has won the world title on three occasions. Though snooker is now reckoned by some to be a young man's game, Spencer, in his fifty-fourth year, has once again climbed up the rankings by one place to number 27. He is also a member of the WPBSA board and a regular commentator for the BBC.

DAVID TAYLOR

World ranking: number 28   *Prize money:* £16,242.18

Full name: David Taylor
Date of birth: 29 July 1943
Star sign: Leo
Height: 5 feet 11 inches
Weight: 11 stone 4 lbs
Colour of eyes: Olive green
Family: Wife Janice and three sons
Home: Seven-bedroom detached house in 2 acres with a snooker room and three reception rooms
Turned pro: 1968
Hobbies: Swimming, walking the dog, reading
Music: Neil Diamond, Simon and Garfunkel, Cher

Commentary man: David Taylor.

Car: Jaguar XJS
Favourite food: Roast goose
Favourite film stars: Bob Hope, Basil Rathbone as Sherlock Holmes, Humphrey Bogart
Favourite colour: Aquamarine
Greatest achievement: Getting to the final of the Jameson International in 1982
Biggest disappointment: Getting beaten by Bill Werbeniuk 13–10 in the 1983 World Championship
Ambition: To win a ranking tournament
Favourite TV: 'Fawlty Towers', 'Only Fools and Horses'

Whom do you most admire? In snooker, Steve Davis; otherwise, Martin Luther King
Favourite holiday spot: Puerto de Andraix, Majorca
Previous jobs: Swimming instructor, hairdresser, tomato picker
Do you collect anything? Books
Favourite author: Wilbur Smith
One wish: what would it be? To have world peace
Nickname: Silver Fox
Dislikes: Having to diet, soaps on TV, bad food

David Taylor was for many years an accepted member of snooker's top sixteen but his fortunes have slipped recently. He didn't enjoy the best of times on the ranking tournament circuit last season and dropped three places to number 28. Taylor has been busy in the BBC commentators' box at certain tournaments and will be hoping for an upsurge on the table in his fortunes over the next few months. He failed to qualify for the final stages of the World Championship when he was beaten 10–6 by Canadian Bob Chaperon.

BOB CHAPERON

World ranking: number 29   *Prize money:* £23,415.26

Full name: Robert Denis Chaperon
Date of birth: 18 May 1958
Star sign: Taurus
Height: 5 feet 11 inches
Weight: 13 stone
Colour of eyes: Green
Family: Mother Yvette and brother Claude
Hobbies: Golf, fishing
Music: Supertramp
Car: Ford Sierra
Favourite food: Steak
Favourite film star: Charles Bronson
Favourite colour: Green
Greatest achievement: Becoming the 1981 Canadian amateur snooker and billiards champion
Ambition: To make it to the top eight in the rankings

Moving up: Bob Chaperon.

Favourite TV: Wildlife programmes
Whom do you most admire? Jack Nicklaus, Tom Watson
Favourite holiday spot: Home in Canada

One wish: what would it be? To win a major championship
Nickname: Frenchie

Bob Chaperon competed in the final stages of the World Championship for the first time last season. He also made a jump of twelve places to number 41 in the rankings last season and this season made a similar leap to number 29. He enjoyed an excellent Rothmans Grand Prix before going out in the quarter-final to John Parrott, but was beaten by Mike Hallett at Sheffield. This popular Canadian is now resident in this country.

STEVE LONGWORTH

World ranking: number 30   *Prize money:* £16,787.30

Full name: Stephen Longworth
Date of birth: 27 July 1948
Star sign: Leo
Height: 5 feet 9 inches
Weight: 12 stone
Colour of eyes: Blue
Family: Wife Madeline and two daughters
Home: Large terraced house
Turned pro: 1984
Hobbies: Golf and bowling
Music: Alison Moyet
Car: Datsun
Favourite food: Chinese
Favourite film stars: Steve McQueen, Paul Newman
Favourite colour: Blue
Greatest achievement: Winning the English amateur title in 1984 and being a semi-finalist in the English Professional tournament in 1985
Biggest disappointment: Losing the English Professional semi-final in 1985
Ambition: To get as far as possible in the professional snooker rankings
Favourite TV: 'Alas Smith and Jones'

Steady: Steve Longworth.

Whom do you most admire? Steve Davis for his consistency
Favourite holiday spot: La Calla, Southern Spain
Previous jobs: Time-served engineer, snooker club manager, van driver
One wish: what would it be? To win a major tournament
Dislikes: Indian food, heights

Steve Longworth would be happy to have made a quicker move up the ranking list by now for he still remains one of the game's more consistent professionals. He rose just one place to number 30 this season and reached the last thirty-two of the World Championship where he was beaten by eventual finalist Terry Griffiths. He was a former English amateur champion and turned professional in 1984 at the age of thirty-six. Once again, this season he will be looking for a place in the top twenty.

TONY MEO

World ranking: number 31   *Prize money:* £47,584.18

Full name: Anthony Christian Meo
Date of birth: 4 October 1959
Star sign: Libra
Height: 5 feet 7 inches
Weight: 11 stone
Colour of eyes: Brown
Family: Wife Denise and children Gina, Tony and Sonny
House: Four-bedroom semi in Lower Morden
Turned pro: 1979
Hobbies: Horse racing
Music: Jazz, soul, reggae
Car: BMW 735
Favourite food: Anything good (Italian)
Favourite film star: Robert De Niro, Gene Wilder

Favourite colours: Royal blue, burgundy
Biggest disappointment: Missing the yellow in the Lada Classic final 1984
Ambition: To become world champion
Favourite TV: Any sport and comedy
Whom do you most admire? My mum and my wife
Favourite holiday spot: Barbados
Previous jobs: Restaurant, despatch clerk (one week)
Do you collect anything? Pottery from different countries
One wish: what would it be? To be happy always
Dislikes: Ignorant and rude people

Tony Meo has not enjoyed the best of fortunes for the last two seasons. This popular Londoner dropped to number 20 in 1987/88 and slipped even further to number 31 this season. But Meo was happy just to salvage his place in the top thirty-two. He also lost his World Doubles title with Steve Davis when they were sensationally beaten in the first round and saw his English title disappear at Ipswich. Even so, Meo earned himself a £5,000 bonus for recording a 147 maximum in the Rothmans Matchroom League.

STEVE JAMES

World ranking: number 32   *Prize money:* £40,812.50

Full name: Stephen Paul James
Date of birth: 2 May 1961

Star sign: Taurus
Height: 5 feet 11 inches

Speed fan: Steve James.

Weight: 12½ stone
Colour of eyes: Blue
House: Two-bedroom flat in Cannock
Turned pro: 1986
Hobbies: Motorbikes, taking the dog for a walk
Greatest achievement: Reaching the quarter-final of the 1988 World Championship
Biggest disappointment: Reaching only number 66 in my first season
Ambition: To reach the top sixteen and win the world title
Favourite TV: Pop programmes and motor-bike racing
Whom do you most admire? Jimmy White
Previous jobs: Postman, metal polisher
One wish: what would it be? To be a world champion motorcyclist
Nickname: Jamie
Dislikes: Losing

Steve James achieved nationwide fame as he reached the quarter-final of the Embassy World Championship with a series of impressive displays. But he counted himself lucky to be playing in the championship as just ten days before it started he somersaulted his BMW car four times and ended up in a field. Luckily he escaped with only cuts, bruises and a black eye. James, who is a motorcycle fanatic has a love of speed. It was this World Championship performance that lifted him from number 66 to number 32 in the world rankings.

WHO SAID THIS?

'We have mutually agreed to part company in a business sense but we remain friends. I can do it all myself and handle my own affairs.'

– *Canadian Cliff Thorburn after parting company with manager Robert Winsor.*

'Barry can do a lot for my career. He has a proven track record as a manager and I have just reached my fortieth birthday – now I can get on with my snooker.'

– *Cliff Thorburn after joining Barry Hearn's Matchroom stable.*

'Looking after Jimmy is harder than looking after all my other seven players put together. Of course he gives me sleepless nights – he still does and probably will in the future. I knew managing him would not be easy and you could say we have had a few discussions behind closed doors.'

– *Barry Hearn talking about his first year with Jimmy White.*

'This pain frightened me – I thought I was a goner. I started to tremble and was on the point of collapse, but after five minutes I started to feel better.'

– *Joe Johnson after being taken ill during the Tennents UK Open.*

'I knew it was on from the first red – it was just nice to finally get a maximum in a tournament.'

– *Willie Thorne after his 147 in the Tennents UK Open.*

'I am deeply upset that, after all my efforts for the players, I did not receive one letter from a fellow professional thanking me for all my work over the years. There were letters from other professional people and my friends but not one from a player. That hurt.'

– *Rex Williams after resigning from the board of the WPBSA.*

'I had already decided to concentrate on snooker when I left school. I took eight "O" levels but would have needed to go back to school to find out the results. I didn't bother.'

– *Barry West after reaching the semi-final of the English Professional Championship.*

'I wanted to get out of the whole circuit – I didn't want to play snooker.'

– *Neal Foulds speaking about his personal problems in 1987.*

'I used to play Crown Green Bowls with my dad but one day it was pouring with rain so we went for a game of snooker. I was only twelve but after that I played snooker every night.'

– *John Parrott talking about the start of his career.*

'We have been disappointed with the live crowds at Northampton – they have shown a significant decrease. We have been looking at a few other venues and will continue to do so.'

– *David Apthorp, Foster's World Doubles tournament director, speaking after last year's event in Northampton.*

'I put the cue down at the Winners Club in Southgate and it went missing. We couldn't find it anywhere – somebody must have taken it away thinking it was their cue.'

– *Cliff Thorburn after losing 5–0 to Steve Newbury in the fourth round of the Rothmans Grand Prix without his favourite cue.*

'It ruined what was going to be the best snooker day of my life – I could have cried. We must have had twenty to twenty-five kicks in the game.'

– *Eric Lawlor, at fifty snooker's oldest newest professional, after losing to Joe*

Johnson in the MIM Britannia Unit Trusts British Open.

'I had been watching a video of the film *Alien* where there is a fire-alarm sequence. I started to hear a second fire alarm in stereo and realized it was in the hotel. I grabbed my cue and got out as quickly as possible.'

– *Dennis Taylor, who spent the early hours of one morning walking round Reading before the quarter-final of the Rothmans Grand Prix.*

'He played me like he was a money player – like every ball was life or death.'

– *Cliff Thorburn after a 5–2 win over Paul Medati in the MIM Britannia Unit Trusts British Open.*

'My ambition is to get into the top thirty-two – I honestly believe there are not thirty-two players in the world better than me. I have lost 2 stone in weight and I am determined to finally make my big breakthrough.'

– *Manchester's Paddy Browne.*

'It looks like Hendry in the next round and then Davis in the final. Then I will take the money and the trophy.'

— Jimmy White after his 10–3 success over Australian John Cameron in the first round of the Embassy World Championship.

'Alcoholics Anonymous saved my life. Four days before the event started I did not think I could compete, but I needed the money to get through the summer.'

— Canadian Kirk Stevens after winning his final qualifying round in the Embassy World Championship.

'He doesn't know what losing is all about. His temperament is a bit suspect and there are a couple of weak spots in his game.'

— Dean Reynolds after losing 10–6 to Stephen Hendry in the first round of the Embassy World Championship.

'It was a case of the Crucible collywobbles. Day one is over and I'm still in it. You couldn't play better if you had been knocked out.'

— Steve Davis after a tough 10–8 victory over John Virgo in the first round of the Embassy World Championship.

'That's goodbye to the Irish.'

— A smiling Tony Drago after beating Dennis Taylor in the second round of the Embassy World Championship. Drago had already put out another Irishman, Alex Higgins, in the first round.

'I love winning, but then you have to remember it's only a game. We will be presenting some wheelchairs to some unlucky kids after this championship. That puts everything into perspective.'

— Dennis Taylor after being beaten 13–5 by Tony Drago in the second round of the Embassy World Championship.

THE SEASON IN DEPTH

CARLING CHAMPIONS TOURNAMENT

Dennis Taylor loves nothing better than winning in front of his own Irish snooker fans. And he did just that as he took the £12,500 first prize in the Carling Champions Tournament in the RTE television studios in Dublin. The Carling Champions, formerly known as the Carlsberg Challenge, has now been held for four years and is a four-man invitation event.

Taylor's 8–5 victory over Joe Johnson meant that he retained the title but, more significantly, he also set a new Irish professional record with a break of 140. That tremendous break came in the second frame of his opening match against Stephen Hendry and beat the 138 that Taylor had knocked in on his way to success in 1986.

In this opening match against young Hendry, the Irish champion raced into a 4–1 lead before eventually coming through to the final with a 5–3 victory. The seventh frame was quite remarkable with the young Scot needing three snookers. He got them and then knocked in a respotted black but, unfortunately for him, Taylor's 33 break in the eighth frame was good enough.

The other opening match, between Joe Johnson and Neal Foulds, went to the final frame but Johnson was the man who came out on top with a break of 51.

The final produced a slowish first session with Taylor edging 4–3 in front. At night Johnson levelled, but then a break of 88 regained the lead for Taylor and he quickly took the next two frames to make it 7–4. Johnson's 53 break earned him the twelfth frame but Taylor was in no mood to lose and took the thirteenth frame to collect the £12,500 first prize plus £2,000 for that record break of 140.

Carling Champions Results

SEMI-FINALS

Dennis Taylor (NI) 5
v
S. Hendry (Scot) 3

J. Johnson (Eng) 5
v
N. Foulds (Eng) 4

Losers: £5,825

High break: 140 – Dennis Taylor £2,000

FINAL

Dennis Taylor 8
v
Johnson 5

Loser: £8,500
Winner: £12,500

Previous Years' Results

YEAR	WINNER	RUNNER-UP	SCORE
1984	(Carlsberg) J. White (Eng)	A. Knowles (Eng)	9–7
1985	(Carlsberg) J. White (Eng)	A. Higgins (NI)	8–3
1986	(Carlsberg) Dennis Taylor (NI)	J. White (Eng)	8–3

LANGS SUPREME SCOTTISH MASTERS

Joe Johnson and Howard Kruger were entitled to wear the widest grins in Glasgow after Johnson won the Langs Supreme Scottish Masters trophy. There was certainly no lack of champagne as Johnson ended the Matchroom monopoly in this traditional pipe-opener for the new season. In the previous twelve months Matchroom had won every title that really mattered except the Langs – but then they didn't have a player competing in 1986. This time it was different, with world number 2 Jimmy White leading the Matchroom charge on a tournament that carried a £16,000 first prize. However, it was Johnson who delighted his Framework boss, Kruger, by taking the top prize with a magnificent 9–7 win over Terry Griffiths.

A packed house of more than 1,000 sat back to enjoy what turned out to be a

What a pair: Jimmy White and Alex Higgins before meeting in the Langs Supreme Scottish Masters.

tremendous final. Emotional Johnson planted a kiss on the cup and Kruger said, 'At last – I have waited two long hard years for this, but it has been worth it. We have finally won a tournament.' According to Johnson, 'The crowd out there were just unbelievable and it was like playing in the World Championship final all over again.'

In the final Griffiths led for most of the match, but he could not find the form that had carried him through the rest of the tournament. In the semi-final he had produced one of the most incredible results of the season, overwhelming White 6–2 in just eighty-three minutes. Terry, who opened his new snooker club in Llanelli just after the match, went for every shot that was going. Afterwards he explained why: 'I haven't been able to practise with this new club opening,' he said, 'so I just decided that I would go for everything.'

It certainly worked, and a dazed White could only say, 'I didn't know what was happening out there – Terry had me completely baffled. I was probably a bit over-confident.' In fact, one frame lasted less than seven minutes and three more didn't pass the ten-minute mark.

The other semi-final was not quite as hectic, though Johnson showed again what fine form he was in as he knocked out the title holder, Cliff Thorburn, 6–3. The Canadian number 1 had been looking for his third successive Langs title, but went back home saying, 'My best form is not that far away but I know that you have to work, work and keep on working.'

A tired-looking Dennis Taylor flew in from Dublin after winning the Carling Champions event twenty-four hours earlier and did manage a tournament best break of 125 that earned him a £1,500 bonus. However, Thorburn in this first-round match was much the stronger player and came home an easy 5–2 winner.

There was another sell-out crowd of

At last: Joe Johnson celebrates Framework's first trophy success in the Langs Supreme Scottish Masters together with (left) Howard Kruger and John Rukin.

enthusiastic Glaswegians who turned up to support the man they see as the greatest player in the world – Edinburgh's Stephen Hendry. Hendry had justified their confidence in his first-round match against Johnson by taking the first two frames. But then the young Scot's concentration went and Johnson scored five frames in succession, including a 105 break in frame five, for what proved to be an easy 5–2 win.

Neal Foulds, not knowing that he was going to endure a terrible season, went out 5–4 against Griffiths, then the crowd was packing in yet again as the 'Hurricane' came into town. It was Higgins *versus* White – the Irishman was back in action even though he was in the middle of a five-tournament ban for that now infamous head-butting incident in 1986. Higgins said, 'I have been playing exhibition matches in Ireland but there is just nothing to beat competition. I can't wait to get playing again – it's great playing someone like Jimmy.' But White twice pulled back a big deficit to take frames he looked like losing and finished off the 'Hurricane' with a break of 88 for a 5–3 victory.

There was, inevitably, controversy when tournament referee John Williams was criticized for an incident in frame six. Higgins claimed that Williams asked the fans to be quiet when he was already down on a shot and both Alex and his manager, Kruger, complained bitterly. However, when BBC Scotland showed the incident later, it was virtually proved that Williams did nothing wrong.

The tournament marked the end to Langs sponsorship – a sad loss for Scottish snooker after the company had generously poured in the money for over seven years.

Langs Supreme Scottish Masters Results

FIRST ROUND		SEMI-FINALS		FINAL	
C. Thorburn (Can)	5				
v		Thorburn	3		
Dennis Taylor (NI)	2				
		v		Johnson	9
J. Johnson (Eng)	5				
v		Johnson	6		
S. Hendry (Scot)	2				
				v	
T. Griffiths (Wales)	5				
v		Griffiths	6		
N. Foulds (Eng)	4				
		v		Griffiths	7
J. White (Eng)	5				
v		White	2		
A. Higgins (NI)	3				
Losers: £3,125		Losers: £5,000		Loser: £10,000	
				Winner: £16,000	

High break: 125 – Dennis Taylor £1,500

Previous Years' Results

YEAR	WINNER	RUNNER-UP	SCORE
1981	J. White (Eng)	C. Thorburn (Can)	9–4
1982	S. Davis (Eng)	A. Higgins (NI)	9–4
1983	S. Davis (Eng)	A. Knowles (Eng)	9–6
1984	S. Davis (Eng)	J. White (Eng)	9–4
1985	C. Thorburn (Can)	W. Thorne (Eng)	9–7
1986	C. Thorburn (Can)	A. Higgins (NI)	9–8

FIDELITY UNIT TRUSTS INTERNATIONAL

Steve Davis, in ominous form, began the new season just as he had finished the old one – by winning a major ranking title. In 1986/87 it was the Embassy World Championship; now Davis got into the familiar groove by coming out on top in the Fidelity Unit Trusts International at Trentham Gardens, Stoke-on-Trent. He overwhelmed Canada's Cliff Thorburn 12–5 to pick up the £40,000 top prize and also added £4,000 to his bank balance for the tournament best break – an outstanding 140 in the seventh frame of the final.

Davis and Thorburn are adversaries of old and had met eight times before. Yet in those many meetings Thorburn had managed only the one solitary victory. After the first day's play Davis was 8–5 in front and wasted little time in taking four frames in a row for a 12–5 triumph. Later he said, 'I have started the year in a relaxed mood. That's what happens when you begin the season as world champion and not runner-up. Cliff is a great player but I just made more of my chances. In fact, if we spent a week locked up in a room I would do more damage because I am a better player than he is.' That might sound big-headed but, unfortunately for Cliff, it was just a plain statement of fact.

Yet Thorburn, in the semi-final, had produced arguably the most devastating snooker of this career as he totally demoralized Stephen Hendry 9–1. Hendry, who started the season looking for his first major triumph, had to admit, 'That's the best snooker I have ever faced – Cliff's safety play was inch-perfect and he missed just one shot all day. I never got a chance.'

Davis was totally relaxed throughout the entire tournament and even spent time sitting in the hubbub of the tournament press room, chatting and doing puzzles out of a book. In the other semi-final he despatched Hendry's stablemate, Mike Hallett, 9–3.

In the quarter-finals Thorburn made it look too easy with a 5–1 win against Irishman Eugene Hughes. Hendry had too much know-how for Joe O'Boye and won 5–2. Hallett, however, had to fight all the way for a 5–4 win over Australian veteran Eddie Charlton. Davis, beaten by John Virgo in the Dulux British Open last season, made no mistake in this quarter-final, beating Virgo 5–2.

WHO SAID THAT?

'I am not frightened of anyone when I am playing well – the problem is that over the years I have not produced that form very often.'

▲

– John Virgo after a 5–2 win over Tony Knowles to reach the quarter-final of the Fidelity Unit Trusts International.

'It was an agonizing decision to make,' recalled the referee. 'What made it worse was the fact that while Nigel was weighing up the shot and working out the way to play, I knew it didn't matter because I was going to have to call him for a foul unless he moved the ball. Nigel was trying to win the frame but I knew he had lost it. The decision provided a lot of talk and discussion in the TV commentators' box and in the venue. I heard some believed that the decision was harsh. I know Nigel accepted my ruling, but I didn't get a chance to have a word with him until I saw him at another tournament. He came up to me and said he had watched the replay forty or fifty times on the video and thought I had made the right decision. It was nice of him to say that.'

Professional new boy Martin Clark created all the media interest in the early stages of the tournament. He faced the awesome challenge of Irishman Dennis Taylor for his first ever TV appearance. But that didn't bother the young man from the Midlands, and he scored a stunning 5–0 victory. Taylor had to admit, 'That's got to be the best television debut in the history of the sport.' Then Clark found out about the ups and downs of snooker life when he was beaten 5–2 by O'Boye in the next round.

There was also good news for young Essex man Dave Gilbert who nearly had to quit the game following a horrific car crash seven years ago. His 5–1 win over Welshman Cliff Wilson earned him a place in the last sixteen. Gilbert, ranked 82 in the world, quit the snooker circuit for a year following the frightening accident that claimed the life of his sister Sue and left him with a steel plate in his shattered right arm. He said, 'The elbow is always bent but it doesn't really affect my game.' And then he joked, 'I just need a drop of 3-in-1 oil every so often.' But Gilbert faced Hendry in round five and went down 5–0.

Also in round five another Gilbert, this time Nigel (no relation to Dave), was involved in a strange incident in the opening frame of the match. He forced a respotted black against Charlton but lost the frame when he was called for a foul by referee John Street. Street noticed that Gilbert had placed the cue ball outside the 'D' and had no option but to call him for a foul.

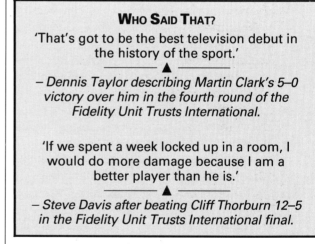

At the end of the day it was that man Davis again, but the world champion was not the only winner. Fidelity, impressive first-time sponsors, produced a unique back-up promotional deal where the quarter-finalists were able to pledge extra money to charities of their choice. £40,000 of unit trusts were given to MENCAP, a fitting gesture at the end of what should prove an exciting new sponsorship on the tournament schedule.

Fidelity Unit Trusts International Results

FOURTH ROUND		FIFTH ROUND		QUARTER-FINALS		SEMI-FINALS		FINAL	
N Foulds (Eng)	2								
v		Hendry	5						
S. Hendry (Scot)	5			Hendry	5				
C. Wilson (Wales)	1								
v		D. Gilbert	0						
D. Gilbert (Eng)	5					Hendry	1		
R. Foldvari (Aust)	4								
v		O'Boye	5						
J. O'Boye (Rep Ire)	5			O'Boye	2				
Dennis Taylor (NI)	0								
v		Clark	2					Thorburn	5
M. Clark (Eng)	5								
J. Wych (Can)	4								
v		E. Hughes	5						
E. Hughes (Rep Ire)	5			E. Hughes	1				
S. Francisco (SA)	5								
v		S. Francisco	4			Thorburn	9		
W. Werbeniuk (Can)	3								
D. Roe (Eng)	3								
v		James	0						
S. James (Eng)	5			Thorburn	5				
C. Thorburn (Can)	5								
v		Thorburn	5						v
S. Newbury (Wales)	3								
J. White (Eng)	5								
v		White	4						
S. Longworth (Eng)	1			Hallett	5				
M. Hallett (Eng)	5								
v		Hallett	5			Hallett	3		
J. Spencer (Eng)	2								
W. Jones (Wales)	4								
v		N. Gilbert	0						
N. Gilbert (Eng)	5			Charlton	4				
T. Griffiths (Wales)	2								
v		Charlton	5					S. Davis	12
E. Charlton (Aust)	5								
A. Knowles (Eng)	5								
v		Knowles	2						
David Taylor (Eng)	2			Virgo	2				
W. Thorne (Eng)	4								
v		Virgo	5			S. Davis	9		
J. Virgo (Eng)	5								
J. Parrott (Eng)	5								
v		Parrott	2						
R. Chaperon (Can)	1			S. Davis	5				
S. Davis (Eng)	5								
v		S. Davis	5						
A. Meo (Eng)	3								

Losers: £1,937.50   Losers: £3,000   Losers: £6,000   Losers: £12,000   Loser: £24,000

Winner: £40,000

High break: 140 – S. Davis £4,000

Previous Years' Results

YEAR	WINNER	RUNNER-UP	SCORE
1981	(Jameson) S. Davis (Eng)	Dennis Taylor (NI)	9–0
1982	(Jameson) A. Knowles (Eng)	David Taylor (Eng)	9–6
1983	(Jameson) S. Davis (Eng)	C. Thorburn (Can)	9–4
1984	(Jameson) S. Davis (Eng)	A. Knowles (Eng)	9–2
1985	(Goya) C. Thorburn (Can)	J. White (Eng)	12–10
1986	(BCE) N. Foulds (Eng)	C. Thorburn (Can)	12–9

The first of four: Steve Davis receives the Fidelity Unit Trusts International trophy from Fidelity's managing director, Barry Bateman. Davis went on to win three more ranking tournaments.

ROTHMANS GRAND PRIX

Stephen Hendry started his professional snooker life as a young man destined to rewrite the record books. He was the youngest Scottish amateur and professional champion, the game's youngest professional at sixteen, and he went into the Rothmans Grand Prix final at Reading's Hexagon Theatre aiming to be the youngest ever professional winner. That honour had been claimed by Jimmy White who, at nineteen, took the Langs Supreme Masters in 1981. But all was about to change as eighteen-year-old Hendry stepped out to face Irishman Dennis Taylor in the nineteen-frame final.

Hendry romped to a 10–7 win, picked up £60,000 and then learnt that he was the first Scot to win a major tournament since Walter Donaldson became world champion way back in 1950. Hendry's potting ability had never been questioned – there was that flair and innovation that made him one to watch wherever he played. But now impressive safety play and a steady nerve were to take him all the way to this title.

In the first session Taylor opened a 4–1 lead and his experience looked as though it was going to prove too much for Hendry. By the end of the first afternoon, however, the scores were level at 4–4. At night Hendry quickly knocked in four frames in a row to go 8–4 ahead and, despite Taylor's eventually fighting back to 7–9, this super-cool youngster claimed the title with a break of 49 in the seventeenth frame.

Hendry was almost speechless at the prize-giving ceremony, although he did say with pure understatement, 'I am just delighted to win.' Watching in the audience was proud father Gordon who just glowed with pleasure at his son's triumph. 'Stephen has been setting records since the day he started,' he said.

The video recorder played a significant part in Hendry's victory. Manager Ian Doyle and Hendry had sat back watching master cueman Steve Davis in action time after time on the small screen. Doyle and Hendry worked out a new plan for attack against Davis and it worked in this tournament as Hendry despatched the world champion 5–2 in round five.

The semi-finals had been marred by yet another overnight trip to the local police station after a second bombscare. The BBC even managed to find a smile as they put up on the internal TV monitors at the Hexagon Theatre: 'Ramada Nightowls – party at Reading police station 3 am. Nobody barred.' That was a reference to the nightly exodus from the Ramada Hotel where this madman had phoned through saying there was a bomb in the place.

Taylor had easily shrugged off Peter Francisco 9–4 to reach the final, but Hendry had to battle all the way to knock out John Parrott 9–7. Taylor, who had had to leave the hotel for two hours following a bombscare at 1 am, had spent the early hours before his quarter-final match with Welshman Steve Newbury walking around Reading with a snooker cue in his hand.

He recalled, 'I had been sitting down watching a video of the film *Alien* and in it there was a fire-alarm sequence. I started to hear another alarm in stereo and realized it was in the hotel. I grabbed my cue and just got out of the place as quickly as possible. I even forgot to put my socks on. I looked as though I had escaped from a lunatic asylum, carrying a snooker cue and wearing no socks!' But he still proved too strong for Newbury and came home 5–2.

Parrott was also worn out after the early-morning alarm call. 'I just grabbed my cash and car keys and ran,' he said. And he also came up with the great line: 'The £9,000 money for getting through to the semi-final will allow me to pay my rates in Liverpool now.' Parrott saw off Canada's Bob Chaperon 5–2, Hendry overturned Tony Knowles by the same score and Peter Francisco completed the last four by knocking out Willie Thorne 5–3.

WHO SAID THAT?

'The £9,000 prize money for getting through to the semi-final will allow me to pay my rates in Liverpool now.'

▲

John Parrott after beating Bob Chaperon in the quarter-final of the Rothmans Grand Prix.

The tournament was riddled with shocks from day one. 'Don't blink or you will miss it,' was the advice from one press-room correspondent when talking about the match between Tony Drago and Jimmy White. The match occupied eight frames but lasted just eighty-five minutes and 'Tornado' Tony hammered 'Whirlwind' White 5–3. Certainly late nights didn't worry the young Maltese Falcon, who said, 'I stayed up until 4 am to watch Mike Tyson's world heavyweight fight on television – I just can't sleep before an important match.'

'Every shot is like life or death,' remarked Kirk Stevens after he had been humiliated 5–0 by John Parrott. And he added, 'If it goes on like this, I would rather not play and get a day job instead.'

World number 5 Joe Johnson departed for Bradford after he went down 5–2 to Peter Francisco.

Tournaments wouldn't be complete without the odd refereeing row and the Rothmans was no exception as big Bill Werbeniuk lost 5–3 to Dennis Taylor. John Street was the man in the middle of the commotion after ruling that the Canadian had hit the pink instead of a red. Werbeniuk said, 'That's the worst refereeing decision that I have had in my career. There is no way I could have hit the pink first. Dennis should have backed me up but he said he hadn't seen what had happened even though he must have known where the balls were on the table.'

There was more drama at Reading as Canadian Cliff Thorburn could not find a cue that he had left at the Winners Club in Southgate near his North London home. Even the BBC asked their viewers if any club member had seen the cue. Thorburn went out against Welshman Steve Newbury in the fourth round, apparently unable to get to grips with a borrowed cue. Meanwhile, the lost cue had been found, but despite a motorway dash down the M4, it arrived at the stage door ten minutes after the match was over. Thorburn declared, 'I will never let this cue out of my sight again.'

WHO SAID THAT?

'That's the worst refereeing decision that I have had in my career . . . Dennis [Taylor] should have backed me up but he said he hadn't seen what happened.'

▲

– Canadian Bill Werbeniuk after being called for a foul during a 5–3 defeat in the Rothmans Grand Prix.

Hitting out: Bill Werbeniuk.

On to round five and Thorne, hardly a slow player himself, put out Drago 5–2, while Parrott scored an impressive 5–4 win over Terry Griffiths. That meant that Parrott could have a day off because his personal manager, Phil Miller, had promised him a day at Newbury racecourse.

'Frenchie' Chaperon knocked out Mick Fisher 5–2 to go through to the first quarter-final of his career. Chaperon, one of the nicest characters on the circuit, said,

'I won't be satisfied with getting this far. I've got £9,000 now, but if I don't win I don't eat.'

The biggest shock, however, was yet to come when Davis lined up against Hendry in the fifth round. Hendry had met Davis on eight previous occasions and lost the lot. But he didn't bat an eyelid as Davis went 56–0 and 45–2 ahead in the first two frames. Hendry took the first frame by 1 point and made it 2–0 when he knocked in a 33. The next two frames were shared and then Hendry made it 4–1. Davis did take frame six, but Hendry's 72 break gave him the most important and most satisfying win of his career. The young Scot said, 'I had to change my game completely because in the other matches I wasn't even getting close to Davis.' He was certainly close to Davis in this match, in fact a lot better on the night. The season was now stretching before Hendry and he could only get better.

WHO SAID THAT?

'I had to change my game completely because in the other matches I was not even getting close to Davis.'

▲

– *Stephen Hendry after his 5–2 Rothmans Grand Prix win over Steve Davis.*

Previous Years' Results

YEAR	WINNER	RUNNER-UP	SCORE
1982	(Professional Players Tournament)		
	R. Reardon (Wales)	J. White (Eng)	10–5
1983	(PPT)		
	A. Knowles (Eng)	J. Johnson (Eng)	9–8
1984	Dennis Taylor (NI)	C. Thorburn (Can)	10–2
1985	S. Davis (Eng)	Dennis Taylor (NI)	10–9
1986	J. White (Eng)	R. Williams (Eng)	10–6

Rothmans Grand Prix Results

FOURTH ROUND

J. White (Eng)	3
A. Drago (Malta)	5
W. Thorne (Eng)	5
R. Bales (Eng)	2
P. Gibson (Eng)	4
G. Cripsey (Eng)	5
J. Johnson (Eng)	2
P. Francisco (SA)	5
Dennis Taylor (NI)	5
W. Werbeniuk (Can)	3
C. Wilson (Wales)	5
J. Virgo (Eng)	3
S. Francisco (SA)	3
Gary Wilkinson (Eng)	5
C. Thorburn (Can)	0
S. Newbury (Wales)	5
M. Clark (Eng)	4
M. Fisher (Eng)	5
P. Houlihan (Eng)	0
R. Chaperon (Can)	5
J. Parrott (Eng)	5
K. Stevens (Can)	0
T. Griffiths (Wales)	5
A. Chappel (Wales)	3
A. Knowles (Eng)	5
D. Roe (Eng)	2
R. Edmonds (Eng)	3
E. Charlton (Aust)	5
J. Chambers (Eng)	1
S. Hendry (Scot)	5
S. Davis (Eng)	5
J. Wych (Can)	1

FIFTH ROUND

Drago	2
Thorne	5
Cripsey	1
P. Francisco	5
Dennis Taylor	5
Wilson	2
Gary Wilkinson	3
Newbury	5
Fisher	2
Chaperon	5
Parrott	5
Griffiths	4
Knowles	5
Charlton	0
Hendry	5
S. Davis	2

QUARTER-FINALS

Thorne	3
P. Francisco	5
Dennis Taylor	5
Newbury	2
Chaperon	2
Parrott	5
Knowles	2
Hendry	5

SEMI-FINALS

P. Francisco	4
Dennis Taylor	9
Parrott	7
Hendry	9

FINAL

Dennis Taylor	7
Hendry	10

Losers: £2,906.25

Losers: £4,500

Losers: £9,000

Losers: £18,000

Loser: £36,000
Winner: £60,000

High break: 130 – J. Parrott £6,000

MATCHROOM CHAMPION OF CHAMPIONS

Barry Hearn's Matchroom men certainly like to be beside the seaside. The second Matchroom Champion of Champions event was staged just off the promenade at Southend – a resort famous for its jellied eels and the world's longest pier. Hearn knows that the cynics label this £125,000 tournament as a pure in-house exercise but he couldn't care less: his seven players' snooker was carried all over Europe by Super Channel, the satellite TV company. It was also a chance for the Matchroom men to entertain clients and meet their Essex fans. Whatever the ethics of the event, the competition is fierce with all seven players keen to be known as the Matchroom champion.

Steve Davis, who failed in his bid for the title in 1986, this time beat Tony Meo in his opening match -- but only just, by 6–5. Davis, incredibly, twice had the chance of a 147; no player had ever before achieved two maximums in the same match. In frame three Davis missed the twelfth red, and then five frames later blew it on the fourteenth red. But the win put him into the semi-finals and he was joined by Neal Foulds who wasted little time in beating Terry Griffiths 6–2.

Dennis Taylor and Jimmy White attracted a sell-out crowd to the Cliffs Pavilion, but it was Taylor who produced the class winning 6–2. He just happened to knock in a 141 that earned him the high break prize of £2,500 and he said, 'That's my fourth break of more than 120 this season.'

In the semi-finals, when defending champion Willie Thorne was at the table for the first time, he delighted his band of travelling Leicester family supporters by overcoming Foulds 6–5. One proud watcher was Thorne's eighty-seven-year-old grandad, Walter.

The other semi-final was between Davis and Taylor with Davis more than keen to exact revenge for Taylor's 5–1 thrashing in the Canadian Masters. When Davis led 3–1 his hopes looked good, but Taylor, cueing as well as any player in the game, reeled off five successive frames for a 6–3 win. It was Taylor's seventh win in ten meetings against the world champion, and no other player can boast such a good record.

The final proved an anti-climax as Taylor beat Thorne with ease 10–3 to take the £50,000 first prize. It was Taylor's fourth title of the season and in just ten weeks he had banked a staggering £170,000.

Previous Years' Results

YEAR	WINNER	RUNNER-UP	SCORE
1986	W. Thorne	S. Davis	10–9

Matchroom Champion of Champions Results

FIRST ROUND		SEMI-FINALS		FINAL	
S. Davis (Eng)	6				
v		S. Davis	3		
A. Meo (Eng)	5				
		v		Dennis Taylor	10
Dennis Taylor (NI)	6				
v		Dennis Taylor	6		
J. White (Eng)	2			v	
N. Foulds (Eng)	6				
v		Foulds	5	Thorne	3
T. Griffiths (Wales)	2				
		v			
		W. Thorne (Eng)	6		
Losers: £7,500		Losers: £12,500		Loser: £25,000	
				Winner: £50,000	

High break: 141 – Dennis Taylor £2,500

TENNENTS UK OPEN

Steve Davis earned his fourth successive title in the Tennents UK Open at Preston's Guild Hall as he and Jimmy White put on a snooker masterpiece in a final which twisted and turned with almost every shot. Davis won 16–14 to take the UK crown for the sixth time and collect £70,000: these were the stark facts of the final. But BBC cameras were there to record every compelling moment of a match that will go down in snooker history as one of the great finals of all time – it was that good.

Davis produced five century breaks and White responded with his own special brand of snooker magic. White led 5–2, was never behind on day one and finished at 7–7 – the highlight coming in the fourth frame when the Whirlwind cracked in a 139 to take the £7,000 high break prize.

Davis loves Preston, he loves the seventeen-frame format and, above all, he loves winning. That was the challenge that Londoner White faced and he matched

At last: Willie Thorne after achieving his dream of a 147 in tournament play.

Davis virtually all the way until it came to the climax. Davis led 11–10 but White, to the delight of a sell-out crowd, fought back to edge in front at 12–11. Then three of those Davis century breaks gave the world number 1 a 15–14 lead and he finished it off with a pink into the middle pocket.

Davis earned the cash, White collected the sympathy and snooker was once again the outright winner. 'Jimmy was brilliant,' said an exhausted Davis. 'His safety play was probably better than mine. That is possibly the best match I have ever been involved in. The 1985 world final was more exciting, but I don't think there has been a better game for sheer quality.'

White commented, 'In the end I made too many mistakes. Steve started to wobble at the end but I never pushed him hard enough. It was a great scrap.'

The other major newsworthy point was the 147 by Willie Thorne, the renowned Mr Maximum. Thorne has been knocking in 147s with frightening regularity for years, but he had never been able to do one in a match. That all changed when maximum number 80 went in against Ireland's Tommy Murphy in the fourth round and history was made in frame two when Thorne polished off every ball on the table. That maximum was worth a modest £6,750 – £5,000 for the 147 and £1,750 for the high break in the non-televised stages. Even in his moment of glory, Thorne was unlucky. If he had waited until the cameras arrived, he would have been able to put £50,000 in his bank! 'I knew it was on from the first red. The money

doesn't worry me – it was just a good feeling to finally get a 147 in a tournament,' he said.

There have been three previous 147s under tournament conditions: Steve Davis's in 1982, Cliff Thorburn's in 1983 and Kirk Stevens's in 1984.

The action in the UK Open started at the third-round stage with six tables in action. It's a tough job being a journalist, trying to guess which table is going to provide the story; it's a bit like tennis at Wimbledon – without the sunshine!

Stephen Hendry, after winning the Rothmans Grand Prix, was expected to go a long way in the UK Open. He did – all the way back to Edinburgh after a surprise 9–7 defeat by Canadian Jim Wych. It was a great win by Wych who was celebrating the birth of his son just twelve days earlier. 'No excuses – Jim was a worthy winner,' said an honest Hendry.

Essex kid Martin Smith dumped out Doug Mountjoy, Neal Foulds failed again – this time against Worksop's Danny Fowler – and Dennis Taylor came back from 2–8 down to beat Les Dodd 9–8. The latter is now known as 'Less' Dodd after losing an incredible 7 stone in weight!

Rex Williams, who had struggled all season, bowed out 9–7 to Derby's David Roe, seventy-one places below him on the world ladder, while in the fourth round Alex Higgins, back at the venue where twelve months earlier he had head-butted tournament director Paul Hatherell, beat David Taylor 9–6. Davis was next for Higgins and the Hurricane said, 'I took liberties against Taylor – I will treat Davis with more respect.'

There is a two-day break to change the arena and set it up for the TV cameras and a two-table format. Higgins commented meanwhile, 'I fancy beating Davis and going all the way to the title.'

Davis responded, 'Alex is one of the few snooker greats – there is something special about playing him even though we have met many times.' Davis went into the match with 17 victories out of their 21 meetings, and easily made it win number 18 as he destroyed Higgins 9–2. He said, 'You did not see the best of Alex but that might be down to me,' while Higgins admitted, 'It was a big occasion and I failed miserably.'

The quarter-finals had begun to sort themselves out with Davis up against John Parrott, Thorne taking on Cliff Thorburn, Joe Johnson tackling Mike Hallett and White meeting Welshman Terry Griffiths. Davis had to struggle to beat Parrott – a self-confessed Davis fan – who kicked off the match with a break of 101; but the drama all happened when Johnson beat Mike Hallett 9–7. Johnson started to suffer pain during the sixth frame and in the interval a doctor was summoned to the Crest Hotel. A heart attack was suspected but the doctor gave Joe the all-clear after examining him thoroughly. John Rukin, Johnson's manager, said, 'I was very, very worried – he said it felt like a vice across his chest.' Johnson himself was even more explicit: 'Those pains petrified me,' he said, 'and I thought I was a goner. I was on the point of collapse, but after a few minutes I started to feel better.' He returned to finish off Hallett, thus ensuring his place in the semi-final.

White and Thorne had to be at their best to book their semi-final places. The London Whirlwind was trailing Griffiths 7–4 but then, in sixty-five minutes of breathtaking snooker, totally transformed the game. For the record, White knocked in breaks of 65, 98, 70, 57 and 81 to leave Griffiths baffled and beaten. 'The best snooker I have played all season,' commented delighted White, 'It was even better considering I was under a lot of pressure.'

Thorne had to fire in three century breaks to edge out friend Thorburn 9–8. Thorne looked comfortable at 8–5 but Thorburn always refuses to buckle under and breaks of 51, 57 and 79 set up the last frame decider. However, Thorne's burst of 61 gave him victory.

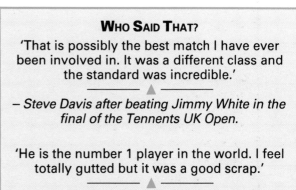

WHO SAID THAT?

'That is possibly the best match I have ever been involved in. It was a different class and the standard was incredible.'

– *Steve Davis after beating Jimmy White in the final of the Tennents UK Open.*

'He is the number 1 player in the world. I feel totally gutted but it was a good scrap.'

– *Jimmy White after losing to Steve Davis in the Tennents UK Open.*

White and Davis both scored comfortable semi-final wins with White ending Johnson's run by a 9–4 scoreline and Davis proving far too good for Thorne and coming home 9–2. Johnson had visited another doctor who diagnosed a trapped nerve in the back – he was certainly trapped by White, though he so nearly took home that £50,000 prize for a televised maximum. It was in the third frame and Johnson confidently put away 15 reds, 15 blacks, yellow, green, brown and blue and lined up a long pink. He missed! 'When I potted the green I was thinking of the Bahamas; when I potted the blue all I could see was pound notes,' said Johnson, who offered no comment on what he thought about the pink which wobbled tantalizingly in the jaws and came out.

Tennents UK Open Results

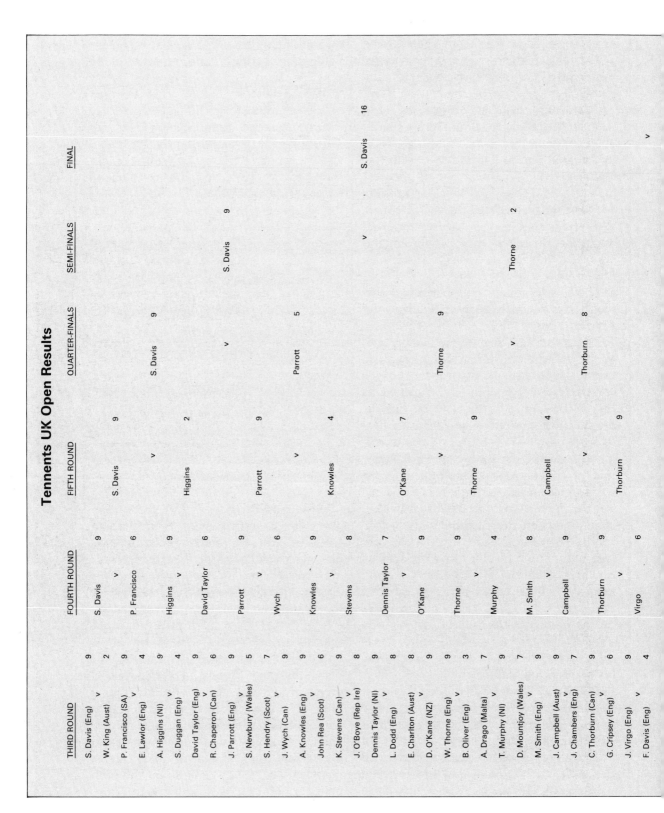

THIRD ROUND		FOURTH ROUND		FIFTH ROUND		QUARTER-FINALS		SEMI-FINALS		FINAL	
S. Davis (Eng)	9										
W. King (Aust)	2	S. Davis									
P. Francisco (SA)	9	P. Francisco	6	S. Davis	9						
E. Lawlor (Eng)	4										
A. Higgins (NI)	9	Higgins				S. Davis	9				
S. Duggan (Eng)	4			Higgins	2						
David Taylor (Eng)	9	David Taylor	6					S. Davis	9		
R. Chaperon (Can)	6										
J. Parrott (Eng)	9	Parrott	9								
S. Newbury (Wales)	5			Parrott	9						
S. Hendry (Scot)	7	Wych	6			Parrott	5				
J. Wych (Can)	9										
A. Knowles (Eng)	9	Knowles	9	Knowles	4						
John Rea (Scot)	6										
K. Stevens (Can)	9	Stevens	8								
J. O'Boye (Rep Ire)	8									S. Davis	16
Dennis Taylor (NI)	9	Dennis Taylor									
L. Dodd (Eng)	8			O'Kane	7						
E. Charlton (Aust)	8	O'Kane	9			O'Kane					
D. O'Kane (NZ)	9							Thorne	9		
W. Thorne (Eng)	9	Thorne	9								
B. Oliver (Eng)	3			Thorne	9						
A. Drago (Malta)	7	Murphy	4			Thorne	9				
T. Murphy (NI)	9									Thorne	2
D. Mountjoy (Wales)	7	M. Smith	8								
M. Smith (Eng)	9			Campbell	4						
J. Campbell (Aust)	9	Campbell	9			Thorburn	8				
J. Chambers (Eng)	7										
C. Thorburn (Can)	9	Thorburn	9								
G. Cripsey (Eng)	6			Thorburn	9						
J. Virgo (Eng)	9	Virgo	6								
F. Davis (Eng)	4										

Round 1		Round 2		Round 3		Quarter-finals		Semi-finals		Final
N. Foulds (Eng)	5									
v										
D. Fowler (Eng)	9	Fowler	9							
J. Spencer (Eng)	5	v		Fowler	4					
v										
G. Miles (Eng)	9	Miles	4							
M. Hallett (Eng)	9	Hallett	9	Hallett	9					
v		v								
A. Jones (Eng)	2					Hallett	7			
A. Meo (Eng)	9	Meo	5							
v										
P. Watchorn (Rep Ire)	1									
D. Reynolds (Eng)	5									
v										
A. Chappel (Wales)	9	Chappel	9	Chappel	4					
S. Longworth (Eng)	9	Longworth	6	v						
v										
W. Werbeniuk (Can)	5									
J. Johnson (Eng)	9	Johnson	9	Johnson	9	Johnson	9	Johnson	4	
v		v		v						
J. Bear (Can)	5							v		
B. West (Eng)	9	West	6							
v										
M. Gauvreau (Can)	6									
T. Griffiths (Wales)	9	Griffiths	9	Griffiths	9					
v		v		v						
Gary Wilkinson (Eng)	5					Griffiths	7			
M. Macleod (Scot)	4									
v										
R. Edmonds (Eng)	9	Edmonds	5							
S. Francisco (SA)	9	S. Francisco	9	S. Francisco	3					
v		v								
R. Reardon (Wales)	3									
C. Wilson (Wales)	9	Wilson	1							
v										
W. Jones (Wales)	6									
R. Williams (Eng)	7									
v										
D. Roe (Eng)	9	Roe	9	Roe	5					
D. Martin (Eng)	7	v		v						
v										
V. Harris (Eng)	9	V. Harris	5							
J. White (Eng)	9	White	9	White	9	White	9	White	9	White 14
v		v		v		v				
J. Dunning (Eng)	0									
E. Hughes (Rep Ire)	9	E. Hughes	4							
v										
N. Gilbert (Eng)	7									

Losers: £1,531.25   Losers: £3,390.62   Losers: £5,250   Losers: £10,500   Losers: £21,000   Loser: £42,000   Winner: £70,000

High break: 139 – J. White £7,000

Politics were again the dominant talking point during the Tennents – beta-blockers (what else?) have provided more column inches, while Williams resigned as chairman of the WPBSA. Snooker even had to deal with a rare case of vandalism on the morning of the final as, two hours before the start on day two, officials found that yobboes had thrown water on to the cloth.

Table-fitter Peter Camm was called in to make emergency repairs and finally replaced the cloth and one cushion, putting the finishing touches just five minutes before kick-off.

However, nothing could stop Davis from making it four UK wins on the trot. White's only consolation is that it was a truly great final.

Previous Years' Results

YEAR	WINNER	RUNNER-UP	SCORE
1977	(Super Crystalate) P. Fagan (Rep Ire)	D. Mountjoy (Wales)	12–9
1978	(Coral) D. Mountjoy (Wales)	David Taylor (Eng)	15–9
1979	(Coral) J. Virgo (Eng)	T. Griffiths (Wales)	14–13
1980	(Coral) S. Davis (Eng)	A. Higgins (NI)	16–6
1981	(Coral) S. Davis (Eng)	T. Griffiths (Wales)	16–3
1982	(Coral) T. Griffiths (Wales)	A. Higgins (NI)	16–15
1983	(Coral) A. Higgins (NI)	S. Davis (Eng)	16–15
1984	(Coral) S. Davis (Eng)	A. Higgins (NI)	16–8
1985	(Coral) S. Davis (Eng)	W. Thorne (Eng)	16–14
1986	S. Davis (Eng)	N. Foulds (Eng)	16–7

FOSTER'S WORLD DOUBLES

Stephen Hendry is a young man with a golden money-filled future. Mike Hallett is a professional who at long last is fulfilling potential that has lain dormant for many years. They are both managed by Scottish businessman Ian Doyle and together they provided a formidable force in the art of doubles play. Before a ball was struck in the Foster's World Doubles at Northampton, Hendry and Hallett were being marked down as possible winners.

The pair had given notice a year earlier of the power of their combined play when they raced through to the final of an event that was then sponsored by Hofmeister. That final appearance ended in disaster when they were trounced 12–3 by holders Steve Davis and Tony Meo. It was a bad result and one they were desperate to erase from their memory. They did just that in the final this time as they took on the experience of Dennis Taylor and Cliff

Thorburn with a £60,000 first prize waiting for the winners.

The winners looked certain to be Taylor and Thorburn as they opened a 5–0 lead. Painful thoughts of the previous final must have been in the mind of Hendry and Hallett. But if there were fears of another final massacre, Hendry didn't let it worry him as he showed what a fearsome potter he has become. Break after break rattled in from his cue and by the end of the first day that 5–0 deficit had been turned into a 7–6 lead. Taylor and Thorburn went away to work out a plan to stem the tide.

Taylor and Thorburn took the first two frames on day two, but these were the last frames they were destined to win as Hendry, once again the dominant partner, rapped in more scintillating breaks. The match finished 12–8 to Hendry and Hallett and there was a £5,000 bonus for the combined high break of 182 and £1,250 for the high break in the non-televised stage. For Hallett memories of the final will linger on as it was his first major success, while Hendry knew it was just another stepping stone that will one day lead him to the individual world crown.

That was the final, but there had been sensations on day one of the event as Davis and Meo embarked on another doubles campaign that has usually seen them go home with the trophy. This time Martin Clark and Jimmy Chambers, rated by bookmakers Coral as a 250-1 shot, dished out a 5–1 third-round hammering to Davis and Meo. Chambers described it as 'the greatest moment of my sporting life'. Davis agreed that the better pair won, commenting, 'They showed better safety play, better positional play and they outpotted us – we probably edged it on the dress suits.'

Doubles can be notoriously slow and Robbie Foldvari and Ian Williamson were warned by referee Alan Chamberlain for slow play. The players were told that they would lose a frame if they didn't start quickening up.

Dene O'Kane, the talented young New Zealander, and Jim Wych, the under-rated Canadian, wasted little time in knocking out the new title favourites, Jimmy White and Willie Thorne, 5–3. The articulate Wych offered a valid reason why White and Davis had both gone out early. 'They have just played a thirty-frame final in the Tennents UK Open – I would have needed a week's vacation to get over that,' he said.

Some of the form horses had managed to get through to the quarter-finals – pairings like John Parrott and Dean Reynolds, Joe Johnson and Tony Knowles, Terry Griffiths and Neal Foulds and the Franciscos (Silvino and Peter).

There were also frantic phone calls to travel agents as Wych and O'Kane had to cancel Christmas trips back home to see their families. Wych remarked, 'I didn't know the event lasted this long and I was really looking forward to seeing my month-old son, Kyle.' But they were both delighted to be in the last eight, even though they then went down 5–4 to the Franciscos.

Johnson and Knowles were fancied as potential winners but they crashed 5–0 to Thorburn and Taylor, while Steve James and David Roe staked a claim for the outsiders as they entered the semi-final with a 5–2 defeat of Parrott and Reynolds. James and Roe had been upset by criticism in some quarters of their attacking policy. But they certainly pleased the crowd despite eventually being overwhelmed 9–1 by Taylor and Thorburn in the semi-final.

Foster's World Doubles Results

THIRD ROUND

S. Davis (Eng)
A. Meo (Eng) — 1
v
J. Chambers (Eng) — 5
M. Clark (Eng

D. Martin (Eng)
J. Spencer (Eng) — 2
v
S. James (Eng) — 5
D. Roe (Eng)

J. Virgo (Eng) — 5
K. Stevens (Can)
v
R. Bales (Eng) — 3
S. Newbury (Wales)

D. Reynolds (Eng) — 5
J. Parrott (Eng)
v
B. West (Eng) — 2
S. Duggan (Eng)

J. Johnson (Eng) — 5
A. Knowles (Eng)
v
M. Bradley (Eng) — 0
L. Dodd (Eng)

M. Macleod (Scot) — 5
J. Campbell (Aust)
v
I. Williamson (Eng) — 4
R. Foldvari (Aust)

David Taylor (Eng) — 5
E. Charlton (Aust)
v
M. Wildman (Eng) — 3
R. Edmonds (Eng)

C. Thorburn (Can) — 5
Dennis Taylor (NI)
v
R. Chaperon (Can) — 1
M. Gauvreau (Can)

J. White (Eng) — 3
W. Thorne (Eng)
v
D. O'Kane (NZ) — 5
J. Wych (Can)

C. Wilson (Wales) — 5
W. King (Aust)
v
M. Smith (Eng) — 3
D. Gilbert (Eng)

D. Mountjoy (Wales) — 5
W. Jones (Wales)
v
G. Cripsey (Eng) — 3
S. Longworth (Eng)

S. Francisco (SA) — 5
P. Francisco (SA)
v
R. Reardon (Wales) — 3
A. Jones (Eng)

A. Higgins (NI) — 5
E. Hughes (Rep Ire)
v
T. Murphy (NI) — 2
A. Chappel (Wales)

M. Hallett (Eng) — 5
S. Hendry (Scot)
v
W. Werbeniuk (Can) — 2
D. Fowler (Eng)

R. Williams (Eng) — 5
G. Miles (Eng)
v
J. O'Boye (Rep Ire) — 1
R. Harris (Eng)

N. Foulds (Eng) — 5
T. Griffiths (Wales)
v
A. Drago (Malta) — 1
K. Owers (Eng)

FOURTH ROUND

Chambers
Clark — 3
v
James
Roe — 5

Virgo
Stevens — 0
v
Reynolds
Parrott — 5

Johnson
Knowles — 5
v
Macleod
Campbell — 1

David Taylor
Charlton — 2
v
Thorburn
Dennis Taylor — 5

O'Kane
Wych — 5
v
Wilson
King — 2

Mountjoy
W. Jones — 3
v
S. Francisco
P. Francisco — 5

Higgins
E. Hughes — 2
v
Hallett
Hendry — 5

Williams
Miles — 3
v
N. Foulds
Griffiths — 5

QUARTER-FINALS

James
Roe — 5
v
Reynolds
Parrott — 2

Johnson
Knowles — 0
v
Thorburn
Dennis Taylor — 5

O'Kane
Wych — 4
v
S. Francisco
P. Francisco — 5

Hallett
Hendry — 5
v
Foulds
Griffiths — 1

SEMI-FINALS

James
Roe — 1
v
Thorburn
Dennis Taylor — 9

S. Francisco
P. Francisco — 4
v
Hallett
Hendry — 9

FINAL

Thorburn
Dennis Taylor — 8
v
Hallett
Hendry — 12

Losers: £2,434 (shared)

Losers: £4,375 (shared)

Losers: £8,750 (shared)

Losers: £17,500 (shared)

Losers: £35,000 (shared)
Winners: £60,000 (shared)

Combined high break: 182 – M. Hallett (66), S. Hendry (116) £5,000 (shared)

In the bottom half of the draw, Hendry and Hallett demolished Griffiths and Foulds 5–1 and then the Franciscos 9–4 to go through to the final.

After Hendry and Hallett's final win, tournament director David Apthorp tried to sound optimistic about an event that was suffering from falling attendances and was known not to be the favourite tournament at ITV. He said, 'The doubles certainly has a future. The top players compete and they wouldn't do that if they didn't like it.' A couple of months later the WPBSA announced that the doubles was to be discontinued. Some of the lesser professionals will be sorry to see the event go as it often provided them with their biggest payday of the season.

Previous Years' Results

YEAR	WINNERS	RUNNERS-UP	SCORE
1982	(Hofmeister)		
	S. Davis (Eng)	T. Griffiths (Wales)	
	A. Meo (Eng)	D. Mountjoy (Wales)	13–2
1983	(Hofmeister)		
	S. Davis (Eng)	A. Knowles (Eng)	
	A. Meo (Eng)	J. White (Eng)	10–2
1984	(Hofmeister)		
	A. Higgins (NI)	C. Thorburn (Can)	
	J. White (Eng)	W. Thorne (Eng)	10–2
1985	(Hofmeister)		
	S. Davis (Eng)	A. Jones (Eng)	
	A. Meo (Eng)	R. Reardon (Wales)	12–5
1986	(Hofmeister)		
	S. Davis (Eng)	S. Hendry (Scot)	
	A. Meo (Eng)	M. Hallett (Eng)	12–3

MERCANTILE CREDIT CLASSIC

Sporting winners can be made on a missed penalty, a dropped catch, a misplaced dart or even the toss of a coin. Liverpool's John Parrott will long remember his failure on a red that cost him the first title of his career in the Mercantile Credit Classic at Blackpool's Norbreck Castle Hotel.

Parrott was up against the toughest challenge in sport – a twenty-five frame battle with defending champion Steve Davis. But Parrott was never overawed in his first major final. At the end of day one, Davis had eased in to a 9–5 lead and the £50,000 winner's cheque looked set to accompany him on his way back home in the Matchroom Cadillac. Parrott had other ideas and soon put these into action, winning frame after frame. The packed crowd were suddenly faced with an absorbing final when at start of play they had probably been anticipating another easy Davis victory.

Then that fatal red came into play with Parrott, now 11–10 in front, 31–16 ahead in the twenty-second frame. He went for that tricky red, missed and Davis was suddenly back with a chance. Parrott found to his cost that it is fatal to give Davis a second bite at a title that he can see rapidly slipping away from him. The world number 1 had an extra bounce in his step as he came to the table, and a break of 83 levelled the scores. Davis was bubbling again, Parrott was downcast and the world champion recorded breaks of 68 and 99 to retain the crown 13–11.

'That was probably the one shot in the match that I didn't play 100 per cent. I threw Davis a lifeline and he grabbed it with both hands,' said Parrott. It proved to be the thirty-seventh title of Davis's career and he had won each of his last nine major finals. It was also his third ranking tournament success of the season but only he knows how close he was to defeat. Parrott had given notice of his intentions on day two in the opening frame which he took with a break of 103.

Parrott had reached the final with an easier-than-expected win over Framework colleague Tony Knowles 9–4. Now Parrott faced Davis – the man he rates as 'the

Guvnor'. He said, 'Steve is the best player that has ever been born but I will not be overawed. I will just go out and enjoy the final.'

Davis was even more clinical than Parrott in his semi-final against Welshman Steve Newbury, and he came through an easy 9–2 victor. This semi-final appearance was to earn Newbury a placing at number 20 in the provisional ranking list, but his earlier performances had probably taken their toll. It was the first time that he

In relaxed mood: Steve Davis after winning the Mercantile Credit Classic.

had contested a major semi-final and he reached that landmark with a 5–4 beating of fellow countryman Terry Griffiths, though the preparation of the world number 6 left a lot to be desired. On the morning of the match, Griffiths had risen at the crack of dawn for a flight to his native Llanelli to make sure that he could obtain a gaming licence for the snooker club he had just opened. He arrived back in Blackpool with forty-five minutes to spare and was brought down to earth by Newbury who assured himself of his biggest ever payday – £15,000.

Davis was in quarter-final action against Stephen Hendry who had beat him 5–2 the last time they met on the way to Hendry's winning the Rothmans Grand Prix. Hendry led 2–1 but Davis didn't make many mistakes and easily wrapped up a 5–3 success even though he was helped by a fluked red in the final frame.

Knowles had ended the giant-killing exploits of Chesterfield's Dave Martin 5–1, while Parrott had scored another personal triumph with a 5–1 hammering of Ireland's Dennis Taylor. It was a victory that gave Parrott immense pleasure and he commented, 'It is the most refreshing win of my career – I rate Dennis the hardest player to beat after Davis.'

The fifth round went virtually according to the form book with one major exception – Martin's 5–2 defeat of Jimmy White, a finalist the previous season. Martin is a player who has many admirers in the pro ranks but he has struggled to stamp his mark on the rankings. His world rating of number 27 was below his capabilities but snooker is judged on results, a commodity in short supply for Martin. That all changed, however, as Martin stepped out against White after just edging home 5–4 against Welshman Doug Mountjoy in the previous round. He won the first frame from 63 points behind and was level 2–2 at the interval but then stunned the Whirlwind by picking up three frames in a row and finishing off in tremendous style with a break of 116.

Yet, seven years ago, Martin had contemplated the end of his career when a bad car accident nearly cost him the sight of his left eye. He vividly remembered the last time he had played White – when the surroundings were less glamorous but the atmosphere was quite incredible. 'It was in the final of the English Amateur nine years earlier down at a club in Helston, Cornwall. The place was unbelievable – the spectators were quite literally hanging from the rafters. Jimmy beat me 13–10,' he said. I can vouch for that: I couldn't even get into the arena but sat outside with White's mother as he went on, at sixteen, to become the youngest ever English amateur champion. How times have changed!

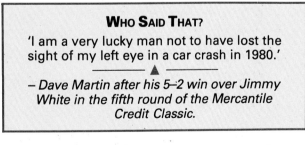

WHO SAID THAT?

'I am a very lucky man not to have lost the sight of my left eye in a car crash in 1980.'

▲

– Dave Martin after his 5–2 win over Jimmy White in the fifth round of the Mercantile Credit Classic.

WHO SAID THAT?

'I will just turn up, hope to play well and pray that Jimmy misses a few.'

▲

– Dave Martin speaking before his victory against Jimmy White in the Mercantile Credit Classic.

Alex Higgins cast a sad shadow as he caved in 5–0 to Davis – only the third time that the Hurricane had been whitewashed in his lengthy career. It was the seventh time in a row that Davis had come out on top and the frame breakdown in that time made embarrassing reading – Davis winning 51 to Higgin's mere 10. 'I feel as if I

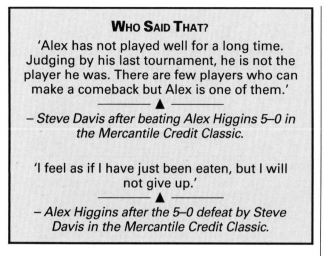

WHO SAID THAT?

'Alex has not played well for a long time. Judging by his last tournament, he is not the player he was. There are few players who can make a comeback but Alex is one of them.'

▲

– Steve Davis after beating Alex Higgins 5–0 in the Mercantile Credit Classic.

'I feel as if I have just been eaten, but I will not give up.'

▲

– Alex Higgins after the 5–0 defeat by Steve Davis in the Mercantile Credit Classic.

with Francisco requiring snookers, and any miss would naturally help the South African's cause. But the golden rule is that the referee can never be wrong! The ball was put back and Taylor argued long and hard that he had made a fair try to escape from the snooker. He then demanded a second opinion, to which Ganley just replied, 'Yes, it is a miss.' Taylor went on to win 5–3, but he was clearly angry at the after-match press conference. 'There is no way I would miss when my opponent needed snookers,' he stated.

In round four, Newbury took on Cliff Thorburn for the third time last season and beat him 5–3. 'Don't tell me that,' was Thorburn's comment when told that he would meet Newbury again in the British Open the following month.

Hendry recovered from 1–3 down to beat Joe Johnson. The former world champion admitted, 'Hendry is brilliant and he has just got to get better and better.'

Tommy Murphy, a former apprentice coffin maker, overcame Dean Reynolds 5–4 and Barry West sent Willie Thorne crashing out 5–2. 'Perhaps I did not practise enough,' said world number 11 Thorne afterwards.

have just been eaten,' said the Irishman, 'but I will not give up.'

There was controversy in the fifth-round encounter between Dennis Taylor and South Africa's Peter Francisco with referee Len Ganley right in the thick of things. Taylor looked home and dry at 4–3 and 65–0 when he was called for a miss by Ganley after failing to hit a red while attempting to wriggle out of a tight snooker. It did seem a strange decision

Previous Years' Results

YEAR	WINNER	RUNNER-UP	SCORE
1980	(Wilsons Classic)		
	J. Spencer (Eng)	A. Higgins (NI)	4–3
1981	(Wilsons Classic)		
	S. Davis (Eng)	Dennis Taylor (NI)	4–1
1982	(Lada)		
	T. Griffiths (Wales)	S. Davis (Eng)	9–8
1983	(Lada) S. Davis (Eng)	W. Werbeniuk (Can)	9–5
1984	(Lada) S. Davis (Eng)	A. Meo (Eng)	9–8
1985	W. Thorne (Eng)	C. Thorburn (Can)	13–8
1986	J. White (Eng)	C. Thorburn (Can)	13–12
1987	S. Davis (Eng)	J. White (Eng)	13–12

Mercantile Credit Classic Results

FOURTH ROUND		FIFTH ROUND		QUARTER-FINALS		SEMI-FINALS		FINAL	
S. Davis (Eng)	5								
v		S. Davis	5						
J. Donnelly (Scot)	0			S. Davis	5				
A. Higgins (NI)	5	v							
v		Higgins	0			S. Davis	9		
A. Meo (Eng)	3			v					
S. Francisco (SA)	5			Hendry	3				
v		S. Francisco	3						
S. Longworth (Eng)	2	v							
J. Johnson (Eng)	3							S. Davis	13
v		Hendry	5						
S. Hendry (Scot)	5					v			
T. Griffiths (Wales)	5								
v		Griffiths	5						
C. Wilson (Wales)	2			Griffiths	4				
W. Thorne (Eng)	2	v							
v		West	2			Newbury	2		
B. West (Eng)	5			v					
M. Clark (Eng)	5			Newbury	5				
v		Clark	2						
M. Bennett (Wales)	2	v							
C. Thorburn (Can)	3								v
v		Newbury	5						
S. Newbury (Wales)	5								
N. Foulds (Eng)	3								
v		Virgo	0						
J. Virgo (Eng)	5			Parrott	5				
J. Parrott (Eng)	5	v							
v		Parrott	5			Parrott	9		
David Taylor (Eng)	0			v					
K. Owers (Eng)	0			Dennis Taylor	1				
v		P. Francisco	3						
P. Francisco (SA)	5	v							
Dennis Taylor (NI)	5							Parrott	11
v		Dennis Taylor	5						
A. Drago (Malta)	0					v			
A. Knowles (Eng)	5								
v		Knowles	5						
C. Roscoe (Wales)	0			Knowles	5				
D. Reynolds (Eng)	4	v							
v		Murphy	3			Knowles	4		
T. Murphy (NI)	5			v					
D. Mountjoy (Wales)	4			Martin	1				
v		Martin	5						
D. Martin (Eng)	5	v							
J. White (Eng)	5								
v		White	2						
J. Spencer (Eng)	1								

Losers: £2,421.87	Losers: £3,750	Losers: £7,500	Losers: £15,000	Loser: £30,000
				Winner: £50,000

High break: 132 – Dennis Taylor £5,000

BENSON AND HEDGES MASTERS

Steve Davis, who has dominated the professional game during the 1980s, had never stamped his mark on the Benson and Hedges Masters – the sixteen-man prestige tournament that traditionally produces the sport's biggest attendances at the Wembley Conference Centre. But he was determined to put that right last season. The world number 1 lives just forty-five minutes away from Wembley and in previous seasons had not thought it necessary to book into the players' hotel right next to the venue. Davis decided on a switch of tactics on this occasion and his change of lifestyle produced a devastating result as he captured the crown for the first time since 1982 with an almost embarrassing 9–0 final demolition of Mike Hallett.

'I thought about the event and decided that perhaps I was lacking a bit of motivation by going after each match. It certainly wasn't doing me any good as I didn't seem to get very far,' he said. 'That made me check into the hotel. Just being with the other players makes you feel part of the tournament. Back home, I never watch snooker on television – but this time I was either watching the matches on the TV in my room or getting in plenty of practice.'

Davis was totally ruthless in the final and never allowed Hallett a chance. Big break followed big break and the unfortunate Hallett could only watch and learn from the Davis onslaught. 'I don't think I have played as well as that for a long time,' said Davis. 'Every time Mike touched the ball it seemed to go wrong for him.' Hallett was gutted at the end and admitted, 'I have never felt such disappointment since I turned professional.'

It was the twenty-fourth time that Davis had whitewashed an opponent – many of them away from the glare of the TV cameras. Sadly for Hallett, the BBC were there to record every shot as Davis twisted the knife with gruesome effect. He even man-

aged a 126 break in the second frame of the final – a 126 total clearance that earned him £5,000 on top of the £56,000 winner's cheque.

In the semi-final, Davis had cleared the formidable obstacle of Joe Johnson 6–3. An interesting statistic was that these two players had met only twice before – both times in World Championship finals!

While Davis progressed smoothly, Hallett met Liverpool's John Parrott in a match that produced a frame which was already being hailed as the Frame of the Season. That came with the scores at 5–5, though Parrott looked a certainty as he sunk the final red to open a 65–22 lead. He was so jubilant that he went for a blazing finish on a green instead of just rolling the ball in. The green flew off the table and that left Hallett requiring just three snookers. If the green had gone in, Hallett later admitted, 'I would have probably called it

Chirpy: John Parrott on his way to the semi-final of the Benson and Hedges Masters.

a day. But that gave me a chance.' The tension was quite remarkable as he chipped away at Parrott's lead. Parrott had cracked up and conceded 18 more penalty points, leaving Hallett to step up to the table needing to clear green to black to win. In went green, brown and blue, but Hallett was still left with a very hard shot on the pink. Many players would have opted for safety at such a crucial time, yet Hallett took the pink and tapped in a simple black for an incredible victory. 'I just hit that green at 100 miles an hour – don't ask me why,' was Parrott's observation at the end.

The quarter-final also produced some memorable moments, like Johnson's 5–3 triumph against Jimmy White. 'If chances appeared, we were both prepared to go for our shots – it was a good game to play in,' said Johnson.

Parrott had recovered from a 2–4 deficit against Cliff Thorburn and then won the final frame with a fluked pink. 'It's the first time I have been beaten on a fluke before,' said a disconsolate Thorburn.

Davis whitewashed Terry Griffiths 5–0 and Hallett took care of Alex Higgins 5–2. The Irishman departed meekly, but there had been nothing meek and mild about his bad-tempered match with Framework stablemate Tony Knowles in the opening round. There was a full house of nearly 2,700 and Knowles had gone 2–0 ahead when Higgins stepped up to referee John Street to complain that Knowles was in his line of sight. Street offered Higgins's opinion to Knowles who obviously disagreed with the Hurricane's assessment of the situation. By the interval Higgins was trailing 3–1 and the bust-up continued in the dressing room area with raised voices that were clearly audible in the nearby pressroom. Journalists listened with interest as tournament director Nick Hill was summoned to the scene. He said, 'Alex has complained that Tony was in his line of sight,' adding wryly, 'there certainly seemed an air of disagreement between them. Tony said he would step away from the table, but he also said that he thought it was Alex who was in fact coming to the table too quickly.'

Knowles resumed play and at times lounged on the arena surround still obviously seething at the earlier events. Higgins won 5–4 and the journalists waited for the usual after-match press conference. Knowles said he would not appear but Higgins arrived insisting, 'We are the best of friends and everything has been sorted out.' Knowles then changed his mind and turned up, sitting next to the Hurricane who tried to make light of the obvious friction. Knowles would only say, 'I have nothing to say.'

Double trouble: Alex Higgins and Tony Knowles during a press conference after their controversial match in the Benson and Hedges Masters.

Neal Foulds's season had been looked on in many quarters as the time when he would perhaps challenge White for his number 2 slot. That was never going to happen after a series of below-par performances. But he looked as though his run of misfortune had subsided when he went into a 4–1 lead against Parrott. Even when Parrott drew level at 4–4, Foulds then swept into a 60–0 lead. Parrott was superb as he took the final frame 66–60.

Defending champion Dennis Taylor was a first round victim – 5–3 against Hallett – while Thorne went down 5–4 to Johnson as the former world champion potted an outstanding pink in the final frame.

The Wembley attendances were down 14 per cent on the previous season and there were only 583 faithfuls in the arena to watch Rex Williams take on Thorburn. Nearly four hours later, the Canadian won 5–3 in a quite dreadful match. But Thorburn cheered up the media afterwards when he said, 'A young kid came up to me in the interval and said that he was disappointed that I hadn't won the car on offer for a 147 maximum break. I thought, "That's nice," and asked why. The kid said if I had won the car I could have given him a lift home because by the time my match was over, he would have missed the last train!'

There were even fewer spectators – just 548 – for Griffiths's 5–3 win over Silvino Francisco who went on to voice his justified anger at being omitted from the Benson and Hedges Irish Masters because he was South African.

However, nothing could detract from the form of Davis who reached a pinnacle of achievement to which poor Hallett had no answer.

Benson and Hedges Masters Results

FIRST ROUND		QUARTER-FINALS		SEMI-FINALS		FINAL	
Dennis Taylor (NI)	3						
v		Hallett	5				
M. Hallett (Eng)	5						
		v		Hallett	6		
A. Higgins (NI)	5						
v		Higgins	2				
A. Knowles (Eng)	4						
				v		Hallett	0
C. Thorburn (Can)	5						
v		Thorburn	4				
R. Williams (Eng)	3						
		v		Parrott	5		
J. Parrott (Eng)	5						
v		Parrott	5				
N. Foulds (Eng)	4						
						v	
J. White (Eng)	5						
v		White	3				
D. Mountjoy (Wales)	0						
		v		Johnson	3		
W. Thorne (Eng)	4						
v		Johnson	5				
J. Johnson (Eng)	5						
				v		S. Davis	9
T. Griffiths (Wales)	5						
v		Griffiths	0				
S. Francisco (SA)	3						
		v		S. Davis	6		
D. Reynolds (Eng)	2						
v		S. Davis	5				
S. Davis (Eng)	5						

Losers: £6,000	Losers: £12,000	Losers: £18,000	Loser: £32,000
			Winner: £56,000

High break: 126 – S. Davis £5,000

Previous Years' Results

YEAR	WINNER	RUNNER-UP	SCORE
1975	J. Spencer (Eng)	R. Reardon (Wales)	9–8
1976	R. Reardon (Wales)	G. Miles (Eng)	7–3
1977	D. Mountjoy (Wales)	R. Reardon (Wales)	7–6
1978	A. Higgins (NI)	C. Thorburn (Can)	7–5
1979	P. Mans (SA)	A. Higgins (NI)	8–4
1980	T. Griffiths (Wales)	A. Higgins (NI)	9–5
1981	A. Higgins (NI)	T. Griffiths (Wales)	9–6
1982	S. Davis (Eng)	T. Griffiths (Wales)	9–5
1983	C. Thorburn (Can)	R. Reardon (Wales)	9–7
1984	J. White (Eng)	T. Griffiths (Wales)	9–5
1985	C. Thorburn (Can)	D. Mountjoy (Wales)	9–6
1986	C. Thorburn (Can)	J. White (Eng)	9–5
1987	Dennis Taylor (NI)	A. Higgins (NI)	9–8

MIM BRITANNIA UNIT TRUSTS BRITISH OPEN

Stephen Hendry, nineteen, picked up his second major ranking tournament of the season with a runaway victory in the MIM Britannia Unit Trusts British Open at the Derby Assembly Rooms. He needed just eleven minutes on the second day to demolish stablemate Mike Hallett 13–2 and collect the £60,000 first prize. Hendry also went back to Scotland an extra £6,000 richer with the highest break of 118 – a break he achieved in the semi-final against Cliff Thorburn.

After seven frames on the first afternoon of the final, Hendry had already established a 6–1 advantage. By the end of the day that gap had stretched to 12–2. Backstage, officials were frantic in case Hendry finished the match off with one day to spare. But Hallett saved their blushes by taking the penultimate frame of the day.

There was a full house for the final day but Hendry needed just one more frame to add the British Open title to his Rothmans Grand Prix success earlier in the season. Afterwards he said happily, 'This has certainly been a tremendous season for me. At the start of the season my ambitions were to win a tournament and get into the world's top eight. I have now won two tournaments and at this stage am provisionally number 3 on the world rankings.' But while Hendry was ecstatic about his success, there was still the World Championship to come and a possible final meeting with Davis. 'I will just go away and get ready for the world event,' he said.

Manager Ian Doyle knows he is sitting on a goldmine. He had already signed a £500,000 five-year deal with Riley Billiards earlier in the week and he knows the sky's the limit for his exciting young protégé. 'If Hendry wins the world title, we can start talking about the £1 million that Steve Davis earns,' said Doyle. Even without that Doyle was looking for £600,000 over the next twelve months.

It was a desperately disappointing final for Hallett, especially after his 9–0 whitewash by Steve Davis in the Benson and Hedges Masters final a month earlier. 'I don't know what went wrong,' he said. 'Against Davis I was probably too tense but against Hendry I was relaxed.'

In the semi-final Hendry had proved too strong for Cliff Thorburn and came home 9–5, while Hallett edged out Liverpool's John Parrott 9–8 in a tremendous match. Hendry had been humiliated 9–1 by Thorburn in the semi-final of the Fidelity Unit Trusts International earlier in the season. There was a score to settle and Hendry produced big break after big break to leave Thorburn 5–2 down at the end of the first session. 'That's the best snooker I have ever played,' commented the young Scot. At night Thorburn tried one of his famous fightbacks, but Hendry was in no mood to miss out on another chance of a ranking tournament victory.

In the other semi-final Hallett led 7–3 but then Parrott, showing great determination, rolled in five frames in a row to go 8–7. However, Hallett was not to be

---

WHO SAID THAT?

'My brain froze out there and my concentration was bad.'

▲

– Cliff Thorburn after losing 9–5 to Stephen Hendry in the semi-final of the MIM Britannia Unit Trusts British Open.

'If Stephen did win the world title, there are so many contracts available that we could even catch up the £1 million earnings of Steve Davis.'

▲

– Ian Doyle, the manager of Stephen Hendry, speaking after Hendry had won the MIM Britannia Unit Trusts British Open.

In line: Stephen Hendry and the MIM Britannia personality girls celebrate his British Open victory.

denied and took the final two frames to go through even though Parrott had his chances to sew the match up. Parrott had lost out 6–5 to Hallett in the semi-final of the Benson and Hedges Masters. Three mistakes on a pink were to cost him dear again as Hallett scraped through. Unfortunately, that determination was missing against Hendry in the final.

The tournament produced some quite remarkable results including the shock of the season in the third round when veteran Ray Reardon handed out a 5–0 whitewash to world champion Steve Davis – the first time he had been whitewashed since he turned professional in 1978. 'I was absolutely amazed,' admitted Reardon, while Davis offered this thought: 'After every defeat, I always try and look on the bright side – there wasn't one.'

Irishman Alex Higgins, now desperately trying to hang on to his place in the world's

top sixteen, and English champion Dean Reynolds were also forced out at the third-round stage, while in the fourth round Irishman Dennis Taylor was another whitewash victim to another veteran player – this time losing 5–0 to three-times world champion John Spencer.

Gary Wilkinson, twenty-one years old and one of the most talented new young players on the circuit, scored a 5–3 victory over world number 10 Silvino Francisco – the same result as when they met at the Rothmans Grand Prix fourth round earlier this season. Wilkinson, from Kirkby-in-Ashfield, has adapted well in his first season on the professional tour and shows all the capabilities of making a big impression in years to come.

World number 7 Tony Knowles was on the end of another surprise result going down 5–4 to Murdo Macleod, but Reardon could not repeat his form against

Davis and crashed 5–2 to local Derby star David Roe.

Round five and Parrott whitewashed the out-of-touch Neal Foulds 5–0. However, New Zealand's Dene O'Kane was on the top of his form to knock out world number 5 Joe Johnson 5–2. O'Kane, who talks sense, is always worth listening to. He said, 'I have given up going to nightclubs and cut out the drinking. I am a much more serious player these days. I am playing nearly as well as when I reached the world quarter-finals in 1987.'

In the quarter-finals of this tournament O'Kane found Parrott in good form and lost 5–2. Thorburn beat Rex Williams 5–2, while Hallett just scraped home 5–4 against Joe O'Boye. The Thorburn *versus* Williams match was hardly one to look forward to – especially after their long-drawn-out encounter in the Benson and Hedges Masters. Thorburn said, 'This is probably one match where it's a shame there has got to be a winner.' He was only joking.

The final quarter-final match saw Jimmy White against Hendry. Though White led 3–1, Hendry showed tremendous potting skills to come back and win the final frame for a 5–4 win.

MIM Britannia must have been pleased with their first sponsorship though, inevitably, the tournament was interspersed with political wranglings, this time between Barry Hearn and the WPBSA. Hearn, who felt some concern that the off-table disputes were detracting from the on-table activities, stated, 'I would like to apologize to MIM for everything that has happened this week. I will pledge the support of my players for their event in the years to come.'

Snooker is now big, big business. Disputes and disagreements are commonplace. But nothing could overshadow the sheer professionalism of Hendry, a nineteen-year-old who made potting look easy while he has obviously added vital new strings like safety play to his bow. The game is entering a new era and Hendry will be at the forefront. But those who try to write Davis off as a fading star are foolish, for one thing is certain: both Hendry and Davis are going to be around for a long time, so there will be plenty of Davis *versus* Hendry to savour in the future.

Previous Years' Results

YEAR	WINNER	RUNNER-UP	SCORE
1980	(British Gold Cup)		
	A. Higgins (NI)	R. Reardon (Wales)	5–1
1981	(Yamaha)		
	S. Davis (Eng)	David Taylor (Eng)	9–6
1982	(Yamaha)		
	S. Davis (Eng)	T. Griffiths (Wales)	9–7
1983	(Yamaha)		
	R. Reardon (Wales)	J. White (Eng)	9–6
1984	(Yamaha) Three-man play-off		
	D. Martin (Eng)	J. Dunning (Eng)	3–2
	S. Davis (Eng)	J. Dunning	4–1
	S. Davis	D. Martin	3–0
	Winner – Davis		
1985	(Dulux)		
	S. Francisco (SA)	K. Stevens (Can)	12–9
1986	(Dulux)		
	S. Davis (Eng)	W. Thorne (Eng)	12–7
1987	(Dulux)	N. Foulds (Eng)	13–9
	J. White (Eng)		

MIM Britannia Unit Trusts British Open Results

FOURTH ROUND		FIFTH ROUND		QUARTER-FINALS		SEMI-FINALS		FINAL	
J. White (Eng)	5								
v		White	5						
S. James (Eng)	1			White	4				
S. Francisco (SA)	3								
v		Gary Wilkinson	1						
Gary Wilkinson (Eng)	5					Hendry	9		
A. Jones (Eng	5								
v		A. Jones	3						
R. Chaperon (Can)	4			Hendry	5				
T. Griffiths (Wales)	1								
v		Hendry	5						
S. Hendry (Scot)	5							Hendry	13
Dennis Taylor (NI)	0								
v		Spencer	4						
J. Spencer (Eng)	5			Williams	2				
R. Williams (Eng)	5								
v		Williams	5						
B. West (Eng)	0					Thorburn	5		
W. Thorne (Eng)	5								
v		Thorne	2						
C. Wilson (Wales)	3			Thorburn	5				
C. Thorburn (Can)	5								
v		Thorburn	5						
P. Medati (Eng)	2							v	
N. Foulds (Eng)	5								
v		N. Foulds	0						
P. Francisco (SA)	3			Parrott	5				
J. Parrott (Eng)	5								
v		Parrott	5						
J. Virgo (Eng)	1					Parrott	8		
D. O'Kane (NZ)	5								
v		O'Kane	5						
P. Browne (Rep Ire)	2			O'Kane	2				
J. Johnson (Eng)	5								
v		Johnson	2						
B. Rowswell (Eng)	2							Hallett	2
A. Knowles (Eng)	4								
v		Macleod	2						
M. Macleod (Scot)	5			Hallett	5				
M. Hallett (Eng)	5								
v		Hallett	5						
G. Cripsey (Eng)	2					Hallett	9		
J. O'Boye (Rep Ire)	5								
v		O'Boye	5						
J. Campbell (Aust)	1			O'Boye	4				
R. Reardon (Wales)	2								
v		Roe	1						
D. Roe (Eng)	5								

Losers: £2,906.25   Losers: £4,500   Losers: £9,000   Losers: £18,000   Loser: £36,000
                                                                                                        Winner: £60,000

High break: 118 – S. Hendry £6,000

FERSINA WINDOWS WORLD CUP

World champion Steve Davis rescued his England side from the brink of defeat against Australia in the Fersina Windows World Cup at the Bournemouth International Centre with a remarkable four-frame spell of success. Underdogs Australia had surprised everybody by reaching their first ever World Cup final, and veteran Eddie Charlton had been in brilliant form in the first session.

After the first four frames were shared, Charlton came out to face Jimmy 'Whirlwind' White – a match that was expected to give England their supremacy. But Charlton was determined to try to win his first major title in this country. Four frames later, he had beaten White 3–1 and Australia were in the driving seat at 5–3.

At night, Australia and England shared the first four frames which left the Aussies still in charge at 7–5. It was Australia's bi-centennial year and it looked as though they were going to celebrate – and celebrate in style – with an against-the-odds victory over tournament favourites England. But then Davis appeared on the scene. He despatched Charlton 2–0, including a break of 69, and then took on Warren King, the Australian champion. The result was the same, 2–0, as Davis knocked in breaks of 89 and 91 to give England a 9–7 win and the £40,000 first prize.

'I knew we were going to do it as soon as I walked into the dressing room,' said England team member Neal Foulds. 'We were 7–5 down but I looked at Steve and he looked really mean – he was psyched up. I was totally confident after that.'

To this Davis responded, 'Even if I had dropped a frame, I still knew Neal would have pulled us through the decider.'

Foulds himself wasn't so sure. 'If it had been in the decider, I wouldn't have wanted to go out and play,' he said.

In the semi-final England had had a slight run of the balls to overcome the Rest of the World 5–3. Davis and Malta's Tony Drago shared the opening frames 1–1, as did Foulds against New Zealand's Dene O'Kane and Jimmy White against Silvino Francisco of South Africa. But White went straight back into action and clinched the match with a 2–0 win over Francisco.

The other semi-final saw Australia produce a magnificent performance to demolish Scotland 5–1. John Campbell and Warren King recorded respective 2–0 victories over Murdo Macleod and John Rea, while that man Charlton was at it again, taking the one frame that Scotland still needed from the Scottish whizz-kid Stephen Hendry.

It was the first year that Fersina Windows had sponsored the event and they had given the tournament some stability at last after previous sponsors had come and gone. Fersina had given their commitment for three years and certainly the public responded well down at the International

Losers: The Australian trio of John Campbell, Warren King and Eddie Charlton drown their sorrows with a commiserating cup of coffee.

Winners: Steve Davis, Neal Foulds and Jimmy White after their Fersina Windows World Cup success.

Centre. Even for the so-called 'lesser' matches there was always a healthy attendance and this bodes well for larger tournaments which may be held down at this South Coast venue.

The opening match produced the closest snooker of the four days with Scotland edging out Wales 5–4, even though it was another bad day for young Hendry. He could win only one of his four frames which put all the pressure on Macleod in the final match against Cliff Wilson. That frame had been set up when Terry Griffiths beat Hendry 2–0 and Wilson drew 1–1 with the Scottish youngster. But Wilson could not keep it going in the final frame and Macleod deservedly put Scotland through to the last four.

Much mileage had been made of the WPBSA decision to split up the hat-trick-winning Irish side into Northern Ireland and the Republic of Ireland. Before the tournament started Irish skipper Dennis Taylor said: 'I was disgusted that they

didn't approach us to find out our opinion. After all, we had won the title three times in a row and it would have been nice to let the WPBSA know our feelings.' There is logic in having the two Irelands, but surely it would have been easier and more humane to do it if and when the Irish trio of Taylor, Alex Higgins and Eugene Hughes had lost the title rather than just splitting up the squad without consultation. Taylor's new Northern Ireland team didn't survive the first round, going down 5–3 to the Rest of the World, while England put paid to the Republic of Ireland's hope with a 5–1 victory.

Even in this round it was the Australians who were causing the biggest shocks as they whitewashed Canada 5–0. Campbell beat Jim Wych 2–0, King despatched Bill Werbeniuk by the same margin, and then Charlton beat Canadian skipper Cliff Thorburn 1–0.

Now the WPBSA must build on the success of this event for the current season.

Fersina Windows World Cup Results

	QUARTER-FINALS		SEMI-FINALS		FINAL	
S. Davis J. White N. Foulds	England	5				
			England	5		
E. Hughes P. Browne J. O'Boye	Republic of Ireland	1				
					England	9
			v			
Dennis Taylor A. Higgins T. Murphy	Northern Ireland	3				
			Rest of the World	3		
S. Francisco A. Drago D. O'Kane	Rest of the World	5				
					v	
C. Thorburn J. Wych W. Werbeniuk	Canada	0				
			Australia	5		
J. Campbell E. Charlton W. King	Australia	5				
					Australia	7
			v			
S. Hendry M. Macleod John Rea	Scotland	5				
			Scotland	1		
T. Griffiths D. Mountjoy C. Wilson	Wales	4				

| | Losers: £7,500 | | Losers: £12,500 | | Losers: £25,000
Winners: £40,000 | |

High break: 106 – S. Hendry £5,000

Previous Years' Results

YEAR	WINNER	RUNNER-UP	SCORE
1979	(State Express) Wales	England	14–3
1980	(State Express) Wales	Canada	8–5
1981	(State Express) England	Wales	4–3
1982	(State Express) Canada	England	4–2
1983	(State Express) England	Wales	4–2
1985	(Guinness) Ireland A	England A	9–7
1986	(Car Care) Ireland A	Canada	9–7
1987	(Tuborg) Ireland A	Canada	9–2

BENSON AND HEDGES IRISH MASTERS

Steve Davis is a man who refuses to believe in coincidences and accepts that ability and skill will prove the decisive factor in virtually any sporting encounter. But his victory in the Benson and Hedges Irish Masters at the Horse Sales Ring at Goffs, County Kildare, provided some interesting facts.

Davis won this title – the last major event before the World Championship – in 1983, 1984 and 1987. Each year he went on to take the Embassy World Championship too. He won the Irish Masters again last season by beating Neal Foulds 9–4 in a one-sided final and then, despite Davis's reluctance to talk about the good omens, went on to claim the World Championship for the fifth time. Davis said: 'Anybody who thinks about statistics like that is an idiot. Facts and figures do not mean anything to me. I just get on and play the game.'

The Masters is a tournament eagerly awaited by all concerned – players, press and officials. There is a unique family atmosphere about the whole event, even though this year's tournament was tinged with controversy before a ball was struck.

Silvino Francisco, the South African ranked at number 10, should have been invited if Benson and Hedges had maintained the same policy as in previous years. But Francisco was told he was not welcome because of possible problems with anti-apartheid demonstrations. Francisco was far from happy about this. 'I have played in the Benson and Hedges Masters in England and yet I have been stopped from coming to the Masters in Ireland,' he said. 'I have been to Ireland on many occasions and have never had any problems. In fact, I have had only one incident and that was in Basingstoke in 1983 when a man in the crowd still seemed to think that there are elephants and lions on the streets in South Africa.' Benson and Hedges pointed to a clause in the contract

which gave them complete freedom as to whom to invite.

However, once the twelve players had arrived and had been met at the airport, all the aggro was quickly forgotten. Benson and Hedges official Kevin Norton, who is the original 'Jack of all trades', saw to that. He makes sure that everything runs like clockwork from picking up the players at the airport to taking the officials for a day's golf or a trip to the races.

In the first round Rex Williams's first appearance in the Masters ended with a 5–1 hammering by Terry Griffiths, while Tony Knowles beat Willie Thorne 5–3. Alex Higgins and Dennis Taylor were both hopeful of producing a first ever Irish victory. Higgins triumphed 5–3, but Taylor said: 'I was a bit upset with Alex leaving the table for four or five minutes at the end of each frame. I mentioned it in my report.' Higgins was not worried – just delighted with only his second victory over Taylor in two years. The final first round saw Joe Johnson taking the last two frames to knock out Eugene Hughes who, as usual, had brought a large contingent of fans from his native Dun Laoghaire, the seaport of nearby Dublin.

Higgins delighted a sell-out crowd who thronged to Goffs by beating Canadian Cliff Thorburn 5–3. The Irishman, bringing looks of disbelief from the assembled pressmen, announced: 'I am cleaning up my act – I have been going to sauna baths to get in shape.' Thorburn, who we now know must have been worried about the impending drugs investigation, said: 'They could have put in me jail if I had won this match. It would have been a crime.'

Referee John Street had to change the cue ball because of a 'burn' mark, but it did not help Knowles as he lost 5–3 to Neal Foulds. Jimmy White, a 5–2 quarter-finalist to Griffiths, was certainly not happy with the playing conditions. 'The table was too slow and the balls were running off to the right,' he complained. 'It was almost impossible to get the right position and you needed a sledge hammer to hit the ball properly.' Davis wasted little time in whitewashing Johnson 5–0.

In the semi-finals, it was Higgins *versus* Davis, and the Irish fans had high hopes of a famous victory when the scores were level at 2–2. Davis did not bat an eyelid and won four frames in a row to come home 6–2. Griffiths set a new tournament break of 139 to beat the old mark of 133 notched by Davis in 1983. It was also the second highest break ever seen in a professional tournament in Ireland – just failing to pip the 140 of Dennis Taylor in the Carling Champions earlier in the season.

But Griffiths, despite that record, went down 6–4 to Foulds who was happy to be in a major final after such a poor season.

The final itself was an anti-climax and Davis proved an easy winner. He said: 'You cannot have great finals all the time and Neal just did not put me under enough pressure.' Foulds could have gone into the first session 4–3 ahead but instead was 5–2 behind and then lost four of the six frames played at night.

Davis will be back next year and another victory will set up talk of world champion titles again. But that won't worry Davis, who picked up £25,748 – another nice payday for the most enjoyable week in the snooker calendar.

Benson & Hedges Irish Masters Results

FIRST ROUND		QUARTER-FINALS		SEMI-FINALS		FINAL	
R. Williams (Eng)	1						
v		Griffiths	5				
T. Griffiths (Wales)	5	v		Griffiths	4		
		J. White (Eng)	2				
				v		Foulds	4
A. Knowles (Eng)	5						
v		Knowles	3				
W. Thorne (Eng)	3	v		Foulds	6		
		N. Foulds (Eng)	5				
						v	
A. Higgins (NI)	5						
v		Higgins	5				
Dennis Taylor (NI)	3	v		Higgins	2		
		C. Thorburn (Can)	3				
				v		Davis	9
E. Hughes (Rep. Ire)	4						
v		Johnson	0				
J. Johnson (Eng)	5	v		Davis	6		
		S. Davis (Eng)	5				
Losers: £3,969.62		Losers: £6,437.22		Losers: £10,728.69		Loser: £15,449.32	
						Winner: £25,748.86	
High break: 139 – T. Griffiths £3,004.01							

Previous Years' Results

YEAR	WINNER	RUNNER-UP	SCORE
1978	J. Spencer (Eng)	D. Mountjoy (Wales)	5–3
1979	D. Mountjoy (Wales)	R. Reardon (Wales)	6–5
1980	T. Griffiths (Wales)	D. Mountjoy (Wales)	9–8
1981	T. Griffiths (Wales)	R. Reardon (Wales)	9–7
1982	T. Griffiths (Wales)	S. Davis (Eng)	9–5
1983	S. Davis (Eng)	R. Reardon (Wales)	9–2
1984	S. Davis (Eng)	T. Griffiths (Wales)	9–1
1985	J. White (Eng)	A. Higgins (NI)	9–5
1986	J. White (Eng)	W. Thorne (Eng)	9–5
1987	S. Davis (Eng)	W. Thorne (Eng)	9–1

ROTHMANS MATCHROOM LEAGUE

Steve Davis duly retained his title as the Rothmans Matchroom League spread its wings and ventured into Europe for the first time.

In 1987 Davis had to sit and wait at home by a telephone as the final match unfolded in Everton. Neal Foulds could only draw and Davis took the championship. In 1988 Davis was the master of his own destiny as he went to Nottingham to meet Jimmy White – the man who had beaten him 5–3 in the League a year earlier.

There were more than 2,000 fans packed into the Royal Concert Hall. White needed to win to stay in the hunt and Davis was exhausted after a hectic week on the road doing exhibitions for Courage after his World Championship success. The result was remarkable as Davis hammered White 8–0 – only the second whitewash in the League.

'It was nice to win on the table and not wait at home for the phone to ring,' said a delighted Davis, who pocketed a £70,000 cheque to take his season's total to a record £495,000. 'I thought Jimmy would come out with all guns blazing but it never happened.'

However, while Davis was out in front at the top, there was also tension at the bottom with the last two players being relegated. Joe Johnson was a certainty for this after losing eight matches in a row, though he did manage to pick up one point with a 4–4 draw against Davis in the last game in Brighton. Dennis Taylor finally became the second man to drop out when Tony Meo beat Johnson 6–2 and Cliff Thorburn demolished the same player 7–1. Matchroom's Barry Hearn had announced at the start of the League that the bottom two would be relegated – 'even if it is Davis and White'.

The League had increased in size from eight to ten players with the inclusion of Scotland's Stephen Hendry and Johnson. Hendry drew his opening match with Davis in Ostend but it was the match with Willie Thorne in Gateshead that ultimately cost Hendry any chance of the title. Thorne romped home 6–2 – Hendry's only League defeat of the season. Yet, early on, there looked to be just one champion as White won his first four matches in a row. Disaster struck for White in the final five encounters, however, as he managed just two points and lost three matches. In fact,

Aces in the pack: (left to right) Dennis Taylor, Steve Davis, Tony Meo, Barry Hearn and Willie Thorne get in practice as the Rothmans Matchroom League announces Monte Carlo, Europe's gambling capital, as a venue.

his dismal end-of-season form allowed Thorne to move up into third place with Neal Foulds slotting in at number 4.

But what of Europe? Five venues were announced – Finland, Luxembourg, Ostend and Antwerp in Belgium, and Monte Carlo. All attention was fixed on the glamorous setting of Monte Carlo, but on the same day Tony Meo was making League history in the not-so-exotic setting of Chesterfield. Meo lost the match 6–2 but managed to knock in a magnificent 147 – the first maximum in the League. That highest break earned him £5,000, but if he had achieved it one year earlier there would have been a Rolls-Royce waiting for him!

Snooker is now a jet-set sport with players, officials and reporters hopping on and off planes as though they were buses. Certainly top referee John Street had a busy time that he won't forget in a hurry.

It was Helsinki, Finland, one day and Luxembourg city the next. He recalled: 'In Finland waiters were serving the spectators with drinks while the game was going on. That would not be tolerated in the UK but anything, within reason, goes when selling the game overseas.'

Street and the two players, Meo and White, certainly felt at home when they arrived in Luxembourg – the match was being held at the George and Dragon public house! 'The pub was owned by English people and they had a specially built snooker room. In fact, it was the only table in the country,' said Street. 'The room had been converted from an old skittle alley and seated about fifty people. Another seventy watched a video screen in the bar.'

Monte Carlo was next on the agenda, though Cliff Thorburn didn't even leave Heathrow Airport. Apparently the French had changed the rules and Thorburn and wife Barbara now needed a visa to get in. After dashing back to London, Thorburn finally obtained the necessary paper work and arrived a few hours behind the main party.

Some of the party opted out of the coach drive from the airport around the twisting, steep roads of Monaco and were whisked in splendour by helicopter across to Monte Carlo. The Casino was high on the agenda for most people, though some did take in the cultural delights of the Palace and the yacht harbour.

The League has once again been a success with attendances up by 25 per cent. When Hearn began the League he said he wanted to take live snooker back to the people. It has worked beyond his wildest dreams, for it was watched by some of the biggest crowds of the season. The sceptics had said that it wouldn't work; after all, one League had flopped financially and another attempted League had folded up. Certainly snooker fans around Britain and Europe loved the latest format and the future of the League looks rosy. Davis will be there to try to make it a title hat-trick, but Taylor and Johnson are out in the cold. Snooker, they say, is tough at the top, but it is even tougher at the bottom.

On the beach: Cliff Thorburn and wife Barbara enjoy a break during a Rothmans Matchroom League encounter in Monte Carlo.

Rothmans Matchroom League Results: Final Table

	P	W	D	L	F	A	Pts	Prize Money (£)
Steve Davis	9	6	3	0	45	27	21	70,000
Stephen Hendry	9	5	3	1	46	26	18	30,000
Willie Thorne	9	4	3	2	41	31	15	25,000
Neal Foulds	9	4	3	2	40	32	15	20,000
Jimmy White	9	4	2	3	34	38	14	17,000
Terry Griffiths	9	3	4	2	35	37	13	15,000
Cliff Thorburn	9	3	2	4	37	35	11	13,000
Tony Meo	9	2	3	4	34	38	9	11,000
Dennis Taylor	9	1	2	6	30	42	5	9,000
Joe Johnson	9	0	1	8	18	54	1	5,000

High break: 147 – Tony Meo £5,000

EMBASSY WORLD CHAMPIONSHIP

Steve Davis appeared in a predictable pose on the final day of the Embassy World Championship at Sheffield's Crucible Theatre. The Essex millionaire held the famous trophy aloft for the fifth time in his career and acknowledged the cheers of yet another sell-out crowd.

Davis earned the £95,000 first prize with an 18–11 victory over his Matchroom colleague, Terry Griffiths. The final was never a classic but merely emphasized Davis's superiority and grip on the world of professional snooker.

Now Davis is just one title behind Ray Reardon whose six championships make up the best performance in the modern game, but the world champion shrugs off comments that he is becoming a legend in his own lifetime. 'Reardon was a legend to me when I was a kid – he was my hero,' he said as he sipped champagne at the traditional after-match party back at the Grosvenor Hotel. 'But I can't think of myself as a legend even though it is nice that people might be saying that.'

The world in his hands: Terry Griffiths is presented with the Embassy globe after he accidentally knocked it over during his final defeat by Steve Davis.

Griffiths, performing in his first World Championship final since his epic victory in 1979, went back to the Welsh valleys £57,000 richer: a nice lump sum to go towards the cost of the luxury snooker club and house that he has had built. Griffiths was also critical of comments he had heard about Davis being a 'lucky' player. He said: 'I have heard a few of the television commentators and some players say that Davis is lucky and I do not like hearing it. Steve is not a lucky player, just a very, very good one.'

Davis was unaware of the criticism and just dismissed it by saying, 'Me, lucky? I remember the golfer Gary Player once said, "The more I practise, the luckier I get." Perhaps the players who are saying I am lucky should go back to the practice table.'

Davis had started the tournament as favourite and went into the final two days against Griffiths at odds-on with the book-

That's my man: Judy Greig shares the moment of triumph with her boyfriend, Steve Davis, after his win over Terry Griffiths in the Embassy World Championship final at Sheffield.

makers. But after day one, Griffiths was in with a realistic chance of dethroning the 1987 world champion as he fought back to finish at 8–8. Griffiths slept well, knowing that Davis was not at his best, but mistakes in the twenty-second and twenty-fourth frames did his cause no good as Davis eased to a 14–10 advantage. Griffiths was now beaten and two century breaks at the end of the match gave Davis his fourth ranking tournament victory of the season and his sixth individual title of the campaign that again established him as the undisputed world number 1.

The history books pointed against Griffiths as he had beaten Davis on only four occasions in the twenty-three times they had met, but the Welshman certainly lived up to his pre-final promise: 'I am going out there to enjoy myself.'

Griffiths's busy schedule in Wales meant that he had to cut back on his practice time and he has tried to introduce more aggression into his performances. He beat London's Neal Foulds 13–9 in the quarter-final and delighted in the thought that he had avoided Davis on his way to the final: they had met in four previous World Championship quarter-finals and Davis had won them all. Griffiths did not have it all his own way against Foulds and he recalled his feelings when he was losing 3–1: 'I went back to the dressing room and banged my head against the wall, telling myself I could win.'

In the semi-final world number 2 Jimmy White became Griffiths's next victim as the twenty-five-year-old Londoner went down 16–11. White was never at his best while Griffiths just seemed to get stronger and stronger as the match progressed.

In the top half of the draw Davis faced a quarter-final encounter with Malta's Tony Drago – a young man who would have surely beaten him in the quarter-final of the 1986 Tennents UK Open if he had not missed a yellow. Drago, who has now earned his place in the top twenty, had

reached the last eight with memorable victories over Alex Higgins (10–2) and another Irishman, Dennis Taylor (13–5). But Davis was in a mean mood and snuffed out the Drago challenge by an overwhelming 13–4 margin. 'He just bloody too good,' said a still-smiling Drago in his lovely Maltese accent.

Troubled Canadian Cliff Thorburn was the next obstacle in the semi-finals. Thorburn, who would have to face a drugs investigation when the tournament was over, had his chances early on to establish a slender lead but he never took those opportunities and Davis gradually pulled

Well played: Tommy White congratulates Martin Griffiths. Tommy's son Jimmy had just lost to Martin's son Terry in the World Championship semi-final.

away for a 16–8 win. Thorburn had dismissed any questions about the drugs incident but said, 'I thought about retiring in five years' time but I love this sport so much I am going to carry on until I drop dead.'

Thorburn had survived a marathon battle with unseeded Steve James in the quarter-final, coming home 13–11, and that followed on a nine-hour-plus match with Liverpool's John Parrott in the second round which the Canadian won 13–10.

WHO SAID THAT?

'I now feel I have got a chance to win it. When I am playing I have got blinkers on.'

▲

– Cliff Thorburn after his nine-hour-twenty-one-minute 13–10 victory over John Parrott in the Embassy World Championship second round.

James's was the fairytale story that all major sporting championships need. This Cannock youngster, ranked number 66 in the world, despatched Rex Williams 10–6 in the first round and then scored a surprisingly confident 13–9 win over Joe Johnson, the man who had graced the previous two World Championship finals. James arrived with a black eye and pains in his chest, the legacy of a frightening car accident just ten days earlier when he wrote off his £7,000 second-hand BMW. He somersaulted the car four times and ended up in a field. He said: 'I am just lucky to be alive.' Certainly he is a speed fan and frightens his management team by riding a powerful motorbike.

James used to be a postman, delivering letters for £100 a week. He has now experienced snooker's good life but after leaving school he was also on the dole and worked as a labourer. Asthma attacks ruined any chance of his becoming a footballer and his dad bought him his first

Still smiling: Steve James looks happy despite his quarter-final defeat in the World Championship.

snooker cue when he was thirteen. The £14,250 he earned in the World Championship at least helped pay for a new car.

Apart from the defeat of Higgins and Williams, there were no real first-round shocks, though Davis, who always struggles in his opening encounter, could only squeeze home against John Virgo 10–8.

Bill Werbeniuk, the 20-stone Canadian who has to drink lager to combat a nervous ailment, also admitted that he took beta-blockers – the ones banned by the WPBSA this season. 'If they try to ban me, I will take the WPBSA to court because I can get no other tablets,' he threatened. 'I am not going to give up my career without a fight as I have to take the drugs. I take Inderal and the top specialists in the world say this is the right treatment. If I have to pack it in, it would devastate me, but I am not going to die for the game of snooker. I need these tablets to survive.'

Higgins's defeat cost him his place in the top sixteen and he now knows will be missing from this year's Benson and Hedges Masters and Irish Masters. But he could

WHO SAID THAT?

'I ended up with a black eye, a gashed leg and pains in my chest – I am just lucky to be alive.'

▲

– Steve James speaking at the Embassy World Championship after somersaulting his car four times just ten days before the tournament.

---

to take six frames in a row for a 9–6 lead. He was unable to maintain that sort of potting excellence and White retaliated to come through a winner.

Hendry's stablemate Mike Hallett was overwhelmed 13–1 by Steve Davis in the second round and Foulds produced the same margin of victory over Doug Mountjoy. These were the largest wins recorded in a World Championship match at the Crucible.

still receive a 'wild card' for the Irish tournament, a fact which amused him. 'Wild card! I would appear to be an ideal person for that!' he laughed.

There was a lot of pressure on Scottish teenager Stephen Hendry and he was not at his best when he came up against English champion Dean Reynolds, but he finally edged through 10–6. Before a ball was struck, White said: 'Stephen is the boy wonder now – I'm just the old man. We both play the game the same way and it should be a cracking match.'

The 'cracking' matched turned out to be the most exciting game of the entire tournament with White winning a last-frame decider 13–12. It was played on a Saturday morning and produced viewing figures of three times the average. It was also a match that brought a traffic jam to the main road outside the theatre and White needed a policeman to hold up the traffic so that he could get in his car and leave.

Hendry was understandably disappointed but his future in the game is assured and his first World Championship win would appear to be a matter of not 'if' but 'when'.

Certainly he produced one of the most devastating bursts of snooker seen last season as he trailed White 6–3. But in just fifty-nine minutes Hendry knocked in breaks of 125, 101, 79, 56, 52, 51 and 35

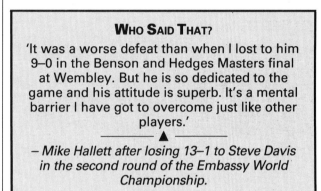

WHO SAID THAT?

'It was a worse defeat than when I lost to him 9–0 in the Benson and Hedges Masters final at Wembley. But he is so dedicated to the game and his attitude is superb. It's a mental barrier I have got to overcome just like other players.'

▲

– Mike Hallett after losing 13–1 to Steve Davis in the second round of the Embassy World Championship.

In the bottom half of the draw Griffiths ended the hopes of Willie Thorne 13–9 and Bolton's Tony Knowles put out Eddie Charlton, the oldest man left in the event, 13–7. But Knowles's run ended at the hands of White 13–6 in the quarter-final.

In the end it all came down to one man yet again, the incomparable Davis. He hardly put a foot wrong and is virtually unbeatable in the longer-frame matches. He lost only twice on the major domestic tournament circuit and his very presence on the table seems to cast fear into the hearts of some of his opponents. The time will come when there will be another Davis but on this evidence that day is a long, long way off.

Embassy World Championship Results

FIRST ROUND		SECOND ROUND		QUARTER-FINALS		SEMI-FINALS		FINAL	
S. Davis (Eng)	10								
v		Davis	13						
J. Virgo (Eng)	8			Davis	13				
M. Hallett (Eng)	10								
v		Hallett	1						
R. Chaperon (Can)	2					Davis	16		
A. Higgins (NI)	2			v					
v		Drago	13						
A. Drago (Malta)	10			Drago	4				
Dennis Taylor (NI)	10								
v		Dennis Taylor	5					Davis	18
W. Werbeniuk (Can)	8					v			
J. Johnson (Eng)	10								
v		Johnson	9						
C. Wilson (Wales)	7			James	11				
R. Williams (Eng)	6								
v		James	13						
S. James (Eng)	10					Thorburn	8		
J. Parrott (Eng)	10			v					
v		Parrott	10						
W. King (Aust)	4			Thorburn	13				
C. Thorburn (Can)	10							v	
v		Thorburn	13						
K. Stevens (Can)	6								
N. Foulds (Eng)	10								
v		N. Foulds	13						
W. Jones (Wales)	7			N. Foulds	9				
D. Mountjoy (Wales)	10								
v		Mountjoy	1						
B. West (Eng)	6					Griffiths	16		
W. Thorne (Eng)	10			v					
v		Thorne	9						
P. Francisco (SA)	6			Griffiths	13				
T. Griffiths (Wales)	10								
v		Griffiths	13					Griffiths	11
S. Longworth (Eng)	1					v			
A. Knowles (Eng)	10								
v		Knowles	13						
D. Fowler (Eng)	8			Knowles	6				
S. Francisco (SA)	7								
v		Charlton	7						
E. Charlton (Aust)	10					White	11		
D. Reynolds (Eng)	6			v					
v		Hendry	12						
S. Hendry (Scot)	10			White	13				
J. White (Eng)	10								
v		White	13						
J. Campbell (Aust)	3								

| Losers: £4,007.81 | Losers: £7,125 | Losers: £14,250 | Losers: £28,500 | Loser: £57,000 |
| | | | | Winner: £95,000 |

High break: 140 – S. James £9,500

World Championship Roll of Honour 1927–87

YEAR	WINNER	RUNNER-UP	SCORE	VENUE
1927	J. Davis (Eng)	T. Dennis (Eng)	20–11	Camkin's Hall, Birmingham
1928	J. Davis (Eng)	F. Lawrence (Eng)	16–13	Camkin's Hall, Birmingham
1929	J. Davis (Eng)	T. Dennis (Eng)	19–14	Lounge Billiard Hall, Nottingham
1930	J. Davis (Eng)	T. Dennis (Eng)	25–12	Thurston's Hall, London
1931	J. Davis (Eng)	T. Dennis (Eng)	25–21	Lounge Billiard Hall, Nottingham
1932	J. Davis (Eng)	C. McConachy (NZ)	30–19	Thurston's Hall, London
1933	J. Davis (Eng)	W. Smith (Eng)	25–18	Joe Davis Billiards Centre, Chesterfield
1934	J. Davis (Eng)	T. Newman (Eng)	25–23	Lounge Billiard Hall, Nottingham
1935	J. Davis (Eng)	W. Smith (Eng)	25–20	Thurston's Hall, London
1936	J. Davis (Eng)	H. Lindrum (Aust)	34–27	Thurston's Hall, London
1937	J. Davis (Eng)	J. Lindrum (Aust)	32–29	Thurston's Hall, London
1938	J. Davis (Eng)	S. Smith (Eng)	37–24	Thurston's Hall, London
1939	J. Davis (Eng)	S. Smith (Eng)	43–30	Thurston's Hall, London
1940	J. Davis (Eng)	F. Davis (Eng)	37–36	Thurston's Hall, London
1941–45	No tournament held			
1946	J. Davis (England)	H. Lindrum (Aust)	78–67	Horticultural Hall, London
1947	W. Donaldson (Scot)	F. Davis (Eng)	82–63	Leicester Square Hall, London
1948	F. Davis (Eng)	W. Donaldson (Scot)	84–61	Leicester Square Hall, London
1949	F. Davis (Eng)	W. Donaldson (Scot)	80–65	Leicester Square Hall, London
1950	W. Donaldson (Scot)	F. Davis (Eng)	51–46	Tower Circus, Blackpool
1951	F. Davis (Eng)	W. Donaldson (Scot)	58–39	Tower Circus, Blackpool

In 1952, a dispute between the Billiards Association and Control Council and the professional players led to a split and two tournaments were held.

The BA&CC tournament attracted just two players in Horace Lindrum and Clark McConachy, while the professionals organized the World Matchplay Championship in which Fred Davis met Walter Donaldson in the final.

BA&CC Tournament

YEAR	WINNER	RUNNER-UP	SCORE	VENUE
1952	H. Lindrum (Aust)	C. McConachy (NZ)	94–49	Houldsworth Hall, Manchester

World Matchplay Championship

YEAR	WINNER	RUNNER-UP	SCORE
1952	F. Davis (Eng)	W. Donaldson (Scot)	38–35
1953	F. Davis (Eng)	W. Donaldson (Scot)	37–34
1954	F. Davis (Eng)	W. Donaldson (Scot)	39–21
1955	F. Davis (Eng)	J. Pulman (Eng)	37–34
1956	F. Davis (Eng)	J. Pulman (Eng)	38–35
1957	J. Pulman (Eng)	J. Rea (NI)	39–34

Between 1958 and 1963 no matches took place. From 1964 the title was decided on a challenge basis which meant that there was often more than one event per year.

YEAR	WINNER	RUNNER-UP	SCORE	VENUE
1964	J. Pulman (Eng)	F. Davis (Eng)	19–16	Burroughes Hall, London
	J. Pulman (Eng)	R. Williams (Eng)	40–33	Burroughes Hall, London
1965	J. Pulman (Eng)	F. Davis (Eng)	37–36	Burroughes Hall, London
	J. Pulman (Eng)	R. Williams (Eng)	25–22	Match series in South Africa
	J. Pulman (Eng)	F. van Rensburg (SA)	39–12	South Africa
1966	J. Pulman (Eng)	F. Davis (Eng)	5–2	Match series at St George's Hall, Liverpool
1967	No tournament held			
1968	J. Pulman (Eng)	E. Charlton (Aust)	39–34	Co-operative Hall, Bolton
1969	Championship again organized on a knockout basis (Players No. 6)			
	J. Spencer (Eng)	G. Owen (Wales)	37–24	Victoria Hall, London
1970	(Players No. 6)			
	R. Reardon (Wales)	J. Pulman (Eng)	37–33	Victoria Hall, London
1971	(actually held Nov 1970 as a round robin)			
	J. Spencer (Eng)	W. Simpson (Aust)	37–29	Sydney, Australia
1972	(reverted to knockout basis)			
	A. Higgins (NI)	J. Spencer (Eng)	37–32	Selly Park British Legion, Birmingham
1973	(Park Drive)			
	R. Reardon (Wales)	E. Charlton (Australia)	38–32	City Exhibition Hall, Manchester
1974	(Park Drive)			
	R. Reardon (Wales)	G. Miles (Eng)	22–12	Belle Vue, Manchester
1975	R. Reardon (Wales)	E. Charlton (Aust)	31–30	Melbourne, Australia
1976	(Embassy until present day)			
	R. Reardon (Wales)	A. Higgins (NI)	27–16	Town Hall, Middlesbrough, and Wythenshawe Forum, Manchester
1977	J. Spencer (Eng)	C. Thorburn (Can)	25–12	Crucible Theatre, Sheffield
1978	R. Reardon (Wales)	P. Mans (SA)	25–18	Crucible Theatre, Sheffield
1979	T. Griffiths (Wales)	Dennis Taylor (NI)	24–16	Crucible Theatre, Sheffield
1980	C. Thorburn (Can)	A. Higgins (NI)	18–16	Crucible Theatre, Sheffield
1981	S. Davis (Eng)	D. Mountjoy (Wales)	18–12	Crucible Theatre, Sheffield
1982	A. Higgins (NI)	R. Reardon (Wales)	18–15	Crucible Theatre, Sheffield
1983	S. Davis (Eng)	C. Thorburn (Can)	18–6	Crucible Theatre, Sheffield
1984	S. Davis (Eng)	J. White (Eng)	18–16	Crucible Theatre, Sheffield
1985	Dennis Taylor (NI)	S. Davis (Eng)	18–17	Crucible Theatre, Sheffield
1986	J. Johnson (Eng)	S. Davis (Eng)	18–12	Crucible Theatre, Sheffield
1987	S. Davis (Eng)	J. Johnson (Eng)	18–14	Crucible Theatre, Sheffield

NATIONAL CHAMPIONSHIPS

ENGLISH CHAMPIONSHIP

Grimsby's Dean Reynolds couldn't conceal his delight after he won his first major title in the English Championship at Ipswich. He had waited a long time for this breakthrough into the snooker big time and he finally made it with a 9–5 final win over world number 3 Neal Foulds.

This twenty-five-year-old left-hander had started the season full of hopes and expectations after coming into the ranking list at number 16. Unfortunately, that optimism wasn't justified as he suffered a series of poor results. However, the Reynolds fortune changed on Christmas Eve with the arrival of a parcel at his home: it contained a brand-new ash cue specially prepared for him by top London cue maker John Parris.

'As soon as I started playing with the new cue I could feel it was that much better. In fact, I don't know how I managed to play with the old one – it was like a piece of driftwood compared to this new cue,' admitted a relieved Reynolds.

Tolly Ales had withdrawn their sponsorship from the English Championship, but the tournament was still worth £63,000 as the WPBSA contributed £1,000 per entry. That gave Reynolds a £15,000 payday but the money didn't matter – it was just the victory that this young man needed.

The final itself was virtually over after the first session when Reynolds's long potting destroyed Foulds as he took the first four frames. Foulds, happy to be in his first final of the season, did stage a fightback, but Reynolds was in no mood to concede defeat and finally came home by a 9–5 margin.

Steve Davis opts out of this English event, so Jimmy White was the tournament favourite. But the Whirlwind didn't last long, going down to an embarrassing 6–2 defeat by the rapidly improving Barry

It's mine: Dean Reynolds lifts aloft the English Professional Championship trophy.

West. In just forty-five minutes this twenty-nine-year-old Yorkshireman had taken a 3–0 lead and White looked very flustered. White had been stuck in traffic and arrived just five minutes before play began. He was in trouble too for not wearing a bow-tie – it had snapped before the start. His form also snapped as West came home to an easy win.

Tony Knowles only managed to scrape through 6–4 against Ken Owers from Fleetwood. And Knowles was quick to say afterwards: 'Yes, I should have been beaten out there – Ken definitely played the better snooker.'

Willie Thorne, defending champion Tony Meo and Joe Johnson all came safely through to the last eight, but there was another shock in store and this time it was

---

WHO SAID THAT?

'It was very nerve racking – I felt like a surgeon doing a brain operation. I broke out in a sweat when I had to cut it in half.'

▲

– *Cue maker John Parris after being given the job of turning Davis's one-piece cue into a two-piece cue.*

John Parrott who found himself deep in trouble. He had enjoyed a tremendous season but he had no answer to the power play of Reynolds who easily won 6–2.

In the quarter-finals Reynolds was again providing the headlines, this time beating Meo 6–4. The latter had been English champion for the past two seasons and, amazingly, still went back to his South London home with a trophy. As Tolly Ales had pulled out of the sponsorship, the WPBSA had to provide a new cup, and that left Meo with the chance to keep the old one – forever!

Mike Hallett, the world number 15, had arrived at this tournament after his 9–0 whitewash against Davis in the final of the Benson and Hedges Masters. He won his first match but then came up against West – a gritty player – who showed tremendous temperament to take the last three frames for a 6–5 win. West also managed to knock in a 134 break – a frame that stunned Hallett and gave the Yorkshireman the high break prize for the tournament.

Foulds – a 6–2 winner over Thorne – and Johnson – beating Knowles 6–4 – made up the last four.

Reynolds and his Framework mate, Johnson, battled to the very last frame before Reynolds took it to win 9–8, while West's impressive run came to an abrupt end when he was beaten 9–6 by Foulds.

The WPBSA obviously have a dilemma

English Championship Results

FIRST ROUND		QUARTER-FINALS		SEMI-FINALS		FINAL	
A. Meo	6						
v		Meo	4				
S. Longworth	4						
		v		Reynolds	9		
D. Reynolds	6						
v		Reynolds	6				
J. Parrott	2						
				v		Reynolds	9
A. Knowles	6						
v		Knowles	4				
K. Owers	4						
		v		Johnson	8		
D. Martin	4						
v		Johnson	6				
J. Johnson	6						
						v	
N. Foulds	6						
v		Foulds	6				
D. Fowler	1						
		v.		Foulds	9		
J. Virgo	0						
v		Thorne	2				
W. Thorne	6						
				v		Foulds	5
R. Williams	3						
v		Hallett	5				
M. Hallett	6						
		v		West	6		
B. West	6						
v		West	6				
J. White	2						
Losers: £1,187.50		Losers: £2,375		Losers: £4,750		Loser: £9,000	
						Winner: £15,000	
High break: 134 – B. West £1,250							

with these national championships with Davis pulling out of the English and Stephen Hendry saying that he will no longer play in the Scottish championship. It is always a proud moment to be called the champion of your country, and it would be nice to think that these events would continue. But without players of the calibre of Davis and Hendry, there is clearly a problem over attracting sponsors, who want to see the strongest line-up.

Reynolds and Meo obviously were thrilled and delighted at their English successes. The tournaments deserve a future, but that remains in the hands of the WPBSA.

SENATOR WINDOWS WELSH CHAMPIONSHIP

Terry Griffiths, later to become a world finalist for the first time since 1979, seems to be making a habit of winning the Welsh title. His 9–3 victory over Wayne Jones in the final was his third championship in four years. Griffiths earned £9,000 towards his new snooker club in Llanelli while Jones, delighted at reaching his first professional final, had the consolation of a £5,500 runner-up prize.

Griffiths's toughest moment came in the semi-final when he was 7–4 down against Cliff Wilson, but he came back strongly and made capital of Wilson's missed chances to take five frames in a row.

In the other semi-final Jones had to meet his snooker friend, Doug Mountjoy.

Mountjoy led 3–2 but was to take just two more frames as Jones came through powerfully, winning the last three frames in succession. Griffiths did not have it all his own way against Tony Chappel in the quarter-final and was behind 2–0 and 4–3 before his eventual victory.

Jones's quarter-final opponent, Ray Reardon, was unhappy about the reflection from the lights and held the game up while registering a complaint. At the end of seven frames Reardon led 4–3, but at 5–4 the match was called off and they had to return before midnight, when Jones took the two frames he needed to go through. Mountjoy won his quarter-final 6–3 against Mark Bennett.

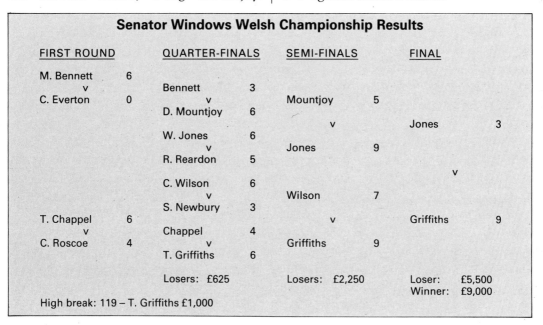

Senator Windows Welsh Championship Results

FIRST ROUND		QUARTER-FINALS		SEMI-FINALS		FINAL	
M. Bennett	6						
v		Bennett	3				
C. Everton	0	v		Mountjoy	5		
		D. Mountjoy	6				
				v		Jones	3
		W. Jones	6				
		v		Jones	9		
		R. Reardon	5				
						v	
		C. Wilson	6				
		v		Wilson	7		
		S. Newbury	3				
T. Chappel	6			v		Griffiths	9
v		Chappel	4				
C. Roscoe	4	v		Griffiths	9		
		T. Griffiths	6				
		Losers: £625		Losers: £2,250		Loser:	£5,500
						Winner:	£9,000
High break: 119 – T. Griffiths £1,000							

SWISH SCOTTISH CHAMPIONSHIP

Stephen Hendry made no mistake as he collected his third Swish Scottish Championship title in a row with a convincing 10–4 win over Murdo Macleod at Marco's Leisure Centre, Edinburgh. Nineteen-year-old Hendry was 5–2 up after the first session and repeated that scoreline at night to come home easily and collect the £9,000 first prize. He also gained a £1,250 bonus for his high break of 106 in the final.

In the semi-final Hendry easily disposed of Matt Gibson 6–1, while Macleod had to scrap all the way to overcome John Rea 6–5. Macleod finished the match in style with a break of 100 – the only other century of the competition.

Macleod had also had to survive a last-frame decider with a 6–5 quarter-final win over Jim Donnelly while Rea enjoyed the same slender margin of success over Eddie Sinclair. There was no such problem for Hendry who beat Burt Demarco without dropping a frame, while Gibson proved too strong for Ian Black at 6–2.

There was good news for Scottish fans in the round-one match between Eddie McLaughlin and Demarco. Demarco won 6–0, but Scottish snooker was just pleased to see McLaughlin back in action after nearly two years out of the game following a serious back injury.

Swish Scottish Championship Results

FIRST ROUND		QUARTER-FINALS		SEMI-FINALS		FINAL	
B. Demarco	6						
v		Demarco	0				
E. McLaughlin	0	v		Hendry	6		
		S. Hendry	6				
				v		Hendry	10
		M. Gibson	6				
		v		M. Gibson	1		
		I. Black	2			v	
		M. Macleod	6				
		v		Macleod	6		
		J. Donnelly	5				
				v		Macleod	4
		John Rea	6				
		v		John Rea	5		
		E. Sinclair	5				
Loser: £750		Losers: £1,250		Losers: £2,250		Loser: £4,500	
						Winner: £9,000	
High break: 106 – S. Hendry £1,250							

IRISH CHAMPIONSHIP

Jack McLaughlin produced one of the shock results of the season when he demolished defending champion Dennis Taylor 9–4 to take the Irish professional title at the Antrim Forum. Before the tournament started Taylor was the undisputed favourite to retain his crown. But McLaughlin, world-ranked number 51, soon destroyed that dream.

At the end of the first session McLaughlin led only 4–3, but at night he was to allow Taylor just one frame as he raced to an impressive win. He was thankful for a brave decision he had made to use a cue

he had had for only four weeks to claim his first professional title. This new hand-made cue was shorter and lighter, but it was a gamble on twenty-nine-year-old McLaughlin's part to use it in a major championship.

There was a shock in the first round when Eugene Hughes was knocked out by his old friend Paul Watchorn, who then went out in the quarter-final to McLaughlin.

Alex Higgins was back in action after serving his ban from last year's Irish event, but he went down to another terrible

Irish Championship Results

FIRST ROUND		QUARTER-FINALS		SEMI-FINALS		FINAL	
		Dennis Taylor	6				
		v		Dennis Taylor	6		
A. Kearney	5	Kearney	3				
v						Dennis Taylor	4
P. Fagan	3			v			
T. Murphy	5	Murphy	5				
v				Browne	5		
B. Kelly	1	v					
P. Browne	5	Browne	6				
v							
Jack Rea	0					v	
E. Hughes	2	Watchorn	5				
v				J. McLaughlin	6		
P. Watchorn	5	v					
J. McLaughlin	5	J. McLaughlin	6				
v				v		J. McLaughlin	9
P. Burke	3						
J. O'Boye	5	O'Boye	6				
v				O'Boye	4		
D. Sheehan	0	v					
		A. Higgins	4				
Losers: £150		Losers: £625		Losers: £1,250		Loser: £2,750	
						Winner: £5,000	
High break: 131 – Dennis Taylor £350							

Bubbling over: Jack McLaughlin celebrates with his mum and dad after his magnificent win in the Irish Professional Championship.

defeat – this time against the 1984 runner-up Joe O'Boye. O'Boye was given his chances by the out-of-touch Higgins and he took virtually every one to come home a 6–4 winner.

Taylor started the tournament by beating Tony Kearney 6–3, while Paddy Browne won a tough match 6–5 against a revitalized Tommy Murphy.

McLaughlin in his semi-final went 2–4 behind against O'Boye but then, including a break of 112, rapped in four frames in a row.

Taylor came up against Browne, now 2 stone lighter after enlisting the help of a Manchester-based boxing trainer. In the fifth frame Browne knocked in a 102 and that helped him to a 4–2 lead, but Taylor hit back immediately and compiled a championship record of 131. Fighting Browne established a lead of 5–4, then Taylor took the last two frames to go through to the final yet again. However, he hadn't reckoned on the spirit of McLaughlin, who scored the greatest win of his career.

CANADIAN CHAMPIONSHIP

Cliff Thorburn might struggle in the Canadian Masters but he has no problems in the Canadian Championship, as he proved by collecting the title for the fourth successive time with an 8–4 win over surprise finalist Jim Bear in Toronto.

Bear, a professional for just two seasons, knocked out Jim Wych in the quarter-final and then hammered Kirk Stevens 7–2 in the semi-final. Thorburn took three frames in a row to beat Gerry Watson 6–3 and then came through a long-drawn-out semi-final with Mario Morra that finished well into the early hours. Thorburn eventually won 7–4.

In the final Bear, an American Indian from Manitoba, looked on the brink of another shock as he led 4–3, but at night could not manage one more frame as Thorburn came through to win.

Canadian champion: Last season saw the fourth successive occasion on which Cliff Thorburn earned this title.

Canadian Championship Results

FIRST ROUND		QUARTER-FINALS		SEMI-FINALS		FINAL	
		C. Thorburn	6				
G. Watson	6	v		Thorburn	7		
v		Watson	3				
P. Thornley	4					Thorburn	8
F. Jonik	6			v			
v		Jonik	2				
W. Saunderson	0	v		Morra	4		
M. Morra	6						
v		Morra	6				v
R. Chaperon	5						
J. Wych	6						
v		Wych	4				
G. Rigitano	4	v		Bear	7		
J. Bear	6						
v		Bear	6			Bear	4
B. Mikkelsen	0			v			
J. Caggianello	6						
v		Caggianello	0				
M. Gauvreau	3	v		Stevens	2		
		K. Stevens	6				

Losers: £471.70	Losers: £801.89	Losers: £1,037.74	Loser: £1,650.94
			Winner: £2,830.18

High break: 84 – C. Thorburn £235.84

AUSTRALIAN CHAMPIONSHIP

Warren King kept hold of his Australian professional title when he beat Eddie Charlton 10–7 in a final that lasted nearly nine hours and finished at 12.30 am in Sydney. King also earned a high break prize with a 120, the only century of the event, which gave him a 5–3 lead at the end of the first session. The first eight frames at night were shared but King sealed success by taking the seventeenth frame.

There were thirteen professionals in the tournament and the semi-final places went according to the seedings as Robbie Foldvari got through to meet King and lanky John Campbell took on Charlton. King overwhelmed Foldvari 8–1, but Charlton had to battle all the way to beat Campbell 8–6.

Aussie defeat: Eddie Charlton.

Australian Championship Results

FIRST ROUND		SECOND-ROUND		QUARTER-FINALS		SEMI-FINALS		FINAL	
		G. Jenkins	6						
		v		Jenkins	4				
		L. Condo	1	v		King	8		
				W. King	6				
						v		King	10
S. Frangie	6								
v		Frangie	6						
W. Potasnik	4	v		Frangie	2				
		P. Morgan	5	v		Foldvari	1		
				R. Foldvari	6				
								v	
		I. Anderson	6						
		v		Anderson	2				
		L. Heywood	4	v		E. Charlton	8		
				E. Charlton	6				
						v		E. Charlton	7
		G. Wilkinson	6						
		v		Wilkinson	4				
		J. Charlton	0	v		Campbell	6		
				J. Campbell	6				

Losers: £333.33   Losers: £555.56   Losers: £888.89   Loser: £1,333.33
                                                          Winner: £2,222.22

High break: 120 – W. King £222.22

SOUTH AFRICAN CHAMPIONSHIP

Francois Ellis earned the South African professional title when he beat Jimmy van Rensburg 9–4 in the final at Germiston.

In the semi-finals Ellis had to survive a last-frame decider against Robbie Grace before winning 9–8, while van Rensburg enjoyed a more comfortable 9–4 success over former WPBSA member Perrie Mans.

South African Championship Results

SEMI-FINALS		FINAL	
F. Ellis	9		
v		Ellis	9
R. Grace	8		
		v	
J. van Rensburg	9		
v		van Rensburg	4
P. Mans	4		

Losers: £2,083   Loser: £3,056
                     Winner: £4,722

OTHER TOURNAMENT RESULTS

Winfield Masters

YEAR	WINNER	RUNNER-UP	SCORE
1983	C. Thorburn (Can)	W. Werbeniuk (Can)	7–3
1984	A. Knowles (Eng)	J. Virgo (Eng)	7–3
1985	A. Meo (Eng)	J. Cambell (Aust)	7–2
1986	S. Davis (Eng)	Dennis Taylor (NI)	3–2
1987	S. Hendry (Scot)	M. Hallett (Eng)	371–226 (5-frame agg.)

Kit-Kat Break for World Champions

YEAR	WINNER	RUNNER-UP	SCORE
1985	Dennis Taylor (NI)	S. Davis (Eng)	9–5

BCE Belgian Classic

YEAR	WINNER	RUNNER-UP	SCORE
1986	T. Griffiths (Wales)	K. Stevens (Can)	9–7

DISCIPLINE, DOYLE AND DAVIS – AND A TARTAN TERROR CALLED HENDRY

by Alexander Clyde

Stephen Hendry is the tartan terror of the table – a snooker genius who makes the game look frighteningly easy and conducts himself with a maturity far beyond his tender years when he is not wielding his deadly cue. The slim youngster from Edinburgh has been rewriting snooker's record books since he collected his first title, the Scottish Amateur Championship, at the age of fifteen. But has it really been that easy or has he just made it look easy?

There is only one man who can supply the answer to those questions and give some clue to the development of the talent, and character, of the most exciting figure to arrive on the snooker scene for a generation. Ian Doyle is to Hendry what Barry Hearn has been to Steve Davis since his early days as an aspiring amateur – friend, confidant, financial adviser, psychologist and, frequently, disciplinarian.

Doyle has managed Hendry's career since the player was sixteen and knows him better than any other person, apart from his family. So who is this man Doyle, what makes him tick and how has he managed to steer his young charge away from the normal temptations which have ruined the promising careers of so many teenage prodigies?

Doyle's face may not be familiar to many snooker followers but the man has rapidly emerged in the last two years as one of the most influential figures in the game. He now manages four players; Hendry; his doubles partner Mike Hallett; fellow Scot Jim Donnelly; and, since the start of the 1988/89 season, world amateur champion Darren Morgan, from Wales. He is also a director of the World Professional Billiards and Snooker Association where he is having more and more say in the planning of the game's future.

Doyle, the epitome of the canny Scot, was born in Glasgow in 1940. A neat, well-organized man, always immaculately turned out with his fine head of grey hair and clipped grey moustache, he talks quietly and deliberately. But he leaves you in no doubt that he is very much the boss, as young Hendry discovered to his cost on several occasions in the early days when he incurred fines for lack of discipline and professionalism.

Well done, Stephen: Manager Ian Doyle and Hendry's MIM Britannia Unit Trusts British Open trophy.

Doyle is low-profile, unlike his great rival, the highly voluble and extrovert Hearn. But the two men have more in common than they may realize. Both have a background in accountancy and both were self-made millionaires at an age when most of us are still struggling to pay the mortgage and the usual household bills.

Doyle takes up the story: 'After I left school, I studied for four years in chartered accountancy. But I didn't complete the course, because I was offered the chance to work for a private limited company, getting some practical and commercial experience. I was offered a position on the selling side at the age of twenty, and by the time I was twenty-three I was general manager of a division of that company. Three years later, I decided to have a go on my own. At that time I had a semi-detached villa, a mortgage and two youngsters. I set up my business on a wing and a prayer with the money I had raised from my pension fund.

'That was my first gamble, but I've been fairly successful. The company, which started in Glasgow and is now in Stirling, covers the distribution of ironmongery, leisure interests and property investments, and now employs forty or fifty people. Over the years we just built up and built up. My partner, Jim Marley, who's a lifelong friend, runs the business now and I'm full-time in snooker. Snooker management has become a full-time job plus.

'I've got very definite ideas on how players should act and behave as professionals. I believe that if you work and apply yourself to the game, both physically and mentally, the rewards are there to be gained. One of the tragedies in snooker is that stardom – as in football or any other sport for youngsters – can go to their heads so quickly. The thing you've got to keep impressing on players is that there is always somebody coming at your back and, if you can make the best of a five- or six-year period, then that is the time when

WHO SAID THAT?

'I've got very definite ideas on how players should act as professionals . . . If you apply yourself to the game, both physically and mentally, the rewards are there to be gained.'

▲

– *Ian Doyle, manager of Stephen Hendry.*

you've really got to set yourself up financially.'

Discipline is a word that keeps cropping up in Doyle's coversation and it is something he drilled into the young Hendry when he first agreed to take on the management of his career.

'My whole strategy revolves round discipline,' he emphasizes. 'If you don't have discipline, you have nothing. When I first started in the management game, I had to look very, very closely at professional snooker. Steve Davis stood out – he was a man apart.

'Whilst there are many, many lovely people on the circuit, such as Terry Griffiths and Dennis Taylor, Steve just stood apart, absolutely apart. Trying to achieve anything less than he has achieved is, for me, really failure. Those are the sort of standards you've got to set yourself.

'In Stephen's case the family background was important. His parents were separated and are now divorced, and I think I came on the scene at a very good time for him, because one might be able to say I had a stabilizing effect on him. He had a friend he could turn to. Like any

WHO SAID THAT?

'Stephen Hendry is the boy wonder now – I'm just the old man.'

▲

– *A joking Jimmy White as he lined up with Stephen Hendry in the second round of the Embassy World Championship.*

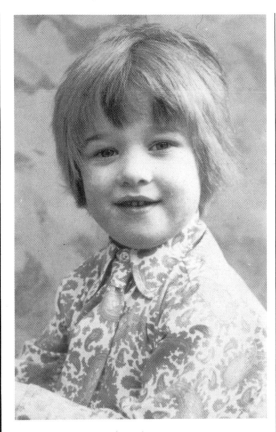

Kid's stuff: Stephen Hendry, aged two.

youngster who has to face this situation, he thought his whole world had been turned upside down when his mum and dad split up.

'His parents, both of them in their own individual way, were a great influence on him. They never, at any time, tried to force snooker on him but let him enjoy his game and things took care of themselves. The most obvious aspect that needed attention when I took him over was that there was a lack of discipline, not in Stephen himself, but in his total approach to the game. Too much had been made of his natural ability. Looking at the professional game, if you consider Jimmy White, his talent and his ability are frightening, but in the individual the whole thing has not been harnessed properly.

'Stephen is already a more mature player than Jimmy and at this point he is very

close to Steve, which is remarkable when you consider that two short years ago he was ranked 108th.'

Doyle is aware of the danger that Hendry could grow away from him as he moves into his twenties and becomes more independent. 'There's always that danger,' he admitted. 'To be perfectly honest, you don't know how a kid will react at sixteen, how he will react at seventeen and so on. But I like to think that, at this moment in time, our relationship is stronger and more mature than it's ever been. The most satisfying feature, from my point of view, is that he's probably enjoying his snooker more now than ever in his life and that's got to be tremendous.

'We've spoken about the World Championship since day one and, although he's set record after record after record, I'll be

Soccer fans: Stephen Hendry (nine) teams up with his six-year-old brother Keith.

Doyle and Hendry: Lee Doyle, son of Hendry's manager, and Stephen in the early days.

honest – three years ago, I didn't think he would be ready to win the World Championship at this early age. He's matured at such speed and all credit to himself. He will start to reach his peak in the next eighteen months to two years. He can honestly be as good as Davis, I'm sure of that.

'The big thing he has over Steve is the flair. He's got this mischievousness within him to play the cheeky shot, to take on the shot that can mean the difference between winning and losing. While a player retains that, he retains the excitement for the public and, after all, they are the most important people in the world.'

Doyle, who lives at Bridge of Allan near Stirling with his wife Irene, three daughters and son Lee – who is the same age as Stephen Hendry – sometimes has to pinch himself when he recalls the slice of good fortune that gave him his first sight of the young Hendry, then aged thirteen.

'Snooker had always been a game I had an awful lot of time for,' he recalled. 'I loved the game. I do play, but not terribly well. My top break is 32 and the night I broke 30 for the first, and possibly the only time, I think I even bought a few drinks. Anyway, I was involved in the amateur game in Scotland and I'd heard of Stephen.

I was approached to see if I'd be prepared to sponsor some tournaments and then I got involved in organizing a junior circuit.

'I came across Stephen purely by accident. I actually saw him for the first time by coincidence. It was as a result of us opening a club in Stirling. It was arranged that a team of our youngsters would play a team from the Locarno club in Edinburgh. My wife and I were going out that particular evening, but we decided to go down and see Lee play in our junior team. As luck would have it, he was drawn on the night to play against Stephen. That night will remain etched in my memory for time immemorial, because what I saw was absolute sheer magic.

'The funny thing was that, as we drove home afterwards, my son suddenly said: "You know, Dad, I've just played the future world champion." I'd been thinking that I'd seen something on that table that I'd never seen in my life, but my wife said that Stephen was just a wee laddie we had been watching, and who could predict that far into the future? She told us we were a couple of nut cases!

'I remember my son broke off in the match and it was a pretty good break – there was just one loose red. Stephen slammed it in and knocked in a break of 49. Bear in mind that he was only 5 foot 2 inches tall and could barely see over the top of the table.

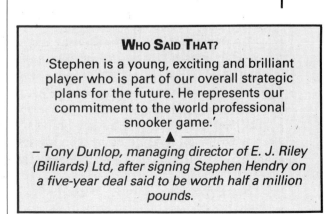

WHO SAID THAT?

'Stephen is a young, exciting and brilliant player who is part of our overall strategic plans for the future. He represents our commitment to the world professional snooker game.'

▲

– *Tony Dunlop, managing director of E. J. Riley (Billiards) Ltd, after signing Stephen Hendry on a five-year deal said to be worth half a million pounds.*

'Anyway, because of my involvement in the amateur game I was fairly well known in the Scottish snooker fraternity. A couple of years passed and the first time Stephen won the Scottish Amateur Championship, one of my companies sponsored the event. He was just fifteen and shortly after that his parents approached me to see if I would manage him. I had to give it fairly serious consideration because I had been thinking of taking life a lot easier. I had it in mind to buy some property in Marbella and spend a bit of time over there. My wife and I were in Marbella looking at some property and I remember her saying to me: "I don't know why you're talking about spending four or six months here. You'll be lucky if you spend four or six days here. You'd better take on Stephen Hendry and see what you can do." I was fairly convinced and I suppose she knew that, but it was her support that I really needed and I got it.'

It certainly wasn't plain sailing from the start and Doyle admits: 'In those early days Stephen had some disastrous results. In fact, one disaster followed another. In the meantime, I had been getting as much information as I possibly could from some friends in Essex on Barry Hearn and how he had managed Davis in the early days. I felt that, rather than bring people into his own club to play him on his own table, it would be much more advantageous to take Stephen out round the clubs and play other people on their tables. We did that and we played in a lot of clubs for money.

'Over three or four months, he played a lot of money matches and he lost more than he won, but I think it gave him a steel which, prior to that, his professional game was missing. Results started to come. He beat Graham Miles and Silvino Francisco in the Mercantile and then he won his first Scottish Professional Championship. The rest is history.'

But Doyle recalls those early days of Hendry's professional career with a shud-

I want to be number 1: Stephen Hendry relaxes on the putting green.

der. He said, 'He was playing at Miller's club in Broxburn and he was popping in there late in the morning or early in the afternoon. He was having a bit of fun on the table and it was not application.

'We had to sit down at that point and say, "Well, okay, this is the position, this is what's going to happen from now on." I brought him into the club every morning at ten o'clock, he practised all the way through to five or six and some nights he was still on the table at eleven o'clock. Ninety per cent of the time he spent just practising on his own. It could have destroyed him but it gave him confidence and built up his character and, most important of all, it gave him the concentration required for pro snooker.

'Initially, he was not terribly happy about it. But he agreed to do it because, when I took him over, he said that whatever I wanted him to do he would do. Within two or three weeks he saw the full merits of what was happening. All of a sudden, from a freewheeling natural-ability snooker player, he had acquired this dedication and application which was essential if he was to go to the top. It all goes back to the discipline again. He had to treat his work seriously, just as anyone who has to go to a factory or an office.

'The differential between the top echelons of snooker and the bottom end is so wide when you consider that more than a third of the players in the 1986/87 season earned less than £3,000. Yet the top players like Steve Davis were earning in excess of £300,000.

'The thing I noticed when I came on to the circuit in 1985 was that there are really no bad players in the game. But, equally, I did recognize that there are so many players who are not prepared to apply themselves. Too many players with ability just want to sit and play cards, or spend their time in the bookies or having fun. If you want success, you've got to be prepared to give these things up. You can appreciate players getting carried away with the glamour of the circuit. In the end, they become quite happy to knock up a result every now and then, which is a tragedy.

'But it's the application of the teenage years that is the important thing. When all your pals are going to the disco, do you want to forgo that? The unfortunate thing is that so many of them drift into oblivion. The disciplinary situation is the most important aspect in a young player. In the first couple of years with me, Stephen was forever falling foul of fines. If he turned up late in the office or at the club in the morning, it would cost him money. One of the great things about him is that he learns quickly, very quickly indeed, and that's got to be good for him and it's got to be good for the game. He hasn't been fined for a long time because the lessons obviously sunk in.'

Doyle admits that he thought he had made a serious mistake when he arranged for Hendry to play Davis six times in six nights on a tour of Scotland in January 1987. 'That tour was the greatest lesson of his life,' he remembers. 'I had phone calls from all sorts of people. For example, Alex Higgins had said: "You're making the biggest mistake in that kid's career, because the Nugget will bury him." And, of course, that's exactly what happened, 6–0. From my point of view, I must admit I was shattered. I really believed I had made the biggest mistake possible . . . I saw Stephen's attitude in the two weeks after the tour and I saw how down he was mentally. His play went to hell, that was the sum and substance of it. Then he came into my office one day – I'll always remember that day: it was to sign an insurance form. He signed it and, as he was going out, he popped his head back round the door and said, "By the way, I know how to beat Steve Davis."

'I just sat there. I couldn't bloody believe it. The difference from that moment on was incredible. I mean, the whole mental burden had been lifted from him. He knew

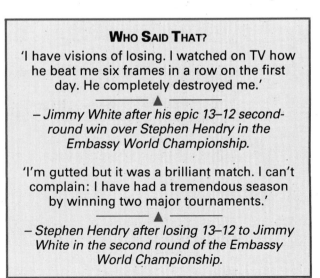

WHO SAID THAT?

'I have visions of losing. I watched on TV how he beat me six frames in a row on the first day. He completely destroyed me.'

▲

– *Jimmy White after his epic 13–12 second-round win over Stephen Hendry in the Embassy World Championship.*

'I'm gutted but it was a brilliant match. I can't complain: I have had a tremendous season by winning two major tournaments.'

▲

– *Stephen Hendry after losing 13–12 to Jimmy White in the second round of the Embassy World Championship.*

exactly what he had to do and, of course, since then he has beaten him 5–2 in the Rothmans Grand Prix. I don't think that's the greatest win over Davis: I think that's still to come, hopefully in a nice long match. In many respects he caught Steve absolutely cold that night. Bear in mind that Steve had beaten him eight or nine times on the trot comprehensively. Steve didn't expect it. He had repeated time after time that there was another element of the game that Stephen had to learn. But I knew it wasn't a question of learning it, just a question of being able to apply it. I don't think Davis believed he could play that type of game. The best of Davis and Hendry is still to come.

'Since he beat Davis, and then again after he lost 5–3 to him in the Mercantile and drew 4–4 with him in the Rothmans League in Ostend, all he has talked about is Davis. It used be Jimmy and Alex. Everything was Jimmy, everything was Alex and the way *they* played snooker.

'The Jimmy-and-Alex syndrome has gone. Stephen has now accepted that Davis is the best player in the world. Once a player accepts that fact, that Davis is the man to beat, then you can really strive for the top.'

Davis, of course, has dominated snooker for the best part of a decade, setting standards for the others to match. So how long will Hendry stay in the game, or will he carry out his well-publicized threat to retire early, when he is still in his twenties?

Doyle commented: 'We've spoken about Stephen retiring early and that could be a distinct possibility. The way it came out initially was a bit of a joke, but so many people have asked about it that we have discussed it a number of times. He is already well set up, but if he came to me at twenty-two or twenty-three and said, "Look, I've had enough, I'm not enjoying it as much as I did," then I'd say, "Fine." '

However, I strongly suspect that the day that happens is a long way off yet. The discipline and application which Doyle has instilled into this talented young man guarantee that he will not be happy until he has at least emulated Davis's unique achievements.

Double success: Stephen Hendry and Mike Hallett after their Foster's World Doubles success. Manager Ian Doyle keeps a watchful eye.

THE OLD AND THE NEW: A YEAR IN THE LIFE OF RAY REARDON AND MARTIN CLARK

RAY REARDON
by John Hennessey

He'd seen it all before; done it all before a thousand times. Yet there was a special smile of satisfaction as Ray Reardon once more faced the inquisitive press corps. This time, however, it was different, because the great man, the superstar who dominated world snooker a decade ago, had just achieved one of the most significant wins of his distinguished career.

After a slightly mystifying absence from the televised stages of snooker's ever-expanding circus, Reardon had bounced back in the MIM Britannia Unit Trusts British Open at Derby with a 5–0 win against world champion Steve Davis, the man who took over his number 1 mantle seven years ago. It was his first professional win against Davis and, not surprisingly, the first whitewash experienced by the Romford millionaire. From missing the cut, so to speak, all season, Reardon was back in his rightful place on the centre stage.

How he loved it. The slick one-liners, the regular banter with reporters, some of whom he recognized, others fairly new to the scene. In the old days he'd have known every face, every name and probably what drink they enjoyed – not that there were that many then – because he was always in the hot seat.

What a difference a year or so makes! Only two seasons ago he was taking on Davis in the Embassy World Championship semi-finals. A day before he had demonstrated his wonderful powers of defence and concentration against John Parrott in an enthralling quarter-final and then thrilled millions of TV viewers with some off-the-cuff chit-chat with Liverpudlian Parrott and interviewer David Vine. All that must have seemed light years away to fifty-five-year-old Reardon last season as he raced back to the British Open at Derby after consulting a London optician about the problems he was having with his new 'permanent' contact lenses.

All smiles: Ray Reardon.

Reardon has never shirked a challenge but the last player he needed between him and the next lucrative round of the Open was the all-conquering Davis, beaten only once on the ranking circuit during the season and looking for his fifth major title of the season. Would it be a whitewash? The bookmakers weren't offering very generous odds, but they were chalked up against the wrong player. The wily old fox, who had last won a title of any significance five years earlier, had Davis in his pocket almost from the first shot.

WHO SAID THAT?

'I am absolutely amazed – it's the first time I have beaten a seeded player for two years.'

▲

– Ray Reardon after beating Steve Davis 5–0 in the MIM Britannia Unit Trusts British Open.

'After a defeat like this you always have to look on the bright side – there isn't one.'

▲

– Steve Davis after losing 5–0 to Ray Reardon in the MIM Britannia Unit Trusts British Open.

A few days later he was heading back to his new Devon home after losing 5–2 to emerging pro David Roe in the next round. 'That's snooker,' said Reardon with a grin, but it was galling, nevertheless, for him to lose to a player he'd once have eaten for breakfast on his way to the practice table. That is no disrespect to Derby youngster Roe, one of a new breed of player no longer standing in awe of the 'Reardons' and 'Spencers'.

Reardon, written off more times than he cares to remember, has always been able to find that extra gear which separates the great from the good. Lately, though, the shadows have been lengthening over one of the most decorated careers in snooker history. Always a leading player on the finest stages, he had, until the Davis spectacular, been lingering among the supporting cast who are forced into the unedifying scramble to emerge from the qualifying rounds and into the televised phase.

For the past twenty years Reardon has worked throughout the summer months at Pontin's, and these days a weekly diet of holiday-camp snooker, where the object first and foremost is to entertain, is hardly the ideal preparation to face the young bloods in the early-season qualifiers.

'It wasn't so bad before we had a full tournament circuit,' said Reardon. 'There were only two or three events and no great pressures at the end of the summer to prepare for them. But now you have to be as sharp as a tack right from the start if you are going to get anywhere.'

Having said that, the Welshman would never dream of giving up his life among the camp-dwellers. 'It's been part of my life for so long, in fact throughout my professional career, that I couldn't possibly turn my back on Pontin's,' he said. 'They gave me a chance when I was a struggling pro and that enabled me to build a successful career because it took care of all my financial worries.'

Nevertheless, the man has immense pride, although he will admit that the desire doesn't always burn as brightly as it did. 'I've done and seen just about everything in the game – and played all over the world,' he said. 'And until now it's been hard to motivate myself at the start of a new season.'

Ruling the world: Ray Reardon as world champion in 1978.

But that hunger for success has returned almost with a gnawing feeling. The reason is simple: the entire tournament circuit has been re-scheduled so that all qualifiers bar those for the World Championship are played in two periods in Blackpool at the start of the season.

'It's the best news I've had for years,' said snooker's elder statesman. 'It means I can concentrate on my game and get it really sharp in time. It also takes the pressure away, because if you miss out on one tournament, you have another six chances to get it right. And if you fail in all seven, then it's your own fault because you are obviously not up to it.'

Not even the turmoil within snooker, with threats of breakaway groups and major rows between the sport's governing body and entrepeneur Barry Hearn, can dampen his enthusiasm. As president of the World Professional Billiards and Snooker Association, Reardon is aware that there must be harmony within the ranks for snooker to continue the enormous growth it has enjoyed in the last decade. 'We have achieved so much in that time and there is still a long way to go,' he said. 'But we must be together.'

There have been breakaway attempts before but always the danger has been averted by commonsense, and the Welshman believes that will prevail again. 'It wasn't so important in the old days because there was so little to play for. But now we're talking about millions of pounds,' he stressed.

His absence from the mainstream has been missed, not only by his close friends on the circuit but in particular by sponsors and officials. And the up-and-coming players all hope to make a name for themselves against the six-times world champion.

'I suppose it is fair to say a lot of television viewers might have thought I'd gone into semi-retirement, especially if they had read that I'd moved down to Devon,' he

Happy day: After their wedding, Ray and wife Carol smile for photos with BBC commentator Ted Lowe.

said. 'But nothing could be further from the truth.' He added with that famous grin, 'I wish I could afford to retire. That would be nice, wouldn't it?' But it's not on. For a start, his many fans around the UK wouldn't allow him to fade away.

Far from sitting on snooker's sidelines, Reardon has been making huge adjustments to his life in the past two years. His first marriage disintegrated amidst much rancour, but even before he had wed again, to long-time friend Carol Covington in 1987, he had been to Buckingham Palace to receive the MBE from the Queen for his services to snooker. An unhappy separation and equally unhappy divorce, well documented in some newspapers, did little for his confidence or form, which resulted in his dropping like a stone down the rankings. But he has no bitterness. His popularity has, if anything, increased and many of the fans he has made in the West Country over the years greet him every summer at Pontin's and all his regular exhibition venues.

'I've got to be honest and say I could be

busier,' said Reardon. 'But I don't get an awful lot of time to myself. I always seem to be playing somewhere or making personal appearances.'

The prize money may have dried up somewhat – he even missed out on playing for Wales in the World Team Cup for the first time – but he's never going to be short of a few bob. I once described Reardon as the player who explored every conceivable commercial avenue in snooker and he would not disagree with that assessment. Old habits die hard and even today there's always something in his car for sale.

'Excuse me, Mr Reardon, but do you still sell cues?' asked a fellow Welshman as we spoke in the car park at Pontin's Brean Sands holiday camp in Devon last summer. 'I'll sell you the car if the price is right,' he quipped, then proceeded to haggle about the price of a cue, produced like magic from the boot. Minutes later the old pro, the super salesman, had clinched another deal after enjoying the fun of being beaten down a few pounds.

'When are you coming back to play at our club in Bury St Edmunds?' shouted a camper as he wrapped up the sale. 'Tomorrow, if they pay me,' he roared back.

There's a lot of life left in Reardon – and a lot of snooker. In 1982, after a barren spell, he whipped himself into shape over a three-month period and finished up in his seventh world final. He lost, narrowly, to Alex Higgins, but proved conclusively that there's no substitute for craft and experience.

Can he do it again? 'If I thought I wasn't ever going to win again, I'd pack up today,' he said. 'Of course, it's a lot harder, especially at my age, but nothing beats the thrill of walking out in front of a packed house and showing spectators just what you are made of.'

He's made of extremely stern stuff and, with the help of his old World Championship cue, rebuilt last season almost from scratch, a settled lifestyle and the magical, all-seeing, hard-wearing contact lenses, Reardon is ready to rise again.

'Snooker is not life or death,' he has always stressed, 'it's only a game.' And he intends to go on playing for many a year. When the curtain finally falls, how about a full-time job as First Ambassador for Snooker? After all the trading he's done over the last twenty years, selling snooker should be a piece of cake for Reardon.

MARTIN CLARK
by Alasdair Ross

Almost unnoticed, Martin Clark stepped warily into the spacious conference room that was bathed in warm August sunshine. Clearly uncertain of his next move, England's youngest professional stood respectfully just inside the door.

A few heads turned. Alex Higgins looked up from the morning papers piled on his lap and instantly returned to the racing pages. Clark shuffled his feet, politely asked if he was in the right place and was immediately rescued by Eugene Hughes.

Making the introductions, Hughes disturbed the Hurricane's thoughtful search for a winner and explained, 'Alex, I'd like you to meet the best young player in Britain.' Higgins briefly looked Clark up and down, shook hands and cracked, 'I didn't know the WPBSA were letting jockeys turn pro now. We'll just have to call you Lester!'

Clark, thankfully, shared the joke with the rest of the Framework camp and set about his first day's work as a professional. 'That was an unnerving experience,' he later admitted. 'I wasn't really sure what to expect when I arrived at the hotel for Framework's pre-season team meeting, and when I walked into that conference room I could have died. I was suddenly surrounded by players like Alex, Joe Johnson, Tony Knowles and John Parrott. They were all heroes of mine but I'd never met any of them before. It hit me as soon as I walked through the door and my mind went blank for a few seconds while it all sunk in. It was a tremendous relief when Eugene spared my embarrassment.

'None of the other lads knew me from Adam, and why should they? I was very conscious of being the office junior, but once Alex broke the ice I realized everything was going to be fine. I've had to live with the "Lester" bit ever since, but I don't mind. It's just great to be accepted as one of the boys – an equal, if you like – and that made me all the more determined to make an impact as soon as possible.'

Clark did that as he quickly qualified for the televised stages of both the Fidelity Unit Trusts International Open and the Rothmans Grand Prix. First Clark, then aged eighteen, from Sedgley, West Midlands, beat Tony Drago to qualify for the Fidelity; he next chalked up a remarkable

On the march: Martin Clark in action.

5–4 extra-time win over world number 3 Neal Foulds to book his place in the last thirty-two of the Rothmans event at Reading. Clark forced the match to go the full distance, but had to wait to play the sudden-death decider as the afternoon session ran into overtime.

He explained: 'I didn't let it bother me. When the match went to 4–4, I knew we would be pulled off and told to come back later that night to play the last frame. I suppose Neal must have fancied his chances. After all, I had no experience in that kind of situation, but I was determined to give it my best shot.'

Clark handled the pressure with a surprising self-assurance, won the final frame and coped with victory in a calm, matter-of-fact manner.

'Obviously I was delighted,' he recalled, 'but I knew it would be stupid to start doing cartwheels. It was only one match and I realized that I had to win many, many more matches like that to break into the game's top sixty-four. I suppose that was my first target, but as I started to get a few good results I aimed even higher. By the time I'd played in the first couple of tournaments I was calculating my chances of making the top thirty-two.'

A couple of days after beating Drago, Clark joined the rest of the Framework pros at the WPBSA's annual awards dinner at the London Hilton. That was plainly another important night in his snooker education.

'It was an occasion when I fully understood exactly how much I had to do to break through,' he said. 'I remember looking around the ballroom and seeing all the familiar faces. I recognized every one of them, but few if any had the slightest idea who I was. Again, it gave me an even greater incentive to go after all that fame and fortune. It's not that I desperately want either of those things, but success in snooker brings them both and I've always been aware of being able to handle them if and when they come along. That night at the Hilton also brought home to me the high-profile image of the game. Perhaps until then I wasn't clued up on the glamorous, showbiz side to snooker. It was a bit of an eye opener.'

Clark recovered sufficiently to mark his first televised appearance with an astonishing 5–0 whitewash over former world champion Dennis Taylor to reach the last sixteen of the Fidelity. The young man barely faltered as he mopped up one of the biggest shocks of the season, but again England's number 1 amateur in 1987 took it all in his stride.

'I couldn't believe it when I came off at the interval leading 4–0,' he recalled. 'I walked into my dressing room in a bit of a daze, but I soon realized I still had plenty to do. I just sat down quietly, had a cup of tea and a chat with Terry Jones, Framework's road manager. Tel told me to stay calm and concentrate on that next frame as if my life depended on it.

'Of course, I knew that was sound advice but talking about it and doing it are two very different matters. Luckily, I kept my nut down and got over the line. I don't think Dennis could believe it – and that made two of us!'

Clark, though, failed to capitalize on those wins over Taylor and Foulds. First, Joe O'Boye sent him packing in the next round of the Fidelity, then Mick Fisher overturned current form to beat him on the opening day of the Rothmans.

Clark commented, 'I suppose a reaction was inevitable, but those losses, particularly the one against Fisher, were really disappointing. I'd only just got over them when Robbie Foldvari beat me in the Tennents UK Open as well. Robbie did my head in. He played so slowly that I just couldn't get into any rhythm, and even when I led 8–5 I still didn't fancy winning. I wasn't that surprised when I lost 9–8, but I was gutted on missing out on a few more precious ranking points.

'Looking back, I suppose those defeats against Fisher and Foldvari ultimately cost me my chance of making it into the top thirty-two, but I'll make it next year. I've made sure I've learned all my lessons well.'

Clark put all that knowledge to good use to clinch yet another 5–4 upset win over world number 16 Mike Hallett in the qualifying stages of the Mercantile Credit Classic in Blackpool. He explained: 'I don't mean to sound flash, but I always fancied winning that one. I knew Mike would give me a few chances, but it was particularly satisfying to take them and beat such a talented player. That gave me a terrific boost.'

The Foster's World Doubles then brought Clark into direct confrontation with Steve Davis for the first time and once again he responded to the challenge, partnering Jimmy Chambers to a shock 5–1 win. That victory over Davis and Tony Meo pushed Clark into the spotlight of mass-media attention, but by now he was learning to live with that added burden.

'From the moment I joined Framework I was made aware of the way I should conduct myself in press interviews and always allow the office to act as a buffer between me and the media,' he said. 'That worked really well until Jimmy and I beat Steve and Tony. Afterwards Howard Kruger decided that it would be best if I kept a low profile and concentrated on our next game.

'That suited me until a local radio reporter walked into the club where I practise and asked for an interview. I told him that I wasn't doing any interviews but if he cleared it with the office then that would be fine. I thought nothing more about it until I read a letter from this guy in one of the snooker magazines slagging Framework off for blocking the interview. It simply wasn't true, and even though the matter was resolved that taught me another important lesson.'

Clark's education continued as he moved back to Blackpool for the final stages of the Mercantile Credit Classic. A 5–2 fourth-round win over Mark Bennett took him into the last sixteen of a major tournament for the second time, but again he failed to cash in, losing to improving Welshman Steve Newbury.

'If I had one real disappointment this season it would be that I failed to take full advantage of my good wins against seeded players,' Clark insisted. 'It was great to beat players like Foulds, Taylor and Hallett, but each time I didn't go on to make a real impact in the tournament. I don't think that has anything to do with a lack of 'killer instinct' but obviously I must make sure I'm absolutely mentally hard for every match – whoever I'm playing.'

Clark's failure to go the distance in the Mercantile was still fresh in the memory when head-on clashes with Jimmy White loomed first in the English Professional Championship and then in the MIM Britannia Unit Trusts British Open. Clark narrowly lost both matches, but the experience was again invaluable. He said: 'I had my chances to beat Jimmy in both of those matches. In the English I came back from 5–1 down to level at 5–5, but I just couldn't finish the job as Jimmy nicked the final frame. I wasn't too disappointed because I knew I had done everything but beat one of the best professionals in the game and that performance gave me a lot of confidence for our match in the British Open at Derby. I really thought I could win that match, and again I had every opportunity. I should have made it 3–3, but Jimmy pinched the sixth frame and from 4–2 down I didn't have much hope.'

That defeat left Clark with the Embassy World Championship to aim at, but he missed out on a Crucible trip in his rookie year, slipping out in the third qualifying round – beaten 10–9 by Australian champion Warren King.

'I really felt low after that match,' he said. 'I thought I had every chance of reaching the final stages at Sheffield, and

Wishing and hoping: Martin Clark looks to the future.

to be honest I should have got past Warren. I was leading 6–3 at the end of the first session and when I won the first frame of the evening to go four frames clear, that should have been that. I did miss a couple of chances I would normally expect to take, but fair play to Warren: he battled really hard and in the end he just about deserved to win.'

Clark's season, though, wasn't quite over. In early April it was off to Peking with the rest of the Framework squad for the £120,000 Kent Cup China International. Victories over Hughes and Knowles carried him to his first final, but then Parrott shattered any title dreams with a high-speed potting display to pocket a 5–1 win.

'It would have been great to win a title in my first season, but I've still done well,' said Clark. 'I've come a long way in a few short months and I've only just started travelling.'

OPERA, UNDIES AND THE MAN WHO CHEATED DEATH: A PROFILE OF ALAN CHAMBERLAIN

Alan Chamberlain knows every joke that has ever been told about men who travel in ladies' underwear. He got used to the sniggers very quickly when he was a travelling salesman for a ladies' lingerie company. But that is now history and Chamberlain is concentrating on his new profession – as an international referee.

Chamberlain was born on 1 January 1943 in Market Harborough, the son of a factory manager, Eric, and his wife Gladys. Home then was a little company house, and baby Chamberlain was used to being woken up by the sound of a bell ringing – in the house! 'Dad used to be in the auxiliary fire service and if there was a fire, a bell rang to tell dad to get down to the station,' he explained.

Snooker was no part of Chamberlain's early sporting diet as he attended a Church of England Junior School.

'Football was my first love. I used to play in goal,' he said. 'I was lucky to be in the best football team we ever had at the school – we had a centre-forward who was 6 feet tall as a ten-year-old. He used to frighten everyone. I let in only eight goals all season.'

In fact, this lethal centre-forward of gigantic proportions once hit the ball so hard that he smashed a crossbar.

After that Chamberlain moved on to the local grammar school where cricket also figured prominently in his day-by-day life. After his goalkeeping performances, it was only natural that he became a wicket-keeper. There was still no sign of snooker and Chamberlain was intent on a career as a veterinary surgeon – that is, until he

discovered one important problem! 'I didn't like the sight of blood,' he said.

While sport figured high on Chamberlain's priority list, there was a deep schoolboy love of music. He said: 'I learnt the piano from the age of six and one year later I was singing in the church choir. Then at sixteen I joined the local operatic society.' To this day he is still a music fan and his car is full of cassettes, though the choice of tape is more likely to be Beethoven than the Beatles or Mozart than Madonna.

Despite the fact that his teachers thought he had a good academic career in front of him, Chamberlain left school at sixteen. His first job was working in the office at the local Symington's Corset Factory – the biggest employer in Market Harborough with just under 1,000 workers. He worked in the production office, but even then wanted to get out on the road to start selling. Instead he was moved to the advertising department. That was in the days when the workplace was rigidly structured. He remembered: 'The advertising department was on the next floor. That got me away from the production office and was a definite step up in status, but I was still inside the office.'

Then suddenly Chamberlain, now seventeen, was called into the boardroom. This was a red-letter day for him: he was asked to take over as secretary of the company's sports and social club. 'It was really good,' he enthused. 'There were 7 acres of fields and we had 1,200 members. I had to organize everything from darts matches to dances. I also had to book all the acts who appeared at the club.'

Now Chamberlain's life was beginning to take shape – especially when he got friendly with Bryan Southwell, a photographer on the *Market Harborough Advertiser and Midland Mail*. Chamberlain switched jobs to work for Olivetti and he finally got on the road – selling typewriters and adding machines. The job had taken him to Leicester and that's where snooker finally came into his life.

'Bryan introduced me to snooker and I used to spend a lot of time down at the Belvoir Billiards Club. I really liked the game. I was down the club most lunchtimes and afternoons when I sneaked some time off work,' he said.

Now came the big career move to Johnson's Wax and a cherished dream. 'I got my first company car – a Vauxhall Viva,' he recalled. Chamberlain was now twenty-two and by now was quite a proficient snooker player with an eventual top break of 75. Every Monday and Friday was spent playing snooker. His first taste of big-time professional snooker came in 1969, when, he remembered, 'I paid out £2 10s – a lot of money in those days – to watch Ray Reardon play John Spencer and I was interested that the referee had come over to Leicester from Northampton. His name was Don Williams. I then phoned up the Billiards and Snooker Control Council and discovered that there was no referee based

in the Leicester area. So I thought this would be good for me to take up as a pastime. I passed my first exam in the early 1970s.'

Chamberlain was soon on the move again, this time across to a place called Keddington in East Anglia where he got a good job – yes, you've guessed it – selling lingerie.

'I have heard all the jokes,' he laughed, 'but it didn't worry me. In fact, it was quite funny. I once remember being stopped in the Aylesbury area around the time of the Great Train Robbery. I was asked what I had in my sample-case and when the policeman took a look he just stepped back and said, "Thank you, sir." I was eventually made redundant and moved back to the Leicester area where I got a job working for another ladies' underwear firm as a salesman.'

Chamberlain had been secretary of the Market Harborough and District Snooker League for four years. He had also passed all the referees' exams and had even become an examiner himself before applying to join the Professional Referees' Association. He was accepted for the 1983/84 season. In 1985 he gave up his job to become a full-time referee, travelling all over the country on the rapidly expanding snooker circuit. He is president of the Leicestershire Referees' Association and vice-president of the Leicestershire Billiards and Snooker Association of which he was a founder member.

It was after the WPBSA dinner in September 1986 that Chamberlain nearly lost his life. He recalled, 'I had been to the dinner and I woke up in the morning with a pain in my chest. I had stopped smoking cigarettes in 1977, but at the dinner I had been getting through quite a few cigars and had been drinking quite a lot. In fact, we were having a great time. But I had to get back to referee the Matchroom Tournament down at Southend and I just put the pain in my chest down to indigestion. I never said anything to my wife about it and we just got in the car and set off.

'I was going quite fast in the outside lane on the motorway when I suddenly had this terrible feeling of heaviness in my arm and severe pressure on my chest which caused me considerable difficulty in breathing. I finally got across the motorway and pulled on to the hard shoulder. It was like a nightmare.

'I had to get into the passenger seat while my wife drove. I don't know how I managed it. We finally made it to the service area and luckily there was a police car there. I don't remember much more because I passed out. I was absolutely drenched with sweat.

'The police phoned for an ambulance and that took about twenty minutes to get there. They didn't know whether to go back to Bristol or on to Gloucester. They gave me oxygen. By this time I had come round. They whipped me off to hospital where they put me into intensive care. Those police were great – they were off duty but they couldn't do enough for me.

'I had had a heart attack – and they kept me on the machine for forty-eight hours. All I could think of was that I must get a message to Barry Hearn to let him know I couldn't do his Matchroom Tournament.

'Luckily I was back at work after six weeks doing the Tennents UK Open. I just had to slow down and take it easy. I feel fine now.'

Chamberlain is one of the up-and-coming referees and is obviously going to be on the circuit for a long time to come. The highlight of his career so far has been doing the Mercantile Credit Classic final between Steve Davis and John Parrott. 'That was an incredible final,' he said, 'a really great match.'

Obviously every referee dreams of doing

a 147. Chamberlain almost achieved that aim in last season's Tennents UK Open at Preston. He recalled: 'Joe Johnson went red, black, red, black all the way through to the colours until finally he lined up on the pink. He missed that pink and bang went my chance.' However, he didn't have to wait too long finally to achieve the 147 dream when he officiated during Tony Meo's magic maximum in a Rothmans Matchroom League match in Chesterfield against Stephen Hendry in February 1988.

Of course, there are lighter moments to the serious side of refereeing and Chamberlain cast his mind back to a qualifying round in a match down at Bristol between Jimmy White and Rex Williams. Jimmy had been taking the frames quite easily and Chamberlain's concentration was not all it should have been. To the delight of the audience, instead of saying, 'Rex Williams to break,' he announced, 'Rex Williams to win.'

Alan still spends a lot of his time on the roads and highways of Britain, but no longer selling women's underwear!

CHAMBERLAIN'S CHALLENGE

Can you match the skill of referee Alan Chamberlain? Answer the questions below, and then turn to page 151 to find out how well you met Chamberlain's challenge.

1 What would happen if an earth tremor moved a ball?

2 Name four occasions when a player incurs a penalty of 7 points, not directly involving the black ball.

3 What is the penalty if a player moves a ball-marker placed by the referee whilst he is cleaning a ball?

4 What happens if, at the end of a stroke, a red ball is left on a cushion rail? (Be very careful!)

5 When is the only time a referee can physically help a player?

6 What options are open to a player if he is angled on the blue ball following a foul stroke?

7 How can a player legally pot a ball that is touching the cue ball?

8 If asked, is the referee allowed to tell a player the colour of a ball?

9 How is it possible for a player legally to pot the yellow ball four times in a break of 8?

10 In a pairs match, who plays the next stroke when requested to play again following a foul?

GOING BATTY BEHIND THE BERLIN WALL

by Bruce Beckett

Bats in the belfry, the Berlin Wall and a magic carpet. What, you may ask, have they got to do with snooker? All will be revealed.

When you turn on your TV set during coverage of a tournament, everything is immaculate – players in best bib and tucker with a neat row of heads behind them in the auditorium; not a speck of dirt on the carpet; and the chalk marks providing the only blemish on the green baize. But go behind the scenes, as I did before last season's MIM Britannia Unit Trusts British Open at the Assembly Rooms, Derby, and you will see an altogether different picture.

You would not believe some of the problems that have to be solved to ensure the smooth running of an event. It's pandemonium as snooker's backroom boys work through the night, all fighting for the same small space in the centre of the arena. Table fitters, television personnel, set designers, scaffolders – each role is as important as the other in making sure that the curtain goes up on time.

Planning for each tournament starts six months in advance, with three or four site meetings to sort out the arrangements. Paul Hatherell, the World Professional Billiards and Snooker Association's tournament director, is the central cog. His job is to link up between the venue, the sponsor, the players and the media, both television and press. Often their demands are diametrically opposed.

The British Open took place at the end of February, but 'We started planning for it in August,' said Hatherell. 'We had a new sponsor this year so we had to make them aware of the commercial advantages such as customer entertaining and media coverage. Commercially a sponsor wants to get the maximum out of his tournament. But, at the same time, there are rules governing advertising on television. We try to find a balance between the two.'

The set is vital. This is where Mike Williams – and the Berlin Wall – come in. Williams is contracted by the WPBSA to design the sets for their tournaments. He

I'm in charge: Tournament director Paul Hatherell.

has to liaise with the TV companies and work within the advertising regulations laid down by the IBA and BBC. 'The first time we did the set for the Embassy World Championship in 1978, we took it all up to Sheffield in a Ford Transit Van,' he recalled. 'This year, we had to use six furniture vans. That's an indication of the way snooker has grown.'

A few years ago at the Crucible, Williams came up with the idea of dividing the two tables by a giant curtain. He remembered: 'We were trying it out when Steve Davis came into the arena and noticed that every time referee Len Ganley walked past the curtain, it moved. Obviously it was going to disturb the players' concentration, so we had to work through the night to replace it with a wooden partition, which is now known on the circuit as the Berlin Wall.'

The third round of the British Open finished at 10.45pm on a Thursday. By 3.40am on Friday, a day set aside for rigging, the Assembly Rooms had been stripped bare and four tables were about to be replaced by two for the televised stage.

Even the colour of the carpet is the result of careful consideration. 'When you lay a carpet it can look very different from how it appears when there is something like three kilowatts of light on it,' explained Hatherell. In the past the organizers have even had to conjure up a 'magic carpet' – out of a paint pot! 'We are only hiring the venue, so we can't use permanent fixtures and fittings,' said Hatherell. 'We have to use tape rather than tacks to fit the carpet. With the weight of the set, and people walking on it, the carpet moves. The joints separate and sometimes we have to paint them in.'

Seating posed a problem or two at the Assembly Rooms, ideal for a single-table set-up but not so good for a two-table one. Television wants faces, not empty spaces, in the background. The organizers were still waiting for some temporary seating to

arrive from Newbury half an hour before the start of play on the Friday. The extra seats were in place with a few minutes to spare.

Strict safety standards must be followed. 'We have to allow for 1.5 metres width in the gangways,' said Hatherell. 'At one World Championship, the fire prevention officer was watching an afternoon performance on his TV set when he noticed that there were people sitting on the stairs. He came down to the Crucible and told us that if we didn't move them, play would be stopped.'

The organizers had only thirty-six hours to get the Assembly Rooms ready for switch-on. But no one pressed the panic button when the new computerized scoreboards, introduced at Derby, arrived without any plugs on! Special cable was hurriedly sent down from Leeds and, despite a hitch or two, they were all wired up in time.

'One year, at the UK Championship, the scoreboards kept blowing up – and we were going live into "BBC Grandstand" that day,' recalled Hatherell. 'We went through three at £210 a time. We sent Len Ganley down to the local Tandy shop and, fortunately, the problem was solved.

'We have always managed to start on time, although there have been a few close calls. We cut it so fine at Sheffield one year that Mike Williams was seen leaving the arena with a paintbrush in his hand as the players were coming down the main gangway!'

Then there was the case of the 'bat in the belfry' at Preston's Guild Hall. Hatherell, relating the 'batty' tale, remembered: 'It kept diving underneath the TV lighting. We all had to put our heads together to catch the little blighter. We tried to blast it out with the public address system, stun it with noise. There was even a suggestion we should try shooting it, but we couldn't do that as bats are a protected species.

'In the end, we closed all the windows,

pulled every curtain, and turned out all the lights. We then left one door open with a light behind it. The bat flew through the door, knocked itself out on a pane of glass, and we were able to catch it!'

The British Open provides the climax to the ITV snooker season. For the first time last season, ITV had two-table coverage from Derby. Trevor East, ITV's executive producer of snooker, said: 'The WPBSA were anxious for a two-table situation to be introduced for both BBC and ITV tournaments to create more space in the calendar. It has increased our coverage costs by a third, but it gives us far greater editorial flexibility. We are not lumbered with one match that does not come up to expectations.'

Miles of multi-coloured cable and thousands of pounds' worth of equipment bring the snooker stars into your living room. ITV have between sixty and seventy people on location, not to mention those back in the studio. Sound, vision, lighting, cameramen, riggers, floor managers, make-up, captions, unit supervisors, videotape engineers, VT editors, electricians, scaffolders – the list is endless.

'Each role is as important as the next,' said East. 'Without one of them fulfilling their job in the overall operation, the whole show could not go on air.'

Some people think snooker is cheap tele-

Electronic wizardry: Above the scoreboard at Wembley.

vision. But East insists: 'It's only cheap in comparison with documentaries, drama and light entertainment. In sporting terms, it is expensive to cover. Snooker is one of the biggest outside broadcast operations either ITV or the BBC mount. The overall cost of covering ten days at Derby is very expensive. It takes up Central TV's entire outside broadcast operation. The main reason it becomes economical is the number of hours (around 400 each year) it is given on television. On an hour-to-hour basis, it's cheap.'

The TV people have to be aware of the finest details, right down to the colour of the players' shirts. East continued: 'Fortunately, we have a terrific working relationship with the WPBSA. They understand both our and the BBC's needs. We have all grown up together in terms of covering the game.'

The BCE tables, with Italian slate 1¾ inches thick and weighing well over a ton, are virtually last to be put in place. It takes two people roughly five hours to put up one table. Andy Williams, of A & D Billiards of Birmingham, who is sub-contracted by BCE to erect the tables and maintain them at Derby, said: 'It's impossible to make a table to suit every player. Some players like a fast table, others slow. Some like easy pockets, others tight. We use templates to get the shape and size of the pock-

Inside: At the Benson and Hedges Masters at Wembley.

ets.' The amount of undercut determines how tight the pocket is. 'A sixteenth of an inch might not make much difference to an ordinary player,' continued Williams, 'but to a professional, it's a lot. It means he can pinch a certain amount on a shot to gain good position for the next.' The tables are brushed and ironed, and the level checked, before each session of play.

Referees, recorders and markers also play a vital part in the running of a tournament. The recorder, as the name implies, records every stroke on a sheet of paper, while the marker works the electronic scoreboard. There are also runners, who keep the press up-to-date with the latest scores and breaks.

John Street, one of the five full-time referees on the circuit, can often be found in the press room before the start of play brandishing a pair of scissors. He scours every newspaper for the tournament cuttings board. 'The referees always get to a tournament the day before it starts to assist with the setting up,' he said. 'We do anything that needs doing to ensure that the event runs smoothly.'

The gadgets used by the players have become very hi-tech. As well as the various rests and spiders, a cue extension and a 'cushaid' (a small, grooved plastic block which fits on to the cross piece of the rest to allow a player to cue more easily over the cushion) are now part of the standard equipment.   The referee is responsible for making sure that all the equipment is there. It is not just a case of putting on the white gloves and racking the balls.

'It's absolutely amazing how things have changed. Whoever thought you would

The all-seeing eye: BBC camera in position at Wembley.

make a living from snooker?' said Street, who – occasionally – lives in Exeter with his family. 'You don't see much of your wife and children during the season. I'm home for a few days, then it's off to another tournament.'

The cameras start rolling and TV coverage of the 1988 British Open is under way. Ten days of sporting drama are about to unfold. Then down come the tables, the set, the lighting and we are off to Bournemouth to start all over again!

THE WORLD SERIES: TOKYO TUMMY, SAM THE SHIRT AND WHO FORGOT THE TROPHY?

Snooker's first World Series arrived in a blaze of publicity. The Series, costing more than £1 million, would take the sport to five continents.

Inevitably, the man behind the scheme was Matchroom's Barry Hearn who had linked up with Barrie Gill, chairman of CSS International. It was a series that would put snooker alongside tennis, athletics and motor racing on a grand prix scale. Eight events were planned – from Toronto to Tokyo, from Rio de Janeiro to Las Vegas. Snooker was planning a massive global take-off. The eleven players invited included the top eight in the world: Steve Davis, Jimmy White, Neal Foulds, Cliff Thorburn, Joe Johnson, Terry Griffiths, Tony Knowles and Dennis Taylor. Tony Meo, Willie Thorne and Stephen Hendry completed the line-up.

Hearn said: 'Make no mistake, this Series is not aimed at giving a living to the also-rans. It's for winners only and every player involved is a champion. This is the biggest breakthrough that snooker has ever made.'

The event had the blessing of the WPBSA and players were geared up for a global explosion. Snooker's top four managers – Hearn, Howard Kruger, Ian Doyle and Robert Winsor (then Thorburn's manager) – all came together for the first time in joint support of the series.

Then came the crash. After just three events in Tokyo, Hong Kong and Toronto, the Series ground to a halt. Hearn blamed the financial collapse in stock markets throughout the world for the delay in setting up the additional events and he also had an international sponsor who pulled out.

Later, when the Series was suspended, Hearn explained, 'The demands on TV time created by the Winter Olympics in Calgary and the Summer Olympics in South Korea, plus the European Football Championship, have made it impossible to obtain sufficient air time for the proposed European and American rounds of the Series. It will be delayed until 1989 – ready for a major relaunch.'

Sign of the times: Jimmy White continues his world travels in Tokyo.

But though the Series hit problems, the three tournaments held produced the usual quota of good stories on and off the green baize. The journey to Tokyo for round one took some of the players twenty-seven hours. It is by visiting the Japanese capital that you realize just how big snooker could become in this paradise for sporting maniacs. Some Japanese golf clubs cost £1 million to join and then the 'lucky' member pays up to £100 a round! Tennis is another Japanese 'must', even if you do have to queue for three hours in temperatures of up to 100°F to book a court you will use in three months' time. Snooker looks like being big, big business in the future despite the fact that there were only two clubs in Tokyo at the time of our visit.

As well as contending with jet-lag, some of the players on the trip were struck down with 'Tokyo tummy', a quaint local bug that leaves you racing to the boys' room every hour or so. Perhaps that raw baby octopus had something to do with it – we should have stuck to the salad.

The Tokyo Masters was sponsored by British Caledonian and held in the Tokyo Prince Hotel, watched by a specially invited audience. The first-round matches between the eight players were held over just three frames – a format the stars do not like. But White accepted the situation: 'Three frames means a lot of pressure, but if this is what we have to do to get the game going in Japan, it's okay by me,' he said.

Davis beat Thorne 2–0, White did the same to Hendry, Taylor squeezed past Meo 2–1 and Foulds lost 2–1 to Griffiths who included a 118 – the first time a century had been scored in a tournament in Tokyo.

The outdoor temperature was around the 100°F mark and Tokyo seemed like a gigantic traffic jam. It's a lot easier to travel by subway than by road: the subway is an ultra-clean efficient way of getting about. Incredibly, a couple of the players were injured – Davis with a back problem

Who's your friend? Referee Len Ganley finds a new pal in Tokyo.

because of cricket duties during the summer, and White with a pulled muscle in his right arm for which he had to see a doctor.

In the semi-finals, Taylor beat Davis 3–2 while Griffiths dumped out White 3–0. Hearn, a late arrival, was now on duty and relaxed with the players around the swimming pool but still kept his business empire ticking over by phone and fax. It turned out that three Japanese TV stations would eventually screen the Masters.

Taylor won the final, £30,000 and a Samurai warrior's helmet by dispatching Griffiths 6–3. 'My best years are yet to come,' he said, 'even though they say snooker is a young man's game.'

Snooker's jet set then hit the road again – this time to Hong Kong for part two of the World Series. On the way, we heard that Riley were to sponsor the event: Hearn was happy.

Tokyo had been a new experience – a land of earthquakes, massive motorway snarl-ups and beer at £8 a pint. Hong Kong was familiar territory, even though the arrival at the airport is one of the most frightening anywhere in the world as the plane soars in between the towering high-rise office buildings. Not a journey for the faint of heart! This British colony is now an accepted stopping point for most of the world's top snooker players. The sport has mushroomed since Davis visited Hong Kong for the first time in 1983: there are now more than 7,000 tables in 200-plus clubs, and it is the local Chinese who are the most enthusiastic players. So much so that Tony Craig, of the Hong Kong and Macau Billiards and Snooker Association, claims: 'These Chinese players are very dedicated – I reckon we will have a Chinese professional within five years.' Brave words, but the Chinese do love a challenge, and when they take up a sport they usually succeed at the highest level: just look at their prowess in table-tennis, athletics and gymnastics.

Steve and friends: Steve Davis and some Chinese fans in Hong Kong.

The Hong Kong venue was the Queen Elizabeth Stadium, where the crowds sometimes numbered around the 3,000 mark. The format was also changed: eight local Chinese players were to do battle with the eight established professionals.

Seven of the players had played in Tokyo, though Meo had flown home to be replaced by Canada's Thorburn.

The Chinese are money-mad. You name it – they bet on it. Thorne, known for his odd wager, loved every minute. Vast amounts of money changed hands during the games, not just on the outcome of the match but often on the outcome of each shot!

There were also other local 'barriers' to overcome. In the UK, press photographers have to obtain equipment that makes the click of their camera inaudible to the human ear, and even then they are sometimes locked away in a sound-proof box. That couldn't happen in Hong Kong. There was a battery of cameramen and camerawomen waiting to snap every shot from every angle. The players had to grit their teeth and get on with it.

Hong Kong's 'gadget-madness' took some getting used to as well. Everyone seems to carry a paging device or a telephone. There were bleeps and rings every night during play.

Thorburn was the only 'star' to drop a frame as he beat billiard hall boss Sunny Tong 3–1, while White knocked out Kenny Kwok, a nineteen-year-old player of immense talent whom the Whirlwind rates as a name to mark down for the future.

Hendry, preparing for what would turn out to be quite a remarkable season, sent his manager, Ian Doyle, into a panic by casually mentioning that he had lost his passport. A frantic search failed to uncover it.

White crushed Thorne 3–0, Hendry beat Foulds 3–2 and Taylor edged out Thorburn 3–2. Griffiths lost 3–0 to Davis, who then expanded his thoughts on globe-trotting – a pastime regarded by many armchair fans as glamorous and exciting. 'I know it sounds great coming to all these exotic locations,' he said, 'but these days there is hardly any time for sight-seeing because there is too much at stake. As soon as we arrive, we have to find a table and get down to hard work.'

The one relaxation for most players in Hong Kong is duty-free shopping, with shirts, suits and shoes the priorities. Sam the Shirt has been looking after snooker players for many years – he is soon down at the Hilton Hotel to take more orders. I decide to get some shirts on the Kowloon side and order three hand-made cotton ones complete with initials. I return ninety minutes later, pick up the shirts and pay out £21. How do they do it?

There was also a brisk demand for fake Rolex watches at £25 each. Some were good value and will last for years. Others would cease to function in a matter of days.

Back on the snooker table, Davis was extended all the way before beating Taylor 5–4. The local fans turned up in force to watch White and Hendry vie for the second final place. There was only one winner and that was Hendry by a comfortable 5–2 margin – a triumph he rated as 'the greatest' of his career so far. That phrase was to be repeated on more than one occasion later in the season.

Davis strolled home 9–3 in the final as Hendry paid the penalty for some silly shots. Davis said: 'There is no doubting Stephen's ability, but now he has got to serve his apprenticeship.'

Hendry then returned to the hotel to continue his search for the missing passport. He finally found it – underneath his suitcase!

At this point Davis and Taylor were level on top of the World Series with thirteen points apiece and there was now a lull before part three of the Series – this time on the other side of the globe in Toronto.

The Toronto event had already been established on the calendar as the Canadian Masters run by the WPBSA. Now Hearn, with WPBSA blessing and £50,000 in cash, was to stage the John Labatt

All at sea: Jimmy White takes it easy after losing to Stephen Hendry in the semi-final of the Riley Hong Kong Masters.

Classic Canadian Masters as part of his Series.

White made a bad start to the trip by missing his flight at London's Gatwick Airport. He finally had to catch a later plane to join up with the main party.

The first morning was spent at one of the most famous sporting stadiums in the whole of North America – the Maple Leaf Gardens, base for the Toronto Maple Leafs ice-hockey squad. The Leafs have been trophy-less for many years, but such is the popularity of ice-hockey that there is a five-year waiting list to get a season ticket.

Davis dropped a bombshell when he just happened to mention in passing that the trophy he had won a year earlier was still back home in Romford. It had to be put on a plane and dispatched in time for the final. Griffiths, the Welshman who can't bear to be away from home too long, lost his opening match 5–4 against Foulds and caught the first plane home . . . after just one night in Canada! Johnson's debut in the Masters ended in a 5–3 defeat by Thorburn, while Knowles's opening match saw him lose 5–1 to White – in just eighty-five minutes.

Davis revealed that his beloved cue had undergone drastic changes. 'First the ferrule worked loose and then the wood split,' he explained. 'I took the cue to John Parris, a top cue repairer, and although the repairs were great, they left the cue a bit short. The weight and balance were all wrong and we added a joint to make it a two-piece. I have got to get used to using it – I was prepared for something to happen to the cue eventually. The funny thing is that I thought someone would have stolen it by now!'

Davis lost 5–1 to in-form Taylor and then told us that he had knocked in a 147 using the new cue down at a local snooker hall.

Journalists on tour have to be prepared for any eventuality, and when Foulds woke up with a bad back, I went along to the local hospital with him. He was fully examined and they couldn't really work out what was wrong, but he was prescribed some tablets and the pain went away. There was, fortunately, no recurrence during his semi-final with White – a truly classic match that saw the Whirlwind scramble home 8–7 after leading 6–2 at one stage.

The second semi-final dragged on for eight and a half hours. Taylor beat Thorburn 8–5, while Davis trudged around the streets and record shops of Toronto looking for more discs for his mammoth collection back home. He managed to cut down his buying and went home with just 300 new records!

Final day and it was White *versus* Taylor. But with less than ten minutes to go to the start of a live broadcast on CBC coast-to-coast across Canada, White could

The master: Dennis Taylor complete with the John Labatt Classic Canadian Masters trophy.

not be found. He finally turned up in the hotel lobby after being delayed at the hairdresser. Tournament director Paul Hatherell was on the brink of a nervous breakdown, while CBC executives were tearing their hair out at the thought of a live show about to go out with 50 per cent of the performers missing. White didn't bat an eyelid as he sprinted all the way to the TV studios and made it with a minute to spare.

The final was superb with a 9–7 win for Taylor and another £25,000 in his bank balance. That gave Taylor a nine-point lead at the top of the table, but it was all to count for nothing as Hearn announced the postponement of the Series.

'You will not see better snooker than that anywhere snooker is played,' said a delighted Taylor, who missed a maximum after failing on the fourteenth red. But he later knocked in a 127.

The World Series events helped explore new markets, protected established venues and gave a whole new direction to the possible explosion of snooker worldwide. Hearn insisted that the World Series is not dead and, at the time of going to press, he had plans for it to be relaunched. Time will tell but, whatever the outcome, the World Series was an imaginative step into the future.

British Caledonian Tokyo Masters Results

FIRST ROUND		SEMI-FINALS		FINAL	
S. Davis (Eng)	2				
v		S. Davis	2		
W. Thorne (Eng)	0	v		Dennis Taylor	6
Dennis Taylor (NI)	2	Dennis Taylor	3		
v					
A. Meo (Eng)	1			v	
T. Griffiths (Wales)	2	Griffiths	3		
v		v		Griffiths	3
N. Foulds (Eng)	1	White	0		
J. White (Eng)	2				
v					
S. Hendry (Scot)	0				
Losers: £7,000		Losers: £12,000		Loser: £18,000	
				Winner: £30,000	

Riley Hong Kong Masters Results

FIRST ROUND		QUARTER-FINALS		SEMI-FINALS		FINAL	
S. Davis (Eng)	3						
v		S. Davis	3				
W. Chi Kuen	0	v		S. Davis	5		
T. Griffiths (Wales)	3	Griffiths	0				
v				v		S. Davis	9
S. Leung	0						
C. Thorburn (Can)	3	Thorburn	2				
v		v		Dennis Taylor	4		
S. Tong	1	Dennis Taylor	3				
Dennis Taylor (NI)	3					v	
v							
F. Chan	0						
J. White (Eng)	3	White	3				
v		v		White	2		
K. Kwok	0	Thorne	0				
W. Thorne (Eng)	3					Hendry	3
v				v			
J. Chan	0						
S. Hendry (Scot)	3	Hendry	3				
v		v		Hendry	5		
G. Kwok	0	Foulds	2				
N. Foulds (Eng)	3						
v							
I. Li	0						
		Losers: £4,000		Losers: £8,000		Loser: £12,000	
						Winner: £30,000	

High break: 92 – J. White £1,000

John Labatt Classic Canadian Masters Results

FIRST ROUND		SEMI-FINALS		FINAL	
N. Foulds (Eng)	5				
v		N. Foulds	7		
T. Griffiths (Wales)	4			White	7
J. White (Eng)	5	v			
v		White	8		
A. Knowles (Eng)	1				v
Dennis Taylor (NI)	5				
v		Dennis Taylor	8		
S. Davis (Eng)	1			Dennis Taylor	9
J. Johnson (Eng)	3	v			
v		Thorburn	5		
C. Thorburn (Can)	5				

Losers: £5,000	Losers: £9,000	Loser: £12,000
		Winner: £25,000

John Labatt Classic Canadian Masters: Previous Years' Results

YEAR	WINNER	RUNNER-UP	SCORE
1985	(BCE)		
	Dennis Taylor (NI)	S. Davis (Eng)	9–5
1986	(BCE)		
	S. Davis (Eng)	W. Thorne (Eng)	9–3

World Series Table

	TOKYO	HONG KONG	TORONTO	POINTS
Dennis Taylor (NI)	9	4	9	22
S. Davis (Eng)	4	9	0	13
J. White (Eng)	3	3	6	12
T. Griffiths (Wales)	6	0	2	8
S. Hendry (Scot)	0	6	–	6
N. Foulds (Eng)	1	1	4	6
C. Thorburn (Can)	–	2	3	5
A. Meo (Eng)	2	–	–	2
J. Johnson (Eng)	–	–	1	1
A. Knowles (Eng)	–	–	0	0
W. Thorne (Eng)	0	0	–	0

HOW DID YOU COPE WITH CHAMBERLAIN'S CHALLENGE?
Answers to the Questions on page 139

1 The referee would replace the moved ball(s) as near to their original position as possible; there would be no penalty. (*Score 3 points.*)

2 (a) When, after potting a red, he commits a foul before nominating a colour. (*Score 3 points.*)
(b) When he uses a ball off the table for any purpose, i.e. to see if a ball will spot before he makes the stroke. (*Score 3 points.*)
(c) When he plays at reds in successive strokes. (*Score 3 points.*)
(d) When he uses as the cue ball any ball other than the white. (*Score 3 points.*)

3 The referee would award a penalty equal to the value of the ball that the ball-marker was replacing, or the value of the ball 'on', whichever is the higher. (*Score 4 points.*)

4 The referee would remove it, place it in a pocket and award a foul of 4 points, unless it had been knocked on to the cushion as a result of the player being on the blue, pink or black, when the penalty would be 5, 6 or 7. (*Score 5 points.*)

5 If requested by the striker, the referee may move and hold in position any light shade which interferes with his stance. (*Score 4 points.*)

6 He can play from where the ball lies, he can request his opponent to play from where the ball lies, or he can lift the cue ball and play the next stroke from in hand (in the 'D'). Note that he cannot have a free ball. (*Score 5 points.*)

7 By playing away from the touching ball, returning after making contact with a cushion or another ball. (*Score 4 points.*)

8 Yes, if the player is colour blind, but he must ask. (*Score 2 points.*)

9 With only one red left on the table, he is snookered after a foul and therefore awarded a free ball. By potting the yellow as a red, then the yellow as a colour, followed by the last red, the yellow, and the yellow again, as the start of the colour sequence. (*Score 8 points.*)

10 The player who made the foul. (*Score 3 points.*)

How did you score?
 0–10: Why don't you take up knitting or darts?
11–20: It's not as easy as it appears, is it?
21–30: Not bad – but read the rules again.
31–40: Very good – get yourself a pair of white gloves.
41–50: Excellent – see you at the Crucible (probably in my place!)

SUFFRAGETTES OF SNOOKER

by Gaye Jones

Imagine the reaction amongst diehard politicians thirty years ago if someone had had the temerity to suggest that a mere woman would one day become Prime Minister! The 'outrageous' behaviour of the suffragettes was, after all, still a vivid memory. Today we have the suffragettes of snooker – women who have decided to dedicate themselves to reaching the top of their chosen sport despite the fact that this has traditionally been a bastion of the male sex.

'It reduces the men to tears, it will kill the women.' These were Barry Hearn's words when he met world champion Ann Marie Farren last year and was asked his opinion about the possibility of women competing on equal terms with men on the professional snooker circuit. But women are already competing on equal terms on the amateur circuit – and winning. So if male amateurs can achieve professional status and fight their way into the upper rankings, why is it that men think that women will not be able to do the same?

It is an acknowledged fact that there is an enormous gap in standards between the top of the men's amateur and professional circuits but some newcomers do make it to the top. There is a similar gap between the male and female amateur circuits, Allison Fisher being the example of someone who

Congratulations: Allison Fisher, the world number 1, with Ann Marie Farren, the girl who has just taken her world title.

has successfully made the transition. So face it, fellas, it can be done and there are a number of ladies, headed by Allison, who are knocking on the door and will soon be challenging the best of you.

Allison competed on the 1987 professional ticket circuit and missed qualifying by a mere three points. Although this must rank as a great personal achievement for Allison, it is also a great step forward for women's snooker because people must now accept that there are women who can produce top-class play and compete on equal terms with the best in the world. This must necessarily open the floodgates for young girls to take up the game in the same way that young boys do, something which has not yet happened simply because many people are still unaware of the fact that women do play serious snooker.

The 1987/88 season has been a year of progress and achievement for the women's game. Kim Shaw from High Wycombe became the first woman to make a century break (104) in a ranking tournament sanctioned by the World Ladies' Billiards and Snooker Association. A number of other players, including Stacey Hillyard and the 1987 world champion, Ann Marie Farren, are now consistently making century breaks in practice. Stacey's highest to date is a total clearance of 137 – no mean achievement in anyone's book.

It is unfortunate that the top female players rarely produce their best except when playing against other women. This is partly because there are only a few players of this calibre at present and it is only when they play each other that they feel sufficiently at risk of defeat to get the adrenalin flowing and produce really high-quality snooker. It is also unfortunate that, to most people, quality is defined by the size of the breaks produced in a match, regardless of the fact that fine safety play is often just as gripping and certainly as skilful.

Anyone who has ever watched live pro-

Ton-up girl: Stacey Hillyard, with a best break of 137.

fessional snooker for any length of time must admit that some matches lead one to wonder whether the word 'live' is actually applicable! It is also true that professional players who are often being paid lots of money – even for losing – cannot always produce high breaks.

The World Championship semi-final match in which Stacey Hillyard came from 1–3 down to beat Allison Fisher 4–3 – a repeat of her achievement at the same stage of the 1984 Championship when she went on to win the title – is an ideal illustration of the point made above regarding safety play. There were several breaks of 40 plus, but no significantly high ones, the majority of the match consisting of extremely high-quality safety play which generated a degree of tension in the auditorium equal to anything I have seen elsewhere. Reporting of the match, however, commented on the fact that neither player had produced the high breaks of which they are both capable: this remark was disappointing and gave a false impression of the quality of the snooker.

The fact that Allison Fisher failed to achieve a hat-trick of world titles was desperately disappointing for her for she is, despite this defeat, undoubtedly the best woman player in the world as denoted by her position 150 points ahead of her nearest rival in the rankings. Allison is aware that, as a champion, she is a target for everyone, and she told me that as she won more and more titles it became more and more difficult to maintain her unbeaten record. Indeed, she was taken to the black ball on several occasions last year. She knew that the run would have to end some time and I think her mother summed it all up when she said to me after Allison's World Championship defeat: 'It's just a pity that it had to be this week and this tournament.'

Allison is a highly motivated player and one of her strongest traits is that a defeat, at any level, only serves to increase her determination to succeed. She has returned to the circuit and won every women's tournament since the World Championship, establishing that she is without doubt the best – even without her World Championship crown. Struggling to gain recognition in a hostile world means that women are continually under the microscope. Our achievements need to be significantly better than those of the men in order to stifle our critics. Allison Fisher almost made it into the professional ranks last year but there are still many influential voices in snooker who are sceptical about her ability to achieve her ambition. The top male amateur players, however, whom she now consistently beats in tournaments, freely admit that she is a very good player and has as much chance as they do of achieving professional status.

The enormous difficulty in raising sponsorship also acts as a barrier to those women who wish to take up snooker full-time. Only the winner and runner-up in any women's event, apart from the World Championship, can expect to take away a three-figure sum; the others are lucky to cover their expenses. Even taking into account the enormous difference in ability, it still seems unfair that Ann Marie Farren's World Championship pay cheque was less than 4 per cent of that won by Steve Davis!

It is interesting to try to envisage the image that many people hold of a female snooker player. One company representative from a major West End clothes supplier, when approached for sponsorship, said that he didn't want the sort of women who play snooker bending over the table in his clothes! What sort of women do people think we are? Suffragettes, certainly, in that we are trying hard to break new ground in a traditionally male domain, but still human beings whose main wish is to play the game of our choice and whose ultimate ambition is to be able to hold our own against all comers in a sport which most people agree to be one of the few that can be played by both sexes on equal terms.

SNOOKER'S NEW QUEEN: ANN MARIE FARREN

When sixteen-year-old Ann Marie Farren won the 1987 Warner World Championship, she looked every inch a champion. Throughout the final she played with a confidence and skill which belied her tender years, taking her chances and winning the title in style.

In fairness, it must be said that Stacey Hillyard, Ann Marie's opponent in the final, was mentally exhausted, having had

Happy family: Ann Marie Farren celebrates her women's world champion success with her proud family.

a dour four-hour struggle against Allison Fisher earlier in the day. Stacey pulled up from 1–3 down to win the match 4–3, thus depriving the odds-on favourite of her third successive title.

Ann Marie was determined not to allow Stacey to complete a replay of the 1984 World Championship in which she had beaten Allison at the same stage and by the same score and then gone on to take the title. Miss Farren is a comparative newcomer to the women's circuit, her first ever appearance having been in the 1985 World Championship when she surprised everyone by reaching the quarter-finals. Since then her game has improved in leaps and bounds, particularly after she left school in 1987 and found a sponsor who provided her with practice facilities and opposition in two of the rising stars of the men's amateur circuit. In the week preceding the world title she took her first major title when she beat fourteen-year-old Lynette Horsburgh to become the first holder of the WLBSA British Open Challenge Trophy. Her timely win built her confidence at just the right moment and she never really looked in danger in any of her World Championship matches.

The big question now for Ann Marie is whether the new pressures of being the world champion will affect her game. She has admitted that she finds it hard to cope with the fact that everyone now expects her to win and people are critical if she doesn't do so. But, like Allison Fisher, Ann Marie is spurred on by ambition. She has her life in front of her and she is one of a new breed of young women who have started the game early enough to have a realistic chance of breaking the men's domination – as long as they can maintain the determination and resilience needed to become a champion.

Slow Coaches but Billiards Battles On

by Mark Wildman

Last season was a period of consolidation and, unfortunately, disappointment for professional billiards. There was an impressive prize fund of over £50,000, more professionals than ever before and record entries for the four ranking tournaments on the circuit. Inevitably, though, after the growing success of the sport in recent years, there had to be setbacks. Some players were warned about slow play; and the loss of television coverage of the BCE World Championship was a sad blow.

On the positive side, hard work meant that sponsors were obtained for all four major tournaments – Strachan, Yorkshire Bank and BCE – the latter backing the World and European Open tournaments. The North East has long given enthusiastic and loyal support to the three-ball game, and it was with optimism that the UK Championship was switched from Stockport to the Marton Hotel and Country Club in Middlesbrough. Local hero Mike Russell was obviously a star attraction for the billiards fans in this area, but even so they supported the Strachan UK Championship in large numbers. The venue proved extremely adaptable and is again scheduled to be used for the UK event this season.

The UK title went to Leeds man Ian Williamson, who beat Australia's Robbie Foldvari 7–3. The final did not live up to expectations, however, and the fans were treated to some rather slow play by both finalists. As a result, referee Alan Chamberlain had to step in and issue a warning for the players to speed up. The

format – based on 150 up over seven frames – was successful once again, even though in some quarters there was criticism. Purists would probably want to go back to the longer frames, but in these days when sponsorship is essential, we must accept that 'fan appeal' is all-important. The new set-up usually makes for brighter matches.

One new member was admitted to the ranks as a billiards-only player – Scotland's Hugh Nimmo. Another newcomer, India's Michael Ferreira, one of the great names in billiards, also showed his worth on the professional circuit. He is a former world amateur champion, and once he gets accustomed to the shorter-frame schedule he will be a threat to be reckoned with. In fact, Ferreira reached the final of the

World beater: Norman Dagley and the BCE World Championship trophy.

Yorkshire Bank Professional Players' Tournament in Leeds but went down 7–3 to Ray Edmonds.

The World Championship attracted a record-breaking twenty-four entries and again the title was taken by Norman Dagley who beat Eddie Charlton 7–4. Dagley, one of the most popular members on the circuit, once more finished top of the ranking list.

Mike Russell was being tipped as a potential winner last season even though he is only eighteen, a prediction which came true in the final event of the season – the BCE European Open in Antwerp. The tournament was organized on a round-robin basis until the semi-final when Russell, who learnt his trade as a youngster because there were no snooker leagues in the area, beat Bobby Close 4–3. In the final Russell scored his greatest win to date, beating world champion Norman Dagley 7–4.

Away from the professional scene, one of the most popular tournaments has been the Pro-Am Mini Prix Series. This tournament, run by Peterborough's Des Heald, has proved extremely popular with professionals and amateurs alike and has grown from strength to strength this season.

STRACHAN UK CHAMPIONSHIP

Ian Williamson produced three tremendous victories as he captured his first professional title – the Strachan UK Championship at Middlesbrough's Marton Hotel and Country Club. Unfortunately, the final against former world champion Robbie Foldvari lasted more than eight hours, with Williamson finally winning 7–3. Both players were warned publicly by referee Alan Chamberlain for slow play and Williamson said afterwards: 'I am sorry it was not a great match but as it was my first final I was very nervous.' He picked up £3,000 and Foldvari went home with £2,000.

Williamson's victim in the semi-final was young local hero Mike Russell, whom he defeated 4–2. In the quarter-finals, Williamson enjoyed a remarkable 4–2 win over world and defending champion Norman Dagley.

Hartlepool's Bob Close had hammered veteran Fred Davis 4–0 in the quarter-final but was then destroyed 4–1 in the next

Well played: Ian Williamson receives his Strachan UK Championship trophy.

round by Foldvari who produced some impressive big breaks.

Strachan's John Giles was pleased with the interest generated by the championship. 'It has been great having the tournament in Middlesbrough in front of such good crowds,' he commented.

One of the highlights of the event was the sportsmanship of young Russell who was trailing Williamson 3–2 in the semifinal but then called himself for a foul which had not been noticed by anyone else. The biggest upset of round one was the 4–2 victory of Scottish newcomer Hugh Nimmo over veteran Jack Karnehm. Karnehm knocked in breaks of 145, 133 and

Aussie number 1: Robbie Foldvari.

139, but Nimmo did not let that worry him and came through a good winner.

Strachan UK Championship Results

FIRST ROUND	QUARTER-FINALS	SEMI-FINALS	FINAL
N. Dagley (Eng) 4			
v	Dagley 2		
C. Everton (Wales) 1			
	v	Williamson 4	
I. Williamson (Eng) 4			
v	Williamson 4		
E. Hughes (Rep Ire) 0			
		v	Williamson 7
E. Charlton (Aust) 4			
v	Charlton 2		
G. Thompson (Eng) 2			
	v	Russell 2	
M. Wildman (Eng) 3			
v	Russell 4		
M. Russell (Eng) 4			
			v
R. Edmonds (Eng) 3			
v	Close 4		
R. Close (Eng) 4			
	v	Close 1	
F. Davis (Eng) 4			
v	F. Davis 0		
G. Cripsey (Eng) 0			
		v	Foldvari 3
J. Karnehm (Eng) 2			
v	Nimmo 0		
H. Nimmo (Scot) 4			
	v	Foldvari 4	
R. Foldvari (Aust) 4			
v	Foldvari 4		
M. Ferreira (Ind) 1			
Losers: £125	Losers: £500	Losers: £1,000	Loser: £2,000
			Winner: £3,000

YORKSHIRE BANK PROFESSIONAL PLAYERS' TOURNAMENT

Ray Edmonds, who was world champion in 1985, collected his first title for three years in the Yorkshire Bank Professional Players' Tournament at the Excelsior Club in Leeds. Edmonds was far too strong for Michael Ferreira, the former world amateur champion from India, and raced home a convincing 7–3 winner to collect £2,250.

Ferreira, a welcome addition to the pro ranks, took on world champion Norman Dagley in the semi-finals and found himself 1–0 in front when Dagley got stuck in a traffic jam on the way to the venue and arrived late! Dagley was predictably not in the right frame of mind to play his best and Ferreira won 4–2.

Edmonds's semi-final was against eighteen-year-old Mike Russell – a young man constantly tipped as a future world champion. But Russell was unable to make any impact against Edmonds who scored a 4–0 whitewash. Edmonds had started the campaign with a 4–0 win over Howard Griffiths and then came from 2–1 behind to beat Geoff Thompson 4–2 in the quarter-final.

England's Bobby Close came home 4–3 against veteran Fred Davis in the first round after a memorable match that included five century breaks. But then the ever-popular Close met Dagley and went down 4–1 in the round of the last eight.

Yorkshire Bank Professional Players' Tournament Results

FIRST ROUND	QUARTER-FINALS	SEMI-FINALS	FINAL
N. Dagley (Eng) 4			
v	Dagley 4		
E. Hughes (Rep Ire) 1		Dagley 2	
F. Davis (Eng) 3			
v	Close 1		
R. Close (Eng) 4			Ferreira 3
I. Williamson (Eng) 3			
v	Nimmo 0		
H. Nimmo (Scot) 4		Ferreira 4	
M. Wildman (Eng) 3			
v	Ferreira 4		
M. Ferreira (Ind) 4			v
R. Edmonds (Eng) 4			
v	Edmonds 4		
H. Griffiths (Wales) 0		Edmonds 4	
J. Karnehm (Eng) 0			
v	Thompson 2		
G. Thompson (Eng) 4			Edmonds 7
E. Charlton (Aust) 4			
v	Charlton 3		
C. Everton (Wales) 0		Russell 0	
R. Foldvari (Aust) 2			
v	Russell 4		
M. Russell (Eng) 4			
Losers: £93.75	Losers: £375	Losers: £750	Loser: £1,500
			Winner: £2,250

BCE WORLD CHAMPIONSHIP

Norman Dagley rediscovered his form at just the right moment as he collected the BCE World Championship at the Albert Hall, Bolton, for the second successive year. Dagley, who had swept all before him in the previous season, had surprisingly been defeated in the first two ranking tournaments. But it all came right in the World Championship final when he beat Australian Eddie Charlton 7–4. The win was worth £7,500 and Charlton collected £5,000.

There was to be no world crown for Ian Williamson to follow on from his success in the UK event. Williamson took on Dagley in the semi-final and lost 4–1, while former world champion Robbie Foldvari suffered a similar margin of defeat at the hands of Charlton.

Ray Edmonds gave Charlton a much tighter scrap in the quarter-final, but Charlton took the final frame for a 4–3 win. There were 4–2 successes for Williamson over Michael Ferreira and Foldvari over Hugh Nimmo; but the most comfortable victory in the last eight came from Dagley who beat Howard Griffiths 4–1.

Dagley made his intentions clear at the start when, in the first round, he despatched Mike Russell 4–0 while Charlton made short work of Irishman Tommy Murphy 4–1.

BCE World Championship Results

FIRST ROUND		QUARTER-FINALS		SEMI-FINALS		FINAL	
N. Dagley (Eng)	4						
v		Dagley	4				
M. Russell (Eng)	0			Dagley	4		
J. Karnehm (Eng)	2						
v		Griffiths	1				
H. Griffiths (Wales)	4					Dagley	7
I. Williamson (Eng)	4						
v		Williamson	4				
B. Close (Eng)	2			Williamson	1		
M. Wildman (Eng)	2						
v		Ferreira	2				
M. Ferreira (Ind)	4						v
R. Edmonds (Eng)	4						
v		Edmonds	3				
E. Hughes (Rep Ire)	0			Charlton	4		
E. Charlton (Aust)	4						
v		Charlton	4				
T. Murphy (NI)	1					Charlton	4
F. Davis (Eng)	2						
v		Nimmo	2				
H. Nimmo (Scot)	4			Foldvari	1		
R. Foldvari (Aust)	4						
v		Foldvari	4				
D. Heaton (Eng)	0						
Losers: £312.50		Losers: £1,250		Losers: £2,500		Loser: £5,000	
						Winner: £7,500	

BCE EUROPEAN OPEN

Mike Russell became professional billiards' youngest ever winner when, at eighteen, he captured the European Open title in Antwerp. Russell, one of the most refreshing young players on the billiards circuit, picked up the £2,200 first prize by beating world champion Norman Dagley 7–4 in the final.

The crowds in Antwerp were particularly disappointing, but that detracted nothing from Russell's impressive success. The early rounds up to the semi-final were organized on a round-robin basis, and though Russell had moments when he thought he might have been out of the competition, he came through with flying colours to reach the semi-final. There he beat Hartlepool's Bobby Close 4–3 to go through to the final against Dagley who despatched Grimsby's Ray Edmonds 4–1. In the final Russell trailed 2–0 and 3–1, but then took six of the next seven frames to record his first ever triumph.

Russell had been looking for a new cue and finally advertised in his local paper. As a result a player in the area offered him an ash cue once used by the immortal Horace Lindrum, and Russell snapped this up for £40. 'The cue is tremendous,' he enthused. 'It is just what I have been looking for. It was a very proud moment for me when I won my first title. I know it is going to be tough making a career in billiards, but I am determined to keep it going.'

Young winner: Mike Russell with the BCE European Open trophy after his victory in Antwerp, Belgium.

There was certainly an unreal atmosphere about the European Open venue when so few spectators turned up to watch, but that didn't detract from the intensity of competition as the world's best billiards players battled it out for a prize fund of £8,700.

BCE European Open Results

FIRST ROUND

Group A
M. Ferreira (India) 4, H. Nimmo (Scot) 0; N. Dagley (Eng) 4, R. Close (Eng) 1; Close 4, Nimmo 1; Dagley 4, Ferreira 1; Close 4, Ferreira 1; Dagley 4, Nimmo 1.

Group B
I. Williamson (Eng) 4, C. Everton (Wales) 0. M. Wildman (Eng) and B. Bennett (Eng) absent.

Group C
G. Cripsey (Eng) 4, H. Griffiths (Wales) 1; R. Edmonds (Eng) 4, Griffiths 0; Edmonds 4, Cripsey 0.
E. Charlton (Aust) absent.

Group D
M. Russell (Eng) 4, G. Thompson (Eng) 0; R. Foldvari (Aust) 4, J. Karnehm (Eng) 2; Thompson 4, Karnehm 2; Foldvari 4, Russell 0; Russell 4, Karnehm 0; Foldvari 4, Thompson 3.

Prize money: £75 – Karnehm, Nimmo; £125 – Ferreira, Griffiths, Thompson

Dagley, Close, Williamson, Everton, Edmonds, Cripsey, Foldvari and Russell qualify for quarter-finals.

QUARTER-FINALS

Group E
Dagley 4, Everton 3; Close 4, Williamson 3; Dagley 4, Williamson 0; Close 4, Everton 1; Dagley 4, Close 2; Williamson 4, Everton 0.

Group F
Russell 4, Edmonds 0; Foldvari 4, Cripsey 0; Edmonds 4, Foldvari 3; Russell 4, Cripsey 0; Edmonds 4, Cripsey 0; Russell 4, Foldvari 3.

Prize money: £500 – Everton, Cripsey; £600 – Williamson, Foldvari.

SEMI-FINALS		FINAL	
Dagley	4	Dagley	4
v			
Edmonds	1		v
Russell	4	Russell	7
v			
Close	3		
Losers: £1,000		Loser: £1,500	
		Winner: £2,200	

BILLIARDS PRIZE MONEY 1987/88 (£)

		Strachan UK	Yorkshire Bank PPT	BCE World	BCE European	Total
1	N. Dagley	500	750	7,500	1,500	10,250
2	I. Williamson	3,000	93.75	2,500	600	6,193.75
3	E. Charlton	500	375	5,000	—	5,875
4	R. Foldvari	2,000	93.75	2,500	600	5,193.75
5	R. Edmonds	125	2,250	1,250	1,000	4,625
6	M. Russell	1,000	750	312.50	2,200	4,262.50
7	M. Ferreira	125	1,500	1,250	125	3,000
8	R. Close	1,000	375	312.50	1,000	2,687.50
9	H. Nimmo	500	375	1,250	75	2,200
10	H. Griffiths	—	93.75	1,250	125	1,468.75
11	F. Davis	500	93.75	312.50	—	906.25
12	C. Everton	125	93.75	—	500	718.75
13=	G. Cripsey	125	—	—	500	625
13=	G. Thompson	125	375	—	125	625
15	J. Karnehm	125	93.75	312.50	75	606.25
16	M. Wildman	125	93.75	312.50	—	531.25
17	E. Hughes	125	93.75	312.50	—	531.25
18=	D. Heaton	—	—	312.50	—	312.50
18=	T. Murphy	—	—	312.50	—	312.50

WITH THE AMATEURS

WORLD AMATEUR CHAMPIONSHIP

Darren Morgan, already guaranteed a place in the professional ranks this season, last year became the fifth Welshman to win the world amateur title in Bangalore, India. Morgan, from Gwent, powered to an easy 11–4 win over Malta's Joe Grech who was already bemoaning his luck after losing in the final of the World Amateur Billiards Championship to India's Geet Sethi. Even Labour leader Neil Kinnock, Morgan's local MP, sent a 'Well done' telegram as the Welsh village of Cwmfelinfach celebrated this outstanding success.

The four other Welshmen to take the world amateur crown were Gary Owen, Doug Mountjoy, Cliff Wilson and Terry Parsons.

King of the world: World amateur champion Darren Morgan after his success in India.

ENGLISH AMATEUR CHAMPIONSHIP

Barry Pinches, the impressive young amateur from Norfolk, earned himself a trip to the World Amateur Championship in Sydney this year when he captured the BCE English Amateur title. Pinches romped to a 13–6 win over Craig Edwards at Bradford and gained a chance to play off for a professional place at the end of this season. But win or lose, Pinches was guaranteed his trip 'Down Under' as beaten opponent Edwards had already earned his professional status this season. Aged only seventeen at the time of his victory, Pinches is one of the most promising players on the circuit and was always in control to take the £1,250 first prize.

Edwards had beaten David Rippon 8–5 in the Northern final, while Pinches's Southern success came with an 8–4 win over South London's Steve Ventham. One of the biggest shocks in an earlier round of the Championship was Paul Davies's 8–4 hammering of Welshman Darren Morgan, the reigning world amateur champion.

WORLD JUNIOR CHAMPIONSHIP

Quietly-spoken teenager Brian Morgan travelled half-way round the world to Bangkok and came back home as world junior champion. Morgan only entered the event when he read in a snooker magazine that all comers were allowed to compete. He borrowed his airfare, thanks to sponsors Radion, and travelled all the way to

Thailand to record a brilliant 6–1 victory over Jason Peplow from Malta in the final.

Morgan had glowing credentials from professional Vic Harris who said: 'I have coached quite a few players over the years but Brian is the best I have seen since Steve Davis. He has got the talent to go right to the top. He is so dedicated.'

WORLD AMATEUR BILLIARDS CHAMPIONSHIP

India's Geet Sethi easily captured the World Amateur Billiards title with a 4,846–3,256 victory over Malta's Joe Grech at the Park Avenue Hotel in Belfast. In the first session twenty-six-year-old Sethi knocked in a World Championship record break of 760 in just thirty-five minutes, and by the end of that session was 1,059 in front with an average break of 103.

AMATEUR RESULTS 1987/88

Snooker

World Championship (India)
Darren Morgan (Wales) 11
Joe Grech (Malta) 4

European Championship (Holland)
Stefan Mazrocis (England) 11
Paul Mifsud (Malta) 7

BCE English Championship
Barry Pinches (Norfolk) 13
Craig Edwards (Humberside) 6
High break: 136 – Pinches

World Junior Championship (Thailand)
Brian Morgan (England) 6
Jason Peplow (Malta) 1

British Isles Under-19
(sponsored by Dudley Snooker)
Joseph Swail (Northern Ireland) 3
Anton Bishop (London) 0

British Isles Under-16
(sponsored by Dudley Snooker)
David Grimwood (Essex) 3
John Lardner (Scotland) 1

BCE Grand Masters
John Griffin (Stockton-on-Tees) 4
Maurice Chapman (Birmingham) 3
High break: 85 – Chapman

San Miguel UK Pairs
Barry Pinches (Norfolk) and David Harold (West Midlands) 3
David Rippon (Cleveland) and Neil Mosley (Cleveland) 1

Inter-Counties
Essex 5 Lancashire 4

Inter-Counties Under-19
Yorkshire 5 Avon 1

Riley/Tournament Champions/Pontin's Home International
Winners: England

Daily Mirror/Pontin's Home International Junior
Winners: Wales

Hainsworth TopTable (Billiards and Snooker Foundation)
Paul King (Northern Ireland) 3
Jason Pusser (London) 1
High break: 59, 39, 36 – King

Billiards

World Championship (Northern Ireland)
Geet Sethi (India) 4,846
Joe Grech (Malta) 3,256

English Championship
Peter Gilchrist (Cleveland) 3,379
David Edwards (Wales) 1,854
High break: 261 – Gilchrist

British Isles Under-19
Michael Stocks (Yorkshire) 218
Nick Hayward (Cleveland) 203

British Isles Under-16
Sacha Journet (Surrey) 221
David Bewick (Cleveland) 220

Inter-Counties
Cleveland 1,042   Devon 556

Billiards and Snooker Foundation Under-16
Karl O'Donnell (Middlesbrough) 288
Conor Morgan (Northern Ireland) 254

THE INTERNATIONAL BILLIARDS AND SNOOKER FEDERATION

The International Billiards and Snooker Federation (IBSF) was set up in 1973 to stage and organize the world billiards and world snooker tournaments. The chairman is elected for a two-year term and the joint vice-chairmen are Stan Brooke (England) and the chairman of the host country for the World Championship being held that year. The B&SCC has given an undertaking to the IBSF that they will be consulted on all major changes affecting the game.

New Zealand's Brian Bennett is the current chairman of the IBSF.

International Billiards and Snooker Federation Member Associations

Australia
John W. Orr,
Secretary,
Australian B&S Council,
PO Box 417,
Spring Hill, Brisbane,
Queensland 4000,
Australia.

Bangladesh
S. Mahboob,
Secretary,
Bangladesh B&SF,
GPO Box 2047,
I/C New Bailey Road,
Dhaka 2,
Bangladesh.

Belgium
Rene Moerman,
Secretary,

Belgium B&SA,
Gerechtsplein 2,
8400 Oostende,
Belgium.

Brunei
J. Chong,
President,
Negara Brunei Darussalam B&SA,
PO Box 1542,
Bandar Seri Begawan 1915,
Negara Brunei Darussalam.

Canada
B. Hargrove,
Secretary,
Canadian B&SCC,
PO Box 1252,
Saint John N.B.,
E2L 4G7 Canada.

Egypt
Hosny Y. Abdel Ghani,
Secretary,
Fédération Egyptienne de Billiard,
83 Rue Ramses,
Le Caire,
Egypt.

England
D. Ford,
Secretary, B&SCC,
Coronet House,
Queen Street,
Leeds LS1 2TN,
England.

Fiji
Kevin Wasson,
Fiji Billiards and Snooker,
United Club,
PO Box 448,
Suva, Fiji.

Germany
M. Henson,
Secretary,
Deutscher Snooker Kontrol Verband,
Trakehnenweg 2,
D-3170 Gifhorn,
Germany.

Ghana
M. A. Kwanena-Poh,
Secretary,
Ghana B&SA,
University of Science and Technology,
Numasi,
Ghana.

Gibraltar
P. DeLa Rosa,
Secretary,
Gibraltar B&SA,
77/13 Irish Town,
Gibraltar.

Hong Kong
The Chairman,
Hong Kong and Macau Amateur Billiards and
Snooker Association,
GPO Box 5798,
Hong Kong.

Iceland
Orn Ingolfsson,
Secretary,
Snooker and Billiards Association of Iceland,
Grundarland 15,
108 Reykjavik,
Iceland.

India
P. N. Roy,
Secretary,
B&S Federation of India,
Bengal Bonded Warehouse,
25 Nataji Subhas Road,
Calcutta 700 001,
India.

Isle of Man
Mrs E. M. M. Colquitt,
Iglen Road Terrace,
Laxey,
Isle of Man.

Israel
Isaac Yavin,
Chairman,
Israeli Billiard Association,
84 Ahad Haam Street,
PO Box 4327,
Tel-Aviv,
Israel.

Japan
Akira Hida,
President,
Japan Snooker and Billiards Association,
Tokumaru 3-1-21,
Itabashi KV,
Tokyo,
Japan 175.

Kenya
J. C. Kinyua,
Secretary,
Kenya BCC,
PO Box 40683,
Nairobi,
Kenya.

Malaysia
W. Y. Chin,
President,
National Snooker Association of Malaysia,
PO Box 1089 Jalan,
Semangat,
46870 Petaling Jaya,
Selengor,
Malaysia.

Malta
David Spiteri,
Secretary,
Malta B&SA,
56 Melita Street,
Valletta,
Malta.

Mauritius
H. Brunel,
Secretary,
Mauritius B&SF,
PO Box 378,
Port Louis,
Mauritius.

Netherlands
John Duymel,
Treasurer,
Snooker and Billiards Association
of the Netherlands,
Van Arembergelaan 8,
2274 BT Voorburg,
The Netherlands.

New Zealand
B. J. Bennett,
President,
New Zealand B&SA,
Box 603,
New Plymouth,
New Zealand.

Northern Ireland
J. R. Williamson,
Secretary,
Northern Ireland B&SA,
105 Glenburn Road,
Dunmurry,
Northern Ireland.

Norway
Bjorn Berntsen,
President,
Det Norske Biljadfordbund,
Lachmannsvei 11,
0495 Oslo 4,
Norway.

Pakistan
C. Kanga,
Secretary,
Pakistan B&SA,
c/o Karachi Club,
Dr Zia Uddin Ahmed Road,
Karachi,
Pakistan.

Papua New Guinea
David Hastings,
President,
Papua New Guinea National B&SA,
PO Box 85,
Rabaul,
East New Britain Province,
Papua New Guinea.

Republic of Ireland
Dermot Dalton,
Secretary,
Republic of Ireland B&SA,
25 Batchelors Walk,
Dublin 1,
Ireland.

Scotland
Peter Bennett,
Secretary,
Scottish B&SA,
130 Woodside Street,
Coatbridge,
Scotland.

Singapore
R. Yap,
Secretary,
c/o Chinese Swimming Club,
21 Amber Road.
Singapore 1543.

Sri Lanka
S. De Alwis,
Secretary,
B&SA of Sri Lanka,
Ministry of Sports Comp.,
Race Course Grand Stand,
Reid Avenue,
Colombo 7, Sri Lanka.

Sudan
I. Tadros,
President,
Sudanese Billiards Association,
PO Box 579,
Khartoum,
Sudan.

Sweden
K. Hartman,
Chairman,
Swedish Snooker Confederation,
Box 49033,
100 28 Stockholm,
Sweden.

Thailand
Sindhu Pulsirivong,
President,
BA&CC of Thailand,
56 Changkolnee Building,
Surawong Road,
Bangkok 10500,
Thailand.

Wales
Mal Hendra,
Chairman,
Welsh Billiards Association,
69 Roman Way,
Neath,
West Glamorgan,
Wales.

Zimbabwe
D. Griffiths,
Secretary,
Zimbabwe B&SA,
PO Box 2722,
Mutare,
Zimbabwe.

THE BILLIARDS AND SNOOKER CONTROL COUNCIL

The Billiards and Snooker Control Council (B&SCC) was set up more than a century ago in 1885 and became the world governing body for games played on an English billiards table. In 1985, however, that responsibility was taken over by the International Billiards and Snooker Federation. Now more than thirty countries have an equal say in the running of the world affairs relating to these games.

The B&SCC duties still include making and revising the rules, certificating referees all over the world, listing official break and championship records, and organizing the English national events for non-professionals.

There are reputed to be more than six million players in the UK, making snooker the largest participant sport. Various categories of membership are available to all – both clubs and individuals. Membership allows players to enter national competitions, while a twice-yearly newsletter keeps members up-to-date with the latest developments. For full details of membership please write to: The Billiards and Snooker Control Council, Coronet House, Queen Street, Leeds LS1 2TN tel: (0532 440586).

There is no doubt that most people see only the glamorous side of professional snooker. But without the administration of the B&SCC and their hard-working team, the game certainly would not be as well organized and smooth-running as it is today.

Billiards and Snooker Control Council County Secretaries

Avon
John Treasure, 7 Stokecliffe, Park Road, Stapleton, Bristol BS16 1DT. (0272 656977) (H); (0272 276866) (B)

Cambridgeshire
E. Newton, 39 Coles Road, Milton, Cambridge CB4 4BZ. (0223 861442) (H); (0223 245191 Ext. 227) (B)

Cheshire
J. Fidler, The Coppice, Tarvin Road, Frodsham, Cheshire. (0928-33014) (H)

Cleveland and South Durham
W. D. Jones, 2 Frobisher Close, Marske, Redcar, Cleveland TS11 7EG. (0642 478748)

Cornwall
Derek Brooks, c/o 1 Rose Meadows, Goonhaven, Truro, Cornwall.

Cumbria
S. Poole, 1 James Watt Terrace, Barrow-in-Furness, Cumbria. (0229 23601)

Derbyshire
E. Gratton, 'Pippenwell', Pippenwell Lane, Chelmorton, Nr Buxton, Derbyshire. (0298 4633) (H); (029885 212) (B)

Devon
Steve Bryant, 8 South View Close, Willand, Cullompton, Devon. (0884 820763) (H)

Essex
R. Johannessen, 2 Bohun Close, Great Leighs, Chelmsford, Essex. (0245 361780) (H); (0245 267111 Ext. 2396) (B)

Gloucestershire
Not functioning

Hampshire
T. Rundle, 100 Cherry Tree Avenue, Cowplain, Hampshire. (0705 252887) (H)

Hereford and Worcester
Not functioning

Hertfordshire
D. Howe, 10 Shelley Close, Hitchin, Hertfordshire. (0462 54338) (H)

Isle of Wight
M. Collingwood, Flat 2, 'Fairholme', New Road, Brading, Isle of Wight. (0983 407777)

Kent
C. Summers, 8 Parkfields, Knights Place, Strood, Kent. (0634 718031) (H); (0634 271681 Ext. 4) (B)

Leicestershire
Ms M. E. Jordan, 48 John Bold Avenue, Stoney Stanton, Leicestershire LE9 6DN. (0455 274071) (H); (0533 50042 Ext. 389) (B)

Lincolnshire and Humberside
K. Kirk, 35 Broughton Gardens, Brant Road, Lincoln LN5 8SW. (0522 33890) (H); (0522 37361) (B)

London
David Saines, Flat 3, 2 Frithwood Avenue, Northwood, Middlesex. (09274 28139) (H); (01 422 3434 Ext. 2303) (B)

Norfolk
Albert Stewart, 16 Porter Road, Long Stratton, Norwich, Norfolk NR15 2TY. (0508 30721) (H)

North East
T. Bell, 'Downlea', Houghton Road, Newbottle, Houghton-le-Spring, Tyne and Wear DH4 4 EF. (091 584 7400)

North West
R. Tonge, 6 Mendip Close, Bolton BL2 6LG. (0204 387144) (H); (061 273 2524) (B)

Northamptonshire
Mrs J. Yule, 87 Westfield Road, Corby, Northamptonshire. (0536 65185)

Nottinghamshire
A. Clowes, 4 Wheatgrass Road, Chilwell, Nottinghamshire NG9 4JN. (0602 227966)

Oxfordshire
Ken Surch, 3 Wellington Street, Thame, Oxfordshire OX3 3BW.

Shropshire
J. Griffiths, 107 Dalelands Estate, Market Drayton, Shropshire. (0630 4757) (H); (0952 503042) (B)

Staffordshire and West Midlands
G. Harding, 140 Hawksford Crescent, Bushbury, Wolverhampton. (0902 725428) (H)

Suffolk
John Disney, 8 Tylers Green, Trimley St Mary, Ipswich IP10 0XF. (0394 275063) (H)

Surrey
R. Mason, 39 Frailey Hill, Maybury, Woking, Surrey GU22 8EA. (04862 66292) (H)

East Sussex
J. F. Summers, 5 Howey Close, Newhaven, East Sussex BN9 0NX.

West Sussex
T. Corio, 22 Kingfisher Lane, Turners Hill, West Sussex RH10 4QP. (0342 715972)

Warwickshire and Midlands Counties
Steve Martin, 73 Blackmare Close, Winyates East, Redditch, Worcestershire. (0527 29739) (H)

Wessex
Barry Tucker, 13 Lark Close, Midsomer Norton, Avon BA3 4PX. (0761 419283)

Wiltshire
D. Lye, 46 Kingsbury Street, Marlborough, Wiltshire. (0672 53464)

Yorkshire
E. Hodgkinson, 3 Eastbury Avenue, Horton Bank Top, Bradford 6. (91 679369) (H)

THE BILLIARDS AND SNOOKER FOUNDATION

The Billiards and Snooker Foundation will be twenty years old in 1989. It was set up under the joint sponsorship of the Billiards and Snooker Trade Association and the Billiards and Snooker Control Council. The main object of the Foundation is to teach young players under eighteen the basic skills of billiards and snooker. In order to achieve this aim it is necessary to train coaches fully by means of courses at Lilleshall National Sports Centre. These courses are usually held four times a year. Coaches who qualify for a certificate are then entitled to organize coaching courses for young players.

The Foundation is aware of the tremendous increase in popularity of the sport throughout the world, particularly in Europe. It can also accommodate prospective coaches from overseas if recommended by their national association.

The national coach of the Foundation is Jack Karnehm, who is a professional billiards player, best-selling author and a senior BBC commentator. He is also a former World Amateur Billiards Champion. The Foundation provides coaches for Pontin's Holidays during the summer and runs the Hainsworth TopTable Snooker event and the B&SF Under-16 Billiards Championship.

The Foundation is controlled by a joint committee made up by members of the Billiards and Snooker Trade Association, officials of the Billiards and Snooker Control Council and the development officer and national coach.

The Coaching Scheme

Each candidate who wishes to become a coach attends a course to be instructed in the basic skills required to coach young persons up to the age of eighteen. After qualifying, a coach is expected to arrange courses in his or her own area.

Qualifications Required

A prospective coach should be a fairly competent player of both billiards and snooker. He should be dedicated to the sport and its advancement, be able to talk freely, clearly and without embarrassment, and be able to communicate easily with others, particularly young people.

Coaching Course Syllabus

Aims and objects of the Billiards and Snooker Foundation.
Instructional techniques.
Basic rules of billiards and snooker.
History, characteristics, care and maintenance of equipment.
Practical demonstration in instruction.

Examination

Written examination on the basic rules of billiards and snooker.
A continuous assessment of candidates takes place during the course.

How to Apply for a Place on the Course

To apply for a place on the course for prospective coaches write to the Development Officer of the Billiards and Snooker Control Council, Coronet House, Queen Street, Leeds LS1 2TN. Every candidate is required to obtain a letter of recommendation from the League or Association with which he or she is connected so that it can be established that he or she conforms to the necessary requirements.

The Billiards and Snooker Foundation Coaches

Devon and Cornwall

AREA COACHES

W. Hopwood, Abbotts-Kabete, 68 Sidford Road, Sidmouth, Devon.
E. Milverton, 2 Barrack Road, Exeter, Devon.
L. Webber, White Dormers, Bole Aller, Westcott, Devon.

Gloucester, Avon, Shropshire and Wiltshire

REGIONAL COACH

C. Handscombe, 8 High Fields Villas, Station Road, Newnham, Gloucestershire. (059 455 429)

AREA COACHES

R. Mytton, 46 Polden House, Windmill Hill, Bristol.

W. D. Curnow, 16 Alton Road, Horfield, Bristol BS7 9PS.

E. W. Nott, 'Ashcroft', Tilley Lane, Farmborough, Bath, Avon.

P. R. May, 144 Silver Street Lane, Trowbridge, Wiltshire.

B. A. Tucker, 13 Lark Close, Midsomer Norton, Avon BA3 4PX.

J. Tomlinson, Yew Tree Lodge, Ogbourne St Andrew, Marlborough, Wiltshire.

D. A. Gilbert, Flat 23b, Spring Gardens, Ditherington, Shrewsbury, Shropshire.

P. I. Howley, 13 Abbey Road, Wellington, Telford, Shropshire.

G. Leddington, 28 Golf Links Lane, Wellington, Telford, Shropshire

S. Humphries, Cloverdale, 1 Church Street, Hampton Lucy, Warwick CV35 8BE.

D. Eels, The Homestead, 32 Charlton Road, Midsomer Norton, Avon.

N. G. Dowie, 29 Buckland Close, Park North, Swindon, Wiltshire.

F. Adamson, 44 Yeo Moor, Clevedon, Avon.

L. Frost, 16 Water Combe Lane, Yeovil, Somerset BA20 2EB.

Hampshire, Dorset, Sussex and Isle of Wight

AREA COACHES

W. Ashdown, 26 Rushlake Road, Coldean, Brighton, Sussex.

E. J. Carroll, 27 Long Water Drive, Gosport, Hampshire.

P. Jennings, 17 Old Manor Close, Bexhill-on-Sea, East Sussex.

A. J. Davies, 63 Shaftesbury Road, Gosport, Hampshire.

N. Harwood, 17 Green Walk, Seaford, Sussex.

D. W. Heaton, 6 Sandwich Drive, Filsham Valley, St Leonards-on-Sea, East Sussex.

J. Hughes, 81 Pevensey Bay Road, Langney, Eastbourne, East Sussex.

W. J. James, 12 St Catherine's Road, Bitterne Park, Southampton, Hampshire.

A. Doughty, 70 Amherst Road, Hastings, East Sussex TN34 1TX.

J. H. Quinn, 8 Meadow View Road, Broadway, Weymouth, Dorset.

T. Rundle, 100 Cherrytree Avenue, Cowplain, Portsmouth, Hampshire.

D. Wells, 'Armwood', 73 Hobb Lane, Hedge End, Southampton, Hampshire.

P. Denham, Ontario Private Hotel, Colwell Common Road, Colwell Bay, Totland, Isle of Wight PO39 0DD.

T. Floate, 115 Broadway, Sandown, Isle of Wight.

F. Sandell, 65 St Lawrence Avenue, West Tarring, Worthing, West Sussex.

H. Excisa, 18 Chalet Road, Ferring, Worthing, West Sussex BN12 5PB.

R. A. K. Nicholson, Flat 1, Glenview, Station Road, Steyning, West Sussex.

R. Hayes, 27 Dumbrills Close, Burgess Hill, West Sussex.

D. C. Torrington, 18 Owen Street, Southsea, Hampshire PO4 9PB.

P. Chalk, 20 Wesley Close, Bewbush, Crawley, West Sussex.

W. Ogg, 10 George Street, Gosport, Hampshire.

P. Fox, 4 Hyde Park House, Hyde Park Road, Portsmouth, Hampshire.

K. Jones, 3 Welles Road, Chandlers Ford, Eastleigh, Hampshire.

R. Spalding, Rozel, 29 Downside, Bridgemary, Gosport, Hampshire PO13 0JJ.

N. Kimmance, 8 Canterbury House, Broomfield Avenue, Worthing, West Sussex BN14 7PT.

Isle of Man, Northern Ireland and Scotland

AREA COACHES

J. J. Herron, 24 Strangeford Park, Londonderry, Northern Ireland.

M. E. McHale, 211 Wellesley Road, Methil, Fife, Scotland.

W. McKerron, 21 Redhill View, Lanark Road, Edinburgh, Scotland.

S. Pavis, Centre Spot Club Ltd, la Lelia Street, Belfast, Northern Ireland.

M. Quine, 52 Barrule Drive, Onchan, Isle of Man.

R. Briggs, c/o Henderson, 107 Yokermill Road, Glasgow, G13 4HL, Scotland.

P. F. Locke, 3 St Catherine's Drive, Douglas, Isle of Man.

P. A. Reynolds, 54 Tromode Park, Douglas, Isle of Man.

R. M. McCabe, 30 Glencairn Street, Camelon, Falkirk, Stirling, Scotland.

E. Gill, 33 Priory Drive, Kylepark, Uddington, Glasgow, Scotland.

H. Brown, Riverford House, Wylie Place, Stewarton, Kilmarnock, Scotland.

G. Manson, 1 Hope Road, Kirk Muir Hill, Lesmahagow, Lanarkshire, Scotland.

J. Caven, 28 Parklands, Coylton, Ayrshire, Scotland.

J. Halcrow, 5 Oak Drive, Larbert, Stirling, Scotland.

D. McGee, 18 Redcliffe Parade, Belfast, Northern Ireland.

J. P. McGowen, 105 Nicol Street, Kirkcaldy, Fife, Scotland.

G. McAleer, The Merchants Snooker Centre, Merchants Quay, Newry, County Down, Northern Ireland.

L. Cameron, Flat 14, House 63, 60 Tarfside Oval, Glasgow G52 3AH, Scotland.

H. Davis, 35 Broomburn Court, Newton Mearns, Glasgow G77 5JJ, Scotland.

J. Wright, 34 Garry Place, Troon, Ayrshire, Scotland KA10 7JD.

I. Wallace, c/o B. Strachan, 43 Cornhill Square, Aberdeen, Scotland.

Lancashire, Merseyside, Greater Manchester and Cheshire

REGIONAL COACH

R. J. Hope, 953 Kingsway, Didsbury, Manchester 20. (061 445 9991)

AREA COACHES

W. L. Lewis, 12 Manor Road, Foxholes, Horwish, Bolton BL6 6AR

D. O'Connor, 29 Rydal Street, Newton-le-Willows, Merseyside.

D. Woodburn, 55 Piccadilly Street, Haslingden, Rossendale, Lancashire BB4 5LU.

B. Neild, 2 Lyndale Avenue, Haslingden, Rossendale, Lancashire BB4 4BP.

A. Davies, 52 Sycamore Lane, Great Sankey, Warrington, Cheshire.

J. Titterington, 20 Grindleton Road, West Bradford, Nr Clitheroe BB7 4TE.

R. Johnstone, 129 Napier Street, Nelson BB9 0RB.

J. W. Hurst, 1 Ardmore Road, Bispham, Blackpool, Lancashire.

H. Lancashire, 32 Oregan Avenue, Oldham, Lancashire.

M. D. Jones, 57 Broughton Lane, Wistaston, Crewe CW2 8JR.

H. McGuire, 96 Irwin Road, St Helens, Merseyside.

F. J. Sheridan, 23 Harrowby Road, Seaforth, Liverpool L21 1DP.

D. M. Williams, 47 Serpentine Road, Wallasey, Merseyside.

D. Rawcliffe, 359 St Anne's Road, Blackpool, Lancashire.

F. Barlow, 36 Goldsworthy Road, Flixton, Manchester M31 2UP.

J. W. Smith, 33 Kirkstone Road South, Litherland, Liverpool.

D. McDonald, 11 Birkbeck Close, Kendal, Cumbria LA9 6AY.

T. Woodward, 944 Oldham Road, Thornham, Rochdale, Lancashire.

W. Smith, 97 Settle Street, Bolton, Lancashire, BL3 3DJ.

D. French, 284 Crescent Road, Bolton, Lancashire.

J. Stephens, Chapel House Farm, Chapel Lane, Rainhill, Merseyside.

W. Moore, 224 Water Street, Accrington, Lancashire.

G. B. Whittaker, 17 Westside, Halton Gardens, Marton, Blackpool, Lancashire.

K. King, 9 Lindwall Close, Northern Moor, Manchester M23 0EF.

R. Davies, 7 Haddon Avenue, New Moston, Manchester M10 0SR.

C. Walton, 70 Brecon Drive, Bury BL9 9LE.

E. Fielding, 24 Goodwood Road, Lancaster LA1 4LZ.

T. Fenton, 1 Wycombe Avenue, South Shore, Blackpool.

London and Home Counties – North

AREA COACHES

M. S. Clarke, 82 Greenway Gardens, Greenford, Middlesex.

J. Brewerton, 40 Green Leas, Sunbury-on-Thames, Middlesex.

H. J. Evans, 4 Glebelands, Headington, Oxford.

H. Wilmot, 340 Cassiobury Drive, Watford, Hertfordshire.

R. T. Ford, 24 Cromwell Avenue, Newport Pagnell, Buckinghamshire MK16 8DQ.

A. Tanner, 923 Green Lanes, London N21 2PB.

J. A. Paton, 45 Bellamy Drive, Stanmore, Middlesex.

G. Armitage, 2 Chessholme Road, Ashford, Middlesex.

K. Rawstron, 104 Laleham Road, Shepperton TW17 0AB.

M. Eaton, 312 Oldfield Lane, Greenford, Middlesex UB6 8PT.

London and Home Counties – South

AREA COACHES

I. A. Murray, 25 Keats House, Porchester Mead, Beckenham, Kent.

J. F. Carter, 'Jamaica', Fullers Road, Holt Pound, Farnham, Surrey.

C. N. Roberts, 41 Lower Gravel Road, Bromley, Kent BR2 8LR.

F. C. R. Wiggins, 7 Petworth Court, Bath Road, Reading, Berkshire.

R. Green, 53 Frythe Way, Cranbrook, Kent TN17 3AT.

E. L. Bailey, 7 Beulah Road, Tunbridge Wells, Kent TN1 2NP.

R. Barrell, 160 Sunningvale Avenue, Biggin Hill, Kent.

R. Field, 9 Parkwood Close, Tunbridge Wells, Kent.

J. E. Waskett, 9 Rothbury Road, Chelmsford, Essex.

J. H. Luker, 435 Ashingdon Road, Ashingdon, Essex.

R. Mason, 39 Frailey Hill, Maybury, Woking, Surrey.

G. Johnson, 163 Albert Road, Horley, Surrey RH6 7HS.

R. Davies, c/o 96 Kinfauns Road, Goodmayes, Ilford, Essex 1G3 9QN.

A. Wix, 99 Merewood Road, Barnehurst, Kent.

J. Pearce, Smithy Cottage, Riseley, Berkshire RG7 1QF.

R. A. Jones, 130 Canberra Road, Charlton, London SE7.

A. Glew, 57 Cantley Crescent, Wokingham, Berkshire.

R. Bacon, 59 Ilfracombe Gardens, Chadwell Heath, Romford, Essex.

P. Webb, 63 Park Lane, Tilehurst, Reading, Berks RG3 5DP.

North East

REGIONAL COACH

A. Hanson, 121 Charles Street, Boldon Colliery, Tyne and Wear NE35 9BH.

AREA COACHES

W. Ormston, 10 Stanmore Avenue, Beechwood Estate, Middlesbrough.

B. Rawlings, 36 Lingfield Drive, Orchard Estate, Eaglescliffe, Stockton-on-Tees, Cleveland.

Mrs V. Selby, 60 Princes Road, Brunton Park, Newcastle-upon-Tyne NE3 5AN.

T. N. Gallagher, 24 Dalton Street, Hartlepool, Cleveland TS26 9EL.

J. Levett, 12 Durham Road, Ferry Hill, County Durham.

W. Jones, 2 Frobisher Close, Marske, Redcar, Cleveland.

G. Crook, 28 Pelaw Road, Chester-le-Street, County Durham.

Staffordshire, Nottinghamshire, Midland Counties and Leicestershire

AREA COACHES

G. O'Halloran, 58 Berkswell Road, Erdington, Birmingham B24 9ED.

M. H. E. Chapman, 15 Wheelers Lane, King's Heath, Birmingham B13 0SB.

P. H. Fisher, 28 Elmsleigh Drive, Midway, Swadlincote, Burton-upon-Trent.

D. L. Rees, 37 Back Lane, Chellaston, Derby S45 9PJ.

D. Hammond, 1 Bonehill Road, Tamworth, Staffordshire B78 3HQ.

E. G. Palmer, 162 Wolverhampton Road, Cannock, Staffordshire.

K. Laverty, 15 Island Close, Hinckley, Leicestershire LE10 1LN.

T. D. Spraggett, 4 Blakeley Avenue, Tettenhall, Wolverhampton, West Midlands.

J. Ridley, 9 Thornhill Drive, Boughton, Nottinghamshire NG22 9JG.

K. Garlick, 16a Wolverhampton Road, Wall Heath, Dudley, West Midlands.

D. Palmer, 46 Walnut Drive, Cannock, Staffordshire WS11 2NF.

D. G. Burton, 'Kimley', 3 Parkside Road, Chadderston, Derby DE2 6QR.

R. M. Hunt, 11 Bader Road, Bentley, Walsall, West Midlands WS2 0BJ.

E. Gratton, 'Pippenwell', Pippenwell Lane, Chelmorton, Nr Buxton, Derbyshire.

K. Gilbert, 113 Regis Heath Road, Rowley Regis, West Midlands.

Suffolk, Norfolk, Cambridge and Lincolnshire

AREA COACHES

E. Brown, 208 Woodbridge Road, Ipswich, Suffolk.

C. Brinded, 51 Kingfisher Close, Bradwell, Great Yarmouth.

A. A. A. Howling, 13 Crown Drive, Spalding, Lincolnshire PE11 2HT.

H. S. Hall, 14 Middleton Way, Leasingham, Sleaford, Lincolnshire.

C. Smith, 5 Manor Close, Walberswick, Suffolk.

A. J. Ampleford, 'Saraja', Chapel Road, Hainford, Norwich, Norfolk NR10 3NA.

A. D. Schofield, 'Wintons', Clover Road, Attleborough, Norfolk NR17 2JQ.

P. J. Sayer, 68 Cedar Drive, Attleborough, Norfolk NR17 2HN.

D. A. Springthorpe, c/o 70 Oakdale Avenue, Stanground, Peterborough PE2 8TD.

N. W. Watson, Old Post Office, Yarburgh, Nr Louth, Lincolnshire LN11 0PN.

R. Barrett, 80 Hillmead, Catton Estate, Norwich NR3 3PF.

F. J. Wilson, 24 Hillcrest, Chedgrave, Loddon, Norwich NR14 6HX

J. Disney, 8 Tylers Green, Trimley St Mary, Ipswich IP10 0XF.

Wales

AREA COACHES

R. O. V. Humphreys, 9 Heaton Place, Colwyn Bay, Llandudno, Gwynedd.

P. Williams, Dwylan, Penrhyndeudraeth, Gwynedd L148 6NP.

J. Carney, 84 Herbert Street, Pontardawe, Swansea, West Glamorgan.

J. Terry, 13 Cherry Grove, Sketty, Swansea SA2 8AS.

J. G. Owen, Browerydd, Caergog Terrace, Aberystwyth, Dyfed.

K. Pask, 87 Brynglas, Hollybush, Cwmbran, Gwent NP44 7LJ.

K. Johnson, Tolcarne, 24 Cefn Road, Rhosnesni, Wrexham, Clwyd LL13 9NH.

Yorkshire and Humberside

REGIONAL COACH

J. Ingleby, 33 Bar-Croft, New Road, Kirkheaton, Huddersfield. (0484 36758)

AREA COACHES

J. H. Bayes, Manor Close, 34 Tower Street, Flamborough, North Humberside.

R. B. England, 27 Horsemarket Road, Malton, North Yorkshire.

B. White, 505 Addy Street, Sheffield S6 3GU.

M. Lockwood, 10 Mount Avenue, Eccleshill, Bradford.

G. Mellor, 78 Fleminghouse Lane, Waterloo, Huddersfield.

W. E. Reed, Laburnum Cottage, The Park, Woodlands, Doncaster.

D. J. Rourke, 7 Portal Crescent, Mirfield, Yorkshire.

K. Steel, 146 Haigh Moor Road, Tingley, Nr Wakefield.

J. Saxby, 60 Sherphaw Avenue, Skipton, Yorkshire BD23 2QE.

R. Stobbs, 115 Ash Road, Headingley, Leeds LS6 3HD.

M. Dawson, 41 Milton Avenue, Peasey Hills, Malton, North Yorkshire.

B. Mizon, 3 Central Avenue, Beverley, North Humberside HU17 3HL.

H. Hodgson, 3 Stonecliffe Walk, Leeds LS12 5BG.

J. Needham, 'Ashlea', Hope Bank, Honley, Huddersfield.

D. J. Sugden, 11 Kingsway Close, Ossett, West Yorkshire WF5 8DY.

D. M. Clarke, 20 Weekes Road, Cleethorpes, South Humberside.

D. Townend, Courtfield, 3 St James's Drive, Harrogate, North Yorkshire.

S. Bennet, 5 Clarendon Street, Barnsley, South Yorkshire S70 6AH.

B. Franks, 31 Westgate, Baildon, Shipley, West Yorkshire BD17 5EH.

D. Marner, 4 Roseacre, Hook, Nr Goole, Yorkshire.

S. Pollard, Topspot Snooker Centre, 38 Wakefield Road, Huddersfield, West Yorkshire.

S. Brooke, 80 Winrose Hill, Leeds 10.

HOW TO FOLLOW IN THE FOOTSTEPS OF WILLIAMS AND CO.

Steve Davis, Jimmy White, Stephen Hendry and the rest of the world's top snooker players are household names. They can't even go shopping without being recognized! Now snooker's top referees are also celebrities in their own right: John Williams, John Street, Len Ganley and Alan Chamberlain are in camera view almost as much as the players.

Ganley has appeared in television commercials even though there is a lot less of him these days. He has lost 5 stone in weight as a result of a strenuous dieting programme. A top referee is in constant demand as he travels all over Britain and across much of the world. Irishman Ganley has been to such exotic places as China, Japan and Hong Kong, while Street spent a couple of weekends last season jetting off to new snooker venues in Finland, Luxembourg and luxurious Monte Carlo.

Clacton's Mike Clarke, a fully qualified referee and coach, might not be one of the game's top officials but he was in Peking last season for the Kent Cup organized by Howard Kruger's Framework outfit.

For years, the Billiards and Snooker Control Council, the organization that runs amateur snooker in the UK, has tested and appointed referees. It ran a qualification system that saw referees earn C, B and A Grade certificates. This is now in the process of change, however, and the B&SCC states: 'It was felt necessary that we should differentiate between 'New' and 'Old' referees, and consequently future grades will be Class 3, Class 2 and Class 1.

'Class 3 referees will have satisfied the examiners that they are fully conversant with the Rules.

'Class 2 referees will be referees of the highest standard. They will have been

Life at the top: Top international referee John Street relaxes before a Rothmans Matchroom League match in Monte Carlo.

observed in action and have indicated that they are fully aware of any amendments to the Rules that may have occurred since their original examination. They will be examined on the table with regard to the intricate situations and special attention will have been paid to their pre-match preparation, positional sense, etc.

'Class 1 referees – this designation will be awarded to Class 2 referees who have satisfied their local Area Assessment Board of their competence and experience at the highest level and who have at least five years' service in the grade. They will be expected to have made a positive contribution to the games of billiards and snooker in general, and to the practice of refereeing in particular, including the training and encouragement of other referees.

'With effect from 1 January 1988, referees' fees will be as follows:
Examination fee: Class 3 and Class 3 to Class 2 – £2 per subject; Class 2 to Class 1 – £5 per subject.
Annual fee (either or both games): all Classes – £5.

'All the above categories will include ordinary membership of the Council, which means the referees will receive membership at a reduced rate. The new scale no longer precludes official examiners from paying fees.'

You are still keen to become a referee? Then your first step is to write to the B&SCC at Coronet House, Queen Street, Leeds LS1 2TN (make sure you enclose a stamped, self-addressed envelope, please). They will write back telling you the name of your local examiner.

As you progress up the refereeing ladder, you may want to apply for membership of the Professional Referees' Association. You will already be officiating at a number of good amateur events and the PRA will monitor your progress. The PRA officiate at all professional tournaments throughout the world sanctioned by the World Professional Billiards and Snooker Association. To become a professional referee your application will be placed before three members of the PRA and three professional players with John Virgo, chairman of the WPBSA, in charge.

It's a long, hard road to the top but it's well worthwhile. Just ask Messrs Williams, Street, Ganley and Chamberlain.

A–Z OF SNOOKER

ANGLED If a direct stroke in a straight line to any part of every ball on is obstructed by a corner of the cushion, then the cue ball is said to be angled.

BALL MARKER A plastic accessory that enables the referee to mark accurately the position of a ball that is to be removed from the table for cleaning or any other purpose.

BALL ON Any ball which may lawfully be struck with the cue ball.

BAULK A straight line drawn 29 inches from the face of the bottom cushion and parallel to it is called the baulk line. The area between this line and the bottom cushion is known as baulk. It is used only in billiards but, even when snooker only is to be played on a table, tradition decrees that this line is still put on the table.

BED CLOTH The green woollen cloth which covers the slate bed of the table and the cushions.

BREAK A number of pots in succession made in any one turn.

CENTRE SPOT This is midway between the top and bottom cushions and midway between the centre pockets. It is used for spotting the blue.

CHALK The material which a player rubs on to his cue tip so that he will get good contact between the tip and the cue ball.

CHINESE SNOOKER A player is said to be in a Chinese snooker when, attempting to strike the cue ball, he is obstructed by another ball directly behind the cue ball.

CLEARANCE A player taking all the balls remaining on the table in one visit.

CROSS REST An aid to a player who cannot place his bridge hand near enough to the cue ball to be able to cue properly.

CUE BALL White ball.

CUE EXTENSION An implement which fits on to the end of a player's own cue, enabling him to reach shots where he would normally be required to use the half-butt cue.

CUSHAID An innovation designed to assist a player when playing a ball near a cushion. Sometimes the line of the shot is such that the shot is difficult to play when using a normal cross rest. The cushaid is a small grooved plastic block which, when fitted on to the cross piece of the rest, allows the player to cue more easily over a cushion.

CUSHIONS The rubber which is covered with bed cloth and which surrounds the playing surface of the table.

DOUBLE When the object ball enters a pocket after first striking a cushion.

EXTENDING CUE A cue with an adjustable shaft which may be used as an alternative to the half-butt or full-butt cues.

EXTENDING REST A cross rest with a shaft of adjustable length which enables a player to play a shot more comfortably when the cue ball is in such a position that it cannot be reached in the conventional manner.

EXTENDED SPIDER REST A version of the spider rest with the grooved portion extended out from the feet to enable a player to bridge over a number of balls.

FOUL An act which contravenes any of the rules of the game.

FREE BALL When a player is snookered after a foul, a free ball is awarded and, for the purposes of the next shot, the ball the striker elects to play receives the value of the ball on.

FULL-BUTTS A cue and rest approximately 9 feet long which have the same function as the half-butts and are used when the player has to stand a long distance from where the cue ball has come to rest.

HALF-BUTTS A cue and rest approximately 7 feet long, which are used when a player cannot play a shot with his own cue as the cue ball is situated in a position that makes it impossible for him to reach it in the normal way.

JUMP SHOT This is a foul shot when the cue ball jumps over any ball, either by accident or design, except when it first strikes the object ball before jumping over another ball.

LONG SPIDER REST A version of the spider rest fitted to a 9-foot shaft.

MAXIMUM BREAK When a player scores 147 points by potting 15 reds, 15 blacks and all the colours.

MISS A miss can be ruled by a referee when he considers that the striker has not endeavoured to hit the object ball.

MULTI-REST A version of the cross and spider rests which combines the characteristics of both implements. It has a single forked end which is adjustable to a variety of positions.

NAP The woollen bed cloth has a pile similar to pile on a carpet. The cloth is fitted so that the nap runs from baulk end to spot end.

NOMINATED BALL The ball which the striker elects to hit with the first impact of the cue ball.

OBJECT BALL Any ball which may lawfully be struck with the cue ball.

PLANT This occurs when an object ball is hit on to another object ball with the second ball going into the pocket. This can be a two-ball plant, three-ball plant, etc.

POT When an object ball enters a pocket without the striker contravening any of the rules of the game.

PUSH SHOT This illegal shot is made when the tip of the cue stays in contact with the cue ball after it begins its forward motion or when the tip of the cue remains in contact with the cue ball when the cue ball makes contact with the object ball.

PYRAMID SPOT Also known as the pink spot, this is situated midway between the centre spot and the face of the top cushion.

SAFETY SHOT A shot played to give one's opponent the least chance possible to make a scoring stroke.

SCREW Striking the white ball in such a way that it will travel backwards after impact with the object ball.

SIDE Striking the cue ball on either the left or right hand side, so that it spins off at an angle after contact with the object ball or cushion.

SNOOKER When a stroke in a straight line to any part of every ball on is obstructed by a ball or balls not on. Then a player is said to be snookered.

SPIDER REST An aid to a player who has to play a shot which he cannot reach with the aid of his normal bridge hand or which, because of the position of other balls, he cannot reach with the normal cross rest. The spider rest has a bridge which is shaped in such a way that it is about 3 inches from the bed of the table.

SPOT 12¾ inches from the face of the top cushion on a point on the centre longitudinal line of the table. The black ball goes on this spot.

STRIKER The person in play or about to play.

STROKE This is made when the person in play strikes the white ball with the tip of the cue.

STUN   Striking the cue ball in such a way that it will stop on impact with the object ball.

SWAN-NECKED SPIDER REST   Sometimes called a goose-necked or billiards spider, which has a single forked end. This implement performs the same function as the ordinary spider rest, but enables the player to play a greater variety of shots from awkward positions.

THE 'D'   This is a semi-circle with a radius of 11½ inches in baulk with its centre at the middle of the baulk line.

TOP CUSHION   The cushion at the spot end of the table. (*See* Spot.)

TOTAL CLEARANCE   A player taking all the balls on the table from the first red to the black with one visit to the table.

TRIANGLE   A three-side frame used by referees to rack the fifteen red balls before the start of a frame with the apex facing the bottom cushion.

Rules of the Game of Snooker *

Authorized by
THE BILLIARDS AND SNOOKER
CONTROL COUNCIL

THE BILLIARDS ASSOCIATION
Established 1885

THE BILLIARDS CONTROL CLUB
Established 1908

AMALGAMATED 1919

Chairman: Stan Brooke
Secretary and Chief Executive: David Ford

SECTION 1. EQUIPMENT

1. Table (Imperial)
1M. Table (Metric)
2. Balls
3. Cue
4. Ancillary

SECTION 2. DEFINITIONS

1. Frame
2. Game
3. Match
4. Balls
5. Striker
6. Stroke
7. In-hand
8. In play
9. On
10. Nominated
11. Pot
12. Break
13. Forced off
14. Foul
15. Snookered
16. Angled
17. Occupied
18. Push-stroke
19. Jump Shot
20. Miss

SECTION 3. THE GAME

1. Description
2. Position of Balls
3. Mode of play
4. Play from in-hand
5. Simultaneous hit
6. Spotting colours
7. Touching balls
8. Edge of pocket
9. Free ball
10. Foul
11. Penalties
12. Movement of ball
13. Stalemate
14. Four handed

SECTION 4. THE PLAYERS

1. Time wasting
2. Unfair conduct
3. Penalty
4. Non-striker
5. Absence

SECTION 5. THE OFFICIALS

1. Referee
2. Marker

SECTION 1.   EQUIPMENT

1.   The Standard Table – Imperial

Dimensions

(a) the playing area within the cushion faces shall measure 11ft 8½ins × 5ft 10ins with a tolerance on both dimensions of ± ½in.

Height

(b) the height of the table from the floor to the top of the cushion rail shall be from 2ft 9½ins to 2ft 10½ins.

Pocket Openings

(c) (i) There shall be pockets at the corners (two at the Spot end known as the top pockets and two at the Baulk end as the bottom pockets) and at the middle of the longer sides.

(ii) the pocket openings shall conform to the templates authorized by the Billiards and Snooker Control Council.

Baulk-line and Baulk

(d) a straight line drawn 29ins from the face of the bottom cushion and parallel to it is called the Baulk-line and the intervening space termed the Baulk.

The 'D'

(e) the 'D' is a semi-circle described in Baulk with its centre at the middle of the Baulk-line and with a radius of 11½ins.

Spots

(f) four spots marked on the centre longitudinal line of the table.

(i) the Spot: 12¾ins from the point perpendicular below the face of the top cushion.

(ii) the Centre Spot: Midway between the centre pockets and equidistant from the faces of the top and bottom cushions.

(iii) the Pyramid Spot: Midway between the centre spot and the face of the top cushion.

(iv) the Middle of the Baulk-line.

1M.   The Standard Table – Metric

Dimensions

(a) the playing area within the cushion faces shall measure 3500 mm × 1750 mm with a tolerance on both dimensions of ± 3 mm.

Height

(b) the height of the table from the floor to the top of the cushion rail shall be from 850 mm to 875 mm.

Pocket Openings

(c) (i) There shall be pockets at the corners (two at the Spot end known as the top pockets and two at the Baulk end as the bottom pockets) and at the middle of the longer sides.

(ii) the pocket openings shall conform to the templates authorized by the Billiards and Snooker Control Council.

Baulk-line and Baulk

(d) a straight line drawn 700 mm (¹/₅th the length of the playing area) from the face of the bottom cushion and parallel to it is called the Baulk-line and the intervening space termed the Baulk.

The 'D'

(e) the 'D' is a semi-circle described in Baulk with its centre at the middle of the Baulk-line and with a radius of 292 mm (¹/₆th the width of the Playing area).

Spots

(f) four spots marked on the centre longitudinal line of the table.

(i) the Spot: 320 mm (¹/₁₁th the length of the playing area) from the point perpendicular below the face of the top cushion.

(ii) the Centre Spot: Midway between the centre pockets and equidistant from the faces of the top and bottom cushions.

(iii) the Pyramid Spot: Midway between the centre spot and the face of the top cushion.

(iv) the Middle of the Baulk-line.

2.   Balls

(a) the balls shall have a diameter of 52.5 mm (2¹/₁₆ins) with a tolerance of +0.05 mm −0.08 mm.

(b) they shall be of equal weight within a tolerance of

(i) 3 gms per Snooker set, and

(ii) 0.5 gms per Billiard set.

NOTE: A SET OF BALLS MAY BE CHANGED WITH THE CONSENT OF THE PLAYERS OR ON A DECISION OF THE REFEREE.

3.   Cue

The cue shall be not less than 910 mm (3ft) in length and shall show no substantial departure from the traditional and generally accepted shape and form.

4.   Ancillary

'Rests' may be used to provide a bridge for the cue.

NOTE: IT IS THE PLAYERS RESPONSIBILITY TO BOTH PLACE THE REST ON AND REMOVE IT FROM THE TABLE.

NOTE: A PLAYER SHALL NOT BE PENALIZED IF A REST HEAD FALLS OFF AND TOUCHES A BALL. THIS DOES NOT, HOWEVER, ABSOLVE A PLAYER FROM THE RESPONSIBILITY TO ENSURE THAT HE DOES NOT TOUCH A BALL WITH OTHER THAN THE TIP OF THE CUE.

SECTION 2.   DEFINITIONS

1. Frame
a frame is completed when
(a) conceded, or
(b) the black is finally potted or fouled.

2. Game
a game is an agreed number of frames.

3. Match
a match is an agreed number of games.

4. Balls
(a) the white ball is the cue-ball.
(b) the 15 reds, and
(c) the 6 colours, are object balls.

5. Striker
The person about to play or in play is the striker and remains so until completion of the stroke or break (Sec. 2 Rules 6 & 12).

6. Stroke
(a) a stroke is made when the striker strikes the cue-ball with the tip of the cue.
(b) for the stroke to be a 'Fair Stroke' the following conditions must be met:
   (i) At the moment of striking, all balls must be at rest, and where necessary, colours correctly spotted.
   (ii) The cue ball must be struck and not pushed.
   (iii) The cue ball must not be struck more than once in the same stroke.
   (iv) At the moment of striking, at least one of the strikers feet must be touching the floor.
   (v) The striker must not touch any ball other than the cue ball as in section (a) above.
   (vi) A ball or balls must not be 'forced off the table'.
(c) a stroke is not completed until all balls have come to rest and the referee has decided the striker has left the table.

7. In-hand
(a) the cue-ball is in-hand when it has entered a pocket or has been forced off the table.
(b) it remains in-hand until played fairly from in-hand or a foul is committed whilst the ball is on the table.

8. Ball in Play
(a) the cue-ball is in play when not in-hand.
(b) object balls are in play when spotted and remain so until pocketed or forced off the table.

NOTE: USING THE CUE TO POSITION THE CUE-BALL
IF THE REFEREE CONSIDERS THE PLAYER IS NOT ATTEMPTING TO PLAY A STROKE, EVEN THOUGH THE TIP OF THE CUE TOUCHES THE CUE-BALL, THE BALL IS NOT IN PLAY.

9. Ball on
Any ball which may be lawfully hit by the first impact of the cue-ball is said to be *on*.

10. Nominated ball
A nominated ball is the object ball which the striker declares, or indicates to the satisfaction of the referee, he undertakes to hit with the first impact of the cue-ball.

NOTE: IF REQUESTED BY THE REFEREE THE STRIKER MUST DECLARE WHICH BALL HE IS ON.

11. Pot
(a) a pot is when an object ball, after contact with another ball, and without any contravention of these rules, enters a pocket.
(b) if a colour, it shall be spotted before the next stroke is made, until finally potted under Sec. 3 Rule 3.
(c) if a stroke is made, with a ball or balls incorrectly spotted, and a foul is not awarded, the ball or balls
   (i) if on the table will be considered to be correctly spotted.
   (ii) if not on the table will be spotted when the foul is awarded.

NOTE:
(I) IT IS THE STRIKERS RESPONSIBILITY TO ENSURE THAT ALL BALLS ARE CORRECTLY SPOTTED BEFORE STRIKING.
(II) SUBJECT TO SEC. 3 RULES 8 & 12, REDS ARE NEVER REPLACED ON THE TABLE DESPITE THE FACT THAT A PLAYER MAY BENEFIT FROM A FOUL.

12. Break
(a) if a ball is potted, the same player plays the next stroke.
(b) a break is a number of pots in succession made in any one turn.

13. Forced off the table
(a) a ball is forced off the table if it comes to rest other than on the bed of the table or in a pocket.
(b) if a colour it shall be spotted as per Sec. 3 Rule 6 before the next stroke is made.

14. Foul
A foul is any act in contravention of these rules.

15. Snookered
(a) the cue-ball is snookered when a direct stroke in a straight line to any part of every ball *on* is obstructed by a ball or balls not *on*.

NOTE: IF THERE IS ANY ONE BALL THAT IS NOT SO OBSTRUCTED, THE CUE-BALL IS NOT SNOOKERED.

(b) if in-hand, the cue-ball is snookered only if obstructed from all positions on or within the lines of the 'D'.

(c) if the cue-ball is obstructed by more than one ball, the one nearest to the cue-ball is the effective snookering ball.

16. Angled

(a) the cue-ball is angled when a direct stroke in a straight line to any part of every ball *on* is obstructed by a corner of the cushion.

NOTE: IF THERE IS ANY ONE BALL THAT IS NOT SO OBSTRUCTED, THE CUE-BALL IS NOT ANGLED.

if angled after a foul,
(b) the referee will state angled ball, and
(c) it may be played from in-hand at the strikers discretion.

17. Occupied

A spot is said to be occupied if a ball cannot be placed on it without it touching another ball.

18. Push Stroke

A push stroke is a foul and is made when the tip of the cue remains in contact with the cue-ball,

(a) when the cue-ball makes contact with the object ball, or

(b) after the cue-ball has commenced its forward motion.

PROVIDED that where the cue-ball and an object ball are almost touching, it shall be deemed a fair stroke if the cue-ball hits the finest possible edge of the object ball.

19. Jump Shot

A jump shot is when the cue-ball jumps over any ball except when it first strikes the object ball and then jumps over another ball.

NOTE: IF THE CUE-BALL FINISHES ON THE FAR SIDE OF THE OBJECT BALL, EVEN THOUGH TOUCHING IT IN THE PROCESS, IT IS CONSIDERED TO HAVE JUMPED OVER.

NOTE: AFTER STRIKING THE BALL *ON* FAIRLY IF THE CUE-BALL SHOULD THEN JUMP OVER THE OBJECT BALL AFTER HITTING A CUSHION, IT SHALL BE DEEMED TO BE A FAIR STROKE.

20. Miss

A miss is when the referee considers the striker has not endeavoured to hit the ball *on*.

SECTION 3. THE GAME

1. Description

The game of Snooker is played on an English Billiard Table and may be played by two or more persons, either as sides or independently.

Points are awarded for scoring strokes and forfeits from an opponents fouls.

The winner is the player or side making the highest score or to whom the game is awarded under Sec. 4 Rule 2.

Each player uses the same WHITE cue-ball and there are twenty-one object balls – fifteen reds each valued 1 and six colours: yellow valued 2, green 3, brown 4, blue 5, pink 6 and black 7.

Scoring strokes are made by potting reds and colours alternately until all reds are off the table and then the colours in the ascending order of their value i.e. – yellow through to black.

2. Position of Balls

At the commencement of each frame the object balls are positioned as follows: BLACK on the SPOT; PINK on the PYRAMID SPOT; BLUE on the CENTRE SPOT; BROWN on the MIDDLE OF THE BAULK-line; GREEN on the LEFT-HAND and YELLOW on the RIGHT-HAND corner of the 'D'.

The reds in the form of a triangle, the ball at the apex standing as near to the pink ball as possible, without touching it, the base being parallel with and nearest to the top cushion.

NOTE: THE POSITIONS FOR THE OBJECT BALLS ARE COMMONLY REFERRED TO BY THE COLOUR, E.G. BLACK SPOT, PINK SPOT, ETC.

3. Mode of Play

(a) the players shall determine the order of play which (subject to Sec. 3 Rule 10) must remain unaltered throughout the *frame*.

NOTE: THE PLAYER TO STRIKE FIRST AT EACH FRAME SHALL ALTERNATE DURING A GAME.

(b) the first player shall play from *in hand* and the frame starts with the first stroke.

(c) the cue ball
   (i) must first hit a ball *on*, and
   (ii) must not enter a pocket.

(d) a ball not *on* must not enter a pocket.

(e) (i) for the first stroke of each turn, until all are off the table, red is the ball *on*.
   (ii) the value of each red potted in the same stroke is scored.

(f) if a red is potted, the next ball *on* is a colour, which if potted is scored. The colour is then re-spotted.

(g) until all reds are off the table the break is continued by potting reds and colours alternately.

(h) if the striker fails to score the next player plays from where the cue-ball comes to rest.

(j) the colours then become *on* in the ascending order of their value (Sec. 3 Rule 1) and when potted remain off the table (except as provided for in the next paragraph).

(k) when only the Black is left the first score or foul ends the frame, unless the scores are then equal,

in which case:
(i) the Black is spotted.
(ii) the players draw lots for choice of playing.

NOTE: AGGREGATE SCORES
NOTE: AGGREGATE SCORES
IN GAMES OR MATCHES WHERE AGGREGATE SCORES ARE RELEVANT IT IS ONLY WHEN THE SCORES ARE EQUAL AS A RESULT OF THE LAST FRAME THAT THE ABOVE APPLIES.

(l) The striker shall to the best of his ability endeavour to hit the ball *on*. If the referee considers the rule infringed he shall call foul and miss.

NOTE: BALL *ON* IMPOSSIBLE TO BE HIT
IN THIS SITUATION IT HAS TO BE CONSIDERED THAT THE STRIKER *IS* ATTEMPTING TO HIT THE BALL *ON*.

4. To play from in-hand
To play from in-hand the cue-ball must be struck from a position on or within the lines of the 'D'.

NOTE: THE REFEREE WILL ANSWER IF ASKED IF THE BALL IS PROPERLY PLACED.

5. Hitting two balls simultaneously
Two balls, other than two reds or a *free ball* and the ball *on*, must not be hit simultaneously by the cue-ball.

6. Spotting colours
(a) if a colour has to be spotted, and its own spot is *occupied*, it shall be placed on the highest value spot available.
(b) if there is more than one colour, and their own spots are *occupied*, the highest value ball takes precedence.
(c) if all spots are *occupied*, the colour shall be placed as near as possible to its own spot between that spot and the nearest part of the top cushion.
(d) if, in the case of the Black and the Pink, the space between its own spot and the nearest part of the top cushion is *occupied*, the colour shall be placed as near as possible to its own spot on the centre line of the table below that spot.

7. Touching Ball
(a) if the cue-ball is touching another ball which is, or can be, *on*, the referee shall state TOUCHING BALL.
(b) the striker must play away from it or it is a *push stroke*.
(c) no penalty is incurred for thus playing away if:
(i) the ball is not *on*.
(ii) the ball is *on* and the striker *nominates* such ball, or
(iii) the ball is *on* and the striker *nominates*, and first hits, another ball.

NOTE: MOVEMENT OF TOUCHING BALL
IF THE REFEREE CONSIDERS THAT A TOUCHING BALL HAS MOVED THROUGH AN AGENCY OTHER THAN THE PLAYER, IT IS NOT A FOUL.

8. Ball on edge of pocket
(a) if a ball falls into a pocket without being hit by another ball it shall be replaced.
(b) if it would have been hit by any ball involved in a stroke, all balls will be replaced and the stroke replayed.
(c) if the ball balances momentarily on the edge and falls in, it must not be replaced.

9. Free ball
(a) after a foul, if the cue-ball is *snookered*, the referee shall state FREE BALL.
(b) if the non-offending player takes the next stroke he may nominate any ball as *on*.
(c) for this stroke, such ball shall (subject to para (e)(i)) be regarded as, and acquire the value of, the ball *on*.
(d) it is a foul, should the cue-ball
(i) fail to first hit, or
(ii) except when only pink and black remain on the table, be *snookered* by, the *free ball*.
(e) if the *free ball* is potted it
(i) is spotted, and
(ii) the value of the ball *on* is scored.
(f) if the ball *on* is potted it is scored.
(g) if both the *free ball* and the ball *on* are potted only the value of the ball *on* is scored (subject to Sec. 3 Rule 3(e)(ii)).

10. Fouls
(a) if a foul is committed:
(i) the referee shall immediately state FOUL and on completion of the stroke announce the penalty.
(ii) unless awarded by the referee or claimed by the non-striker, before the next stroke is made, it is condoned.
(iii) any ball improperly spotted shall remain where positioned, except that if off the table it shall be correctly spotted.
(iv) all points scored before the foul is awarded or claimed are allowed.
(v) the next stroke is made from where the cue-ball comes to rest.
(b) should more than one foul be committed in the same stroke the highest value penalty shall be incurred.
(c) the player who committed the foul:
(i) incurs the penalty prescribed (which is added to the opponent's score), and
(ii) has to play again if requested by the next player. Once such a request has been made it cannot be withdrawn.
(iii) If a breach of Section 3.3(l) occurs, the offending player has to play again from the original position, if requested by the next player.

11. Penalties

The following are fouls and incur a penalty of four points or the higher one prescribed.

(a) value of the ball *on*:

by striking

(i) when the balls are not at rest (Sec. 2 Rule 6).

(ii) the cue-ball more than once (2–6).

(iii) with both feet off the floor (2–6).

(iv) out of turn (3–3).

(v) improperly from *in-hand* (3–4).

by causing

(vi) the cue-ball to miss all object balls (3–3).

(vii) the cue-ball to enter a pocket (3–3).

(viii) a *snooker* with *free ball* (3–9).

(ix) a *jump shot* (2–19).

(b) value of the ball *on* or ball concerned:

by causing

(i) a ball not *on* to enter a pocket (3–3).

(ii) the cue-ball to first hit a ball not *on* (3–3).

(iii) a *push stroke* (2–18).

(iv) by striking with a ball incorrectly spotted (2–11).

(v) by touching a ball with other than the tip of the cue (2–6).

(vi) by forcing a ball off the table (2–13).

(c) value of the ball *on* or higher value of the two balls by causing the cue-ball to hit simultaneously two balls other than two reds or a *free ball* and the ball *on* (3–5).

(d) a penalty of seven points is incurred if:

the striker

(i) after potting a red commits a foul before *nominating* a colour,

(ii) uses a ball off the table for any purpose,

(iii) plays at reds in successive strokes, or

(iv) uses as the cue-ball any ball other than white.

12. Ball moved by other than striker

if a ball, stationary or moving, is disturbed other than by the striker it shall be re-positioned by the referee.

NOTE: THIS COVERS THE CASE IN WHICH ANOTHER AGENCY CAUSES THE STRIKER TO TOUCH A BALL. NO PLAYER SHALL BE RESPONSIBLE FOR ANY DISTURBANCE OF THE BALLS BY THE REFEREE.

13. Stalemate

If the referee considers a position of stalemate is being approached, he should warn the players that if the situation is not altered in a short period of time he will declare the frame null and void. The frame shall be re-started with the same order of play.

14. Four-handed snooker

(a) in a four-handed game each side shall open alternate frames, the order of play shall be determined at the commencement of each frame, and must be maintained throughout that frame.

(b) players may change order of play at the beginning of each frame.

(c) if a foul is committed and a request made to play again, the player who committed the foul plays again, and the original order of play is maintained.

(d) when a frame ends in a tie Snooker Rule 3k applies. The pair who play the first stroke have the choice of which player plays that stroke. The order of play must then be maintained as in the frame.

(e) Partners may confer during a game but not whilst the striker is at the table or after the first stroke of his break.

SECTION 4. THE PLAYERS

1. Time wasting

If the referee considers that a player is taking an abnormal amount of time over a stroke, he should be warned that he is liable to be disqualified.

2. Unfair conduct

For refusing to continue a frame or for conduct which, in the opinion of the referee is wilfully or persistently unfair a player shall lose the game. He is liable to be disqualified from competitions held under the control of The Billiards and Snooker Council and its Affiliated Associations.

3. Penalty

If a game is awarded to a player under this section the offender shall:

(i) lose the game, and

(ii) forfeit all points scored, and the non-offender shall receive the value of the balls still on the table (each red counting eight points).

NOTE: PROVIDED THAT WHERE AGGREGATE POINTS SCORES APPLY, THE OFFENDER SHALL ALSO FORFEIT 147 POINTS FOR EACH UNPLAYED FRAME, TO THE NUMBER REQUIRED TO COMPLETE THE GAME.

4. Non-striker

The non-striker shall, when the striker is playing, avoid standing or moving in the line of sight; he should sit or stand at a fair distance from the table.

5. Absence

In case of his absence from the room he may appoint a substitute to watch his interests, and claim a foul if necessary.

SECTION 5. THE OFFICIALS

1. The Referee
(a) the referee shall
    (i) be the sole judge of fair and unfair play, and responsible for the proper conduct of the game under these Rules.
    (ii) intervene if he sees any contravention.
    (iii) if a player is colour blind, tell him the colour of a ball if requested.
    (iv) clean a ball on a player's request.
(b) he shall not
    (i) answer any question not authorized in the Rules.
    (ii) give any indication that a player is about to make a foul stroke.
    (iii) give any advice or opinion on points affecting play.
(c) if he has failed to notice any incident he may take the evidence of the spectators best placed for observation to assist his decision.

NOTE: THE REFEREE WILL NOT ANSWER A QUESTION REGARDING THE DIFFERENCE IN SCORES.

2. The Marker
The marker shall keep the score on the marking board and assist the referee in carrying out his duties.

NOTE: IF REQUESTED BY THE STRIKER, THE REFEREE OR MARKER MAY MOVE AND HOLD IN POSITION ANY LIGHT SHADE WHICH INTERFERES WITH THE ACTION OF THE STRIKER.

Rules of the Game of English Billiards*

Authorized by

THE BILLIARDS AND SNOOKER CONTROL COUNCIL

THE BILLIARDS ASSOCIATION
Established 1885

THE BILLIARDS CONTROL CLUB
Established 1908

AMALGAMATED 1919

Chairman: Stan Brooke
Secretary and Chief Executive: David Ford

SECTION 1. EQUIPMENT

1. Table (Imperial)
1M. Table (Metric)
2. Balls
3. Cue
4. Ancillary

SECTION 2. DEFINITIONS

1. Game
2. Match
3. Balls
4. String
5. Striker
6. Stroke
7. In-hand
8. Ball in play
9. Hazard
10. Pot
11. In-Off
12. Cannon
13. Miss
14. Break
15. Forced off
16. Foul
17. Occupied
18. Push Stroke
19. Jump Shot

SECTION 3. THE GAME

1. Description
2. Commencement of Game
3. Order of play
4. Spotting the red ball
5. Details of scoring
6. To play from In-hand
7. Limitation of hazards
8. Limitation of cannons
9. Ball on edge of pocket
10. Ball moved by other than striker
11. Balls touching
12. Miss
13. Fouls

SECTION 4. THE PLAYERS

1. Time wasting
2. Unfair conduct
3. Penalty
4. Non-striker
5. Absence

SECTION 5. THE OFFICIALS

1. Referee
2. Marker

SECTION 1. EQUIPMENT

1. The Standard Table – Imperial
Dimensions
(a) the playing area within the cushion faces shall measure 11ft 8½ins × 5ft 10ins with a tolerance on both dimensions of ± ½in.

Height
(b) the height of the table from the floor to the top of the cushion rail shall be from 2ft 9½ins to 2ft 10½ins.

Pocket Openings
(c) (i) There shall be pockets at the corners (two at the Spot end known as the top pockets and two at the Baulk end as the bottom pockets) and at the middle of the longer sides.
(ii) the pocket openings shall conform to the templates authorized by the Billiards and Snooker Control Council.

Baulk-line and Baulk
(d) a straight line drawn 29ins from the face of the bottom cushion and parallel to it is called the Baulk-line and the intervening space termed the Baulk.

The 'D'
(e) the 'D' is a semi-circle described in Baulk with its centre at the middle of the Baulk-line and with a radius of 11½ins.

Spots
(f) four spots marked on the centre longitudinal line of the table.
(i) the Spot: 12¾ins from the point perpendicular below the face of the top cushion.
(ii) the Centre Spot: Midway between the centre pockets and equidistant from the faces of the top and bottom cushions.
(iii) the Pyramid Spot: Midway between the centre spot and the face of the top cushion.
(iv) the Middle of the Baulk-line.

1M. The Standard Table – Metric
Dimensions
(a) the playing area within the cushion faces shall measure 3500mm × 1750mm with a tolerance on both dimensions of ± 3mm.

Height
(b) the height of the table from the floor to the top of the cushion rail shall be from 850mm to 875mm.

Pocket Openings
(c) (i) There shall be pockets at the corners (two at the Spot end known as the top pockets and two at the Baulk end as the bottom pockets) and at the middle of the longer sides.
(ii) the pocket openings shall conform to the templates authorized by the Billiards and Snooker Control Council.

Baulk-line and Baulk
(d) a straight line drawn 700mm ($^1/_5$th the length of the playing area) from the face of the bottom cushion and parallel to it is called the Baulk-line and the intervening space termed the Baulk.

The 'D'
(e) the 'D' is a semi-circle described in Baulk with its centre at the middle of the Baulk-line and with a radius of 292mm ($^1/_6$th the width of the Playing area).

Spots
(f) four spots marked on the centre longitudinal line of the table.
(i) the Spot: 320mm ($^1/_{11}$th the length of the playing area) from the point perpendicular below the face of the top cushion.
(ii) the Centre Spot: Midway between the centre pockets and equidistant from the faces of the top and bottom cushions.
(iii) the Pyramid Spot: Midway between the centre spot and the face of the top cushion.
(iv) the Middle of the Baulk-line.

2. Balls
(a) the balls shall have a diameter of 52.5mm ($2^1/_{16}$ins) with a tolerance of +0.05mm–0.08mm.
(b) they shall be of equal weight within a tolerance of
(i) 3 gms per Snooker set, and
(ii) 0.05 gms per Billiard set.

NOTE: A SET OF BALLS MAY BE CHANGED WITH THE CONSENT OF THE PLAYERS OR ON A DECISION OF THE REFEREE.

3. Cue
The cue shall be not less than 910mm (3ft) in length and shall show no substantial departure from the traditional and generally accepted shape and form.

4. Ancillary
'Rests' may be used to provide a bridge for the cue.

NOTE: IT IS THE PLAYERS RESPONSIBILITY TO BOTH PLACE THE REST ON AND REMOVE IT FROM THE TABLE.

NOTE: A PLAYER SHALL NOT BE PENALIZED IF A REST HEAD FALLS OFF AND TOUCHES A BALL. THIS DOES NOT, HOWEVER, ABSOLVE A PLAYER FROM THE RESPONSIBILITY TO ENSURE THAT HE DOES NOT TOUCH A BALL WITH OTHER THAN THE TIP OF THE CUE.

SECTION 2. DEFINITIONS

1. Game
A game is completed
(a) at the expiry of a specified period of play, or
(b) when the number of points agreed on is first scored.

2. Match
A match is an agreed number of games.

3. Balls
(a) the cue-ball is the ball of the striker.
(b) the other balls are object balls.

4. String
To string is to play together from the Baulk-line to the top cushion with the object of leaving the player's ball as near as possible to the bottom cushion.

5. Striker
The person about to play or in play is the striker and remains so until completion of the stroke or break.

6. Stroke
(a) a stroke is made when the striker strikes the cue-ball with the tip of the cue.
(b) for the stroke to be a 'Fair Stroke' the following conditions must be met:
    (i) At the moment of striking, all balls must be at rest, and where necessary, object balls correctly spotted.
    (ii) The cue-ball must be struck and not pushed.
    (iii) The cue-ball must not be struck more than once in the same stroke.
    (iv) At the moment of striking, at least one of the strikers feet must be touching the floor.
    (v) The striker must not touch any ball other than the cue-ball as in section (a) above.
    (vi) A ball or balls must not be 'forced off the table'.
(c) a stroke is not completed until all balls have come to rest and the referee has decided the striker has left the table.

7. In-hand
(a) A player's ball is in-hand when it is off the table, and
(b) It remains in-hand until played fairly from in-hand or a foul is committed whilst the ball is on the table.
(c) When the non-striker's ball is in-hand it remains so until his turn to play or is spotted as in Sec. 3 Rule 7.

8. Ball in Play
(a) A player's ball is in play when not in-hand.
(b) The red is in play when spotted and remains so until potted or forced off the table.

NOTE:
USING THE CUE TO POSITION THE CUE-BALL
IF THE REFEREE CONSIDERS THE PLAYER IS NOT ATTEMPTING TO PLAY A STROKE, EVEN THOUGH THE TIP OF THE CUE TOUCHES THE CUE-BALL, THE BALL IS NOT IN PLAY.

9. Hazard
a hazard is
(a) A pot, or
(b) An in-off.

NOTE: A POT IS OFTEN REFERRED TO AS A WINNING HAZARD AND AN IN-OFF AS A LOSING HAZARD.

10. Pot
A pot is when an object ball, after contact with another ball, and without any contravention of these rules, enters a pocket.

11. In-Off
An in-off is when the cue-ball, after contact with an object ball, and without any contravention of these rules, enters a pocket.

12. Cannon
A cannon is when the cue-ball hits both the object balls, without any contravention of these rules.

13. Miss
A miss is when the cue-ball fails to hit any other ball.

14. Break
A break is a succession of scoring strokes made in any one turn.

15. Forced off the table
A ball is forced off the table if it comes to rest other than on the bed of the table or in a pocket.

16. Foul
A foul is any act in contravention of these rules.

17. Occupied
A spot is said to be occupied if a ball cannot be placed on it without it touching another ball.

18. Push Stroke
A push stroke is a foul and is made when the tip of the cue remains in contact with the cue-ball,
(a) when the cue-ball makes contact with the object ball, or
(b) after the cue-ball has commenced its forward motion.
    PROVIDED that where the cue-ball and an object ball are almost touching, it shall be deemed a fair stroke if the cue-ball hits the finest possible edge of the object ball.

19. Jump Shot
A jump shot is when the cue-ball jumps over any

ball except when it first strikes the object ball and then jumps over another ball.

NOTE: IF THE CUE-BALL FINISHES ON THE FAR SIDE OF THE OBJECT BALL, EVEN THOUGH TOUCHING IT IN THE PROCESS, IT IS CONSIDERED TO HAVE JUMPED OVER.

SECTION 3. THE GAME

1. Description
The game of English Billiards is played by two or more persons, either as sides or independently. Three balls are used, 'plain' white, 'spot' white and red.

It is a game of *pots*, *in-offs*, *cannons* and positional play.

Points are awarded for scoring strokes and forfeits from an opponents fouls.

The winner is the player, or side, who has scored most points at the expiry of an agreed period, first scores an agreed number of points or to whom the game is awarded under Sec. 4 Rule 2.

2. Commencement of Game
(a) The choice of ball and order of play, unless mutually agreed upon, shall be decided by *stringing*, the winner having the option, and shall remain unaltered throughout the game.
(b) At the commencement of the game the red is placed on the spot, the first player plays from *in-hand* and the game starts with the first *stroke*.

3. Order of Play
The players play alternately unless a score is made, in which case the *striker* continues the *break* playing from where his ball rests, or, after an *in-off* or as in Sec. 3 Rule 11, from *in-hand*.

4. Spotting the Red Ball
(a) If the red is *potted* or *forced off* the table it is placed on the spot. If the spot is *occupied* it is placed on the pyramid spot. If that spot is also *occupied* it is placed on the centre spot.
(b) If the red is potted from the spot or pyramid spot twice in succession in one break, not in conjunction with another score, it is placed on the centre spot. If this spot is *occupied* it is placed on the pyramid spot or if both these spots are *occupied* on the spot.
If again potted it shall be placed on the spot.

NOTE: IF DURING A STROKE THE RED COMES TO REST ON THE SPOT, IT IS NOT CONSIDERED TO BE SPOTTED. IT IS THE STRIKER'S RESPONSIBILITY TO ENSURE THAT ALL BALLS ARE CORRECTLY SPOTTED BEFORE STRIKING.

5. Details of Scoring
Points are awarded as follows:
(a) for a *cannon*, *pot* white and *in-off* white, two.

(b) for a *pot* red and *in-off* red, three.
(c) if more than one *hazard* or a combination of *hazards* and a *cannon* are made in the same *stroke* all are scored.
(d) when an *in-off* is combined with a *cannon* it shall score two or three according to whether the white or red was first hit.
(e) should both be hit simultaneously the *in-off* shall count two.

6. To Play from In-hand
The cue-ball must
(a) be struck from a position on or within the lines of the 'D'.

NOTE: THE REFEREE WILL ANSWER, IF ASKED, IF THE BALL IS PROPERLY PLACED.

(b) be played out of baulk, except that it may be played against a cushion in baulk to hit a ball out of baulk.
(c) hit a ball or cushion out of baulk before hitting a ball in baulk.

NOTE: A BALL IS IN BAULK WHEN IT RESTS ON THE BAULK-LINE OR BETWEEN THAT LINE AND THE BOTTOM CUSHION.
IF A BALL IS OUT OF BAULK ANY PART OF ITS SURFACE MAY BE PLAYED ON FROM IN-HAND: IF A BALL IS IN BAULK NO PART OF ITS SURFACE MAY BE PLAYED ON DIRECTLY FROM IN-HAND. THE REFEREE WILL ANSWER, IF ASKED, IF A BALL IS IN OR OUT OF BAULK.

7. Limitation of Hazards
Consecutive *hazards*, not in conjunction with a *cannon*, are limited to fifteen.

If more than one *hazard* is made in the same *stroke* it shall count as one for the purpose of this rule but all points shall be scored.

After ten *hazards*, or on request, the referee shall inform the *striker*.

Should the non-striker's ball be off the table as a result of the non-striker's last stroke, it shall be spotted after the fifteenth *hazard* on the middle spot of the 'D', or if *occupied* on the right hand corner of the 'D'.

NOTE: SHOULD THE REFEREE FAIL TO INFORM THE STRIKER AFTER TEN HAZARDS THE STRIKER IS ENTITLED TO PLAY A FURTHER FIVE HAZARDS AFTER HE IS INFORMED.

8. Limitation of Cannons
Consecutive *cannons*, not in conjuntion with a *hazard*, are limited to seventy-five.

After seventy *cannons*, or on request, the referee shall inform the *striker*.

NOTE: SHOULD THE REFEREE FAIL TO INFORM THE STRIKER AFTER SEVENTY CANNONS THE STRIKER IS ENTITLED TO PLAY A FURTHER FIVE CANNONS AFTER HE IS INFORMED.

9. Ball on Edge of Pocket
(a) if a ball falls into a pocket without being hit by another ball it shall be replaced.
(b) if it would have been hit by any ball involved in a *stroke*, all balls will be replaced and the *stroke* replayed.
(c) if the ball balances momentarily on the edge and falls in, it must not be replaced.

10. Ball moved by other than striker
If a ball, stationary or moving, is disturbed other than by the *striker* it shall be repositioned by the referee.

NOTE: THIS COVERS THE CASE IN WHICH ANOTHER AGENCY CAUSES THE STRIKER TO TOUCH A BALL. NO PLAYER SHALL BE RESPONSIBLE FOR ANY DISTURBANCE OF THE BALLS BY THE REFEREE.

11. Balls Touching
When the *striker's* ball remains touching another ball, red shall be placed on the spot, the non-striker's ball, if on the table, shall be placed on the centre spot, and the striker shall play from *in hand*.

12. Miss
(a) For a *miss* the striker incurs a penalty of two points.
(b) a *miss* is a foul except when the striker is *in hand* and there is no ball out of baulk.

13. Fouls
(a) if a foul is committed
   (i) the referee shall immediately state foul.
   (ii) unless awarded by the referee or claimed by the non-striker, before the next stroke is made, it is condoned.
   (iii) any ball improperly spotted shall remain where positioned, except that if off the table it shall be correctly spotted.
   (iv) all points scored before the foul is awarded or claimed are allowed.
(b) the player committing the foul incurs a penalty of two points, which are added to his opponent's score.
(c) the next player has the option of playing
   (i) from where the balls are at rest (the red if off the table having been spotted), or
   (ii) from *in-hand*, the red and white being spotted on the spot and centre spot respectively.
(d) the following acts are fouls:
   by striking
   (i) when the balls are not at rest (Sec. 2 Rule 6).
   (ii) the *cue-ball* more than once (2–6).
   (iii) with both feet off the floor (2–6).
   (iv) out of turn (3–3).
   (v) improperly from *in-hand* (3–6).
   (vi) with a ball incorrectly spotted.
   (vii) a ball other than the *cue-ball* (2–6).
   by making (viii) a *jump shot* (2–19).
   (ix) a *push stroke* (2–18).
   (x) more than fifteen *hazards* (3–7).
   (xi) more than seventy-five *cannons* (3–8).
   (xii) by touching a ball with other than the tip of the cue (2–6).
   (xiii) by forcing a ball off the table (2–6).
   (xiv) by using a ball off the table for any purpose.

SECTION 4. THE PLAYERS

1. Time wasting
If the referee considers that a player is taking an abnormal amount of time over a stroke, he should be warned that he is liable to be disqualified.

2. Unfair conduct
For refusing to continue a frame or for conduct which, in the opinion of the referee, is wilfully or persistently unfair a player shall lose the game. He is liable to be disqualified from competitions held under the control of The Billiards and Snooker Council and its Affiliated Associations.

3. Penalty
If a game is awarded to a player under this section the offender shall:
   (i) lose the game, and
   (ii) if the game was to be decided on a number of agreed points he shall forfeit all points scored and the non-offender shall receive the agreed number of points, or
   (iii) if the game be decided at the expiry of a specified period of play and forms part of a team match the whole match shall be forfeited.

4. Non-striker
The non-striker shall, when the striker is playing, avoid standing or moving in the line of sight; he should sit or stand at a fair distance from the table.

5. Absence
In case of his absence from the room he may appoint a substitute to watch his interests, and claim a foul if necessary.

SECTION 5. THE OFFICIALS

1. The Referee
(a) the referee shall
   (i) be the sole judge of fair and unfair play, and responsible for the proper conduct of the game under these Rules.
   (ii) intervene if he sees any contravention.
   (iii) if a player is colour blind, tell him the colour of a ball if requested.
   (iv) clean a ball on a player's request.

(b) he shall not
    (i) answer any question not authorized in the Rules.
    (ii) give any indication that a player is about to make a foul stroke.
    (iii) give any advice or opinion on points affecting play.
(c) if he has failed to notice any incident he may take the evidence of the spectators best placed for observation to assist his decision.

NOTE: THE REFEREE WILL NOT ANSWER A QUESTION REGARDING THE DIFFERENCE IN SCORES.

2. The Marker

The marker shall keep the score on the marking board and assist the referee in carrying out his duties.

NOTE: IF REQUESTED BY THE STRIKER, THE REFEREE OR MARKER MAY MOVE AND HOLD IN POSITION ANY LIGHT SHADE WHICH INTERFERES WITH THE ACTION OF THE STRIKER.